Unlocking the Emperor's Door

Unlocking the Emperor's Door

Success, Tradition, and Innovation in China

CHRISTOPHER SHEEDY

nb

NICHOLAS BREALEY
PUBLISHING

London • Boston

theemperorsdoor.com

First published in Great Britain in 2020 by Nicholas Brealey, an imprint of John Murray Press, a division of Hodder & Stoughton Ltd. An Hachette UK company.

British Library Cataloguing in Publication Data: a catalogue record for this title is available from the British Library.

Library of Congress Catalog Card Number: on file.

ISBN: 978 1 473 69839 0

eBook ISBN: 978 1 473 69837 6

Typeset by Cenveo® Publisher Services.

Printed and bound in Great Britain by Clays Ltd, Elcograf S.p.A.

John Murray Press policy is to use papers that are natural, renewable and recyclable products and made from wood grown in sustainable forests. The logging and manufacturing processes are expected to conform to the environmental regulations of the country of origin.

John Murray Press
Carmelite House
50 Victoria Embankment
London EC4Y 0DZ, UK

Nicholas Brealey Publishing
Hachette Book Group
Market Place, Center 53, State Street
Boston, MA 02109, USA

www.nicholasbrealey.com

Contents

About the author

A respected author and professional writer, Christopher Sheedy has enjoyed a career that has taken him around the globe. He has written countless feature articles, books, travel stories, blogs, annual reports, profiles and more for publications, businesses, and universities in the USA, UK, Australia, and New Zealand, as well as throughout Asia and Europe.

He has produced content in New York City, London, Rome, Paris, Sydney, Singapore, Canberra, Auckland and Beijing for brands as varied as Guinness World Records, GQ, McDonald's, Virgin Australia, American Institute of CPAs, Westpac Bank, Salesforce, Volvo, Institute of Chartered Accountants of Scotland, and more.

Sheedy's fascination with everything connected to business has led to relationships of trust with thought leaders across numerous areas of corporate knowledge, making him one of the business world's most in-demand writers. His interest in the landscape-altering effect of a China-focused international business environment led to his researching and writing of this book.

Married to novelist Jenny Bond, Sheedy has two young sons, a dog, and a strong but manageable obsession with the sport of football.

Preface by Li Jinyuan

I have learned much from the stories of others. I have learned from ancient philosophers, from leaders of government, from leaders of business, and from everyday people. I continue to listen and to learn, because we can only move forward if we continue to learn. And we should help others to learn and move forward also, whenever possible.

This book came about in part because others, including people in Western countries, were asking about my story, which I think is a simple one of belief, persistence, and respect. I have been fortunate to grow my company through its first stage of focus on China, its second stage of international business, and now its third stage of progressive globalization while staying true to the traditions, values, and aspirations of my country, the People's Republic of China.

Tiens Group has had its share of challenges and difficulties, but those events have given us energy and heightened our efforts to succeed. True success, of course, comes from helping others, especially in the areas of health and education, and Tiens tries to do that through creating harmony, assuming responsibility, and fostering prosperity.

Fortunately, we were able to engage the author, Christopher Sheedy, to spend time with us to gather the material used for this book. Although an experienced business writer, he knew little about China, about Chinese business, or about my company when he started on this work. That is exactly what I wanted, someone who wanted and needed to learn about it all, and someone who could then tell others, especially readers outside China, what he had discovered.

To the many people who freely gave their time to speak with him, I am grateful. These people – including professors, Tiens management, university students, Tiens employees and business partners, consultants and everyday people – provided him with a balanced and informed view that comes across clearly.

I am grateful to Professor Kevin McConkey who coordinated the preparation of this book, and with whom I authored *Achieving Your*

Dream: Words from Li Jinyuan (Li Jinyuan & Kevin McConkey, 1 Plus Books, 2017) from which you will find various quotes at the beginning of the chapters in this book.

Finally, I am grateful to those who take the time to read this book, which gives a portion of my story until now, a sense of the achievements and directions of Tiens, and an understanding of the culture and possibilities of my country within itself and its influence around the world. I say "until now" because, for me and I hope for all of us, there will be more to come. This will come through education and health, through gratitude and respect, and through belief, effort, and good relationships. Those are the attributes that we need to achieve our future as individuals, as businesses, and as societies.

I hope you enjoy this book, and I hope you find something that will assist in furthering your own life and creating the future that you desire.

Li Jinyuan
Chairman, Tiens Group

Preface by Christopher Sheedy

Navigating business rules, relationships, and regulations in a new territory is always a challenge. Even those moving around similar cultures – American or British people who visit an Australian workplace, for example – find they must recalibrate at least a little to do business positively and successfully.

When the cultural shift is a major one, as it is for most during their first (or twenty-first) visit to China, much more than a recalibration around behavioral and procedural issues is required.

There are surface-level considerations, such as where and when to sit at a conference table, how to refer to individuals in formal and informal situations, and the basic differences between collective and individualistic societies. There are mid-level matters, such as the meaning and significance of "face," the influence of politics and the complicated relationships between those of varying seniority and age. And there are deeper issues around motivation, faith, family, philosophy, history, generational attitude shifts, and business purpose.

This book informs around all of these topics and more. Along the way it explains the complicated relationship between Chinese politics and business, dissects the problems China has with its own brand, analyzes the culture and processes within organizations in China, discusses how Chinese businesses view the Western landscape, and outlines the many differences between Western and Chinese business cultures.

Most importantly, to bring this knowledge to life it tells the rich narrative of Li Jinyuan, who came from almost nothing to create a business worth billions of dollars during a period in China that originally offered little to no support for entrepreneurs. The challenges he faced and the lessons he learned sometimes feel as if they are borrowed directly from a movie script, with themes around rags to riches, triumph over tragedy, overcoming insurmountable odds, the individual against the system, loyalty and self-belief, and the courage to never, ever consider retreat.

It all unfolds against the stunning and almost surreal backdrop of the development of modern China.

Welcome to a deep experience of business in China, a journey that not only offers profound insight into a people and a culture, but also tells the compelling story of one man, one company, and one country.

Christopher Sheedy

Acknowledgements

A brilliant story, as I often tell students of my writing courses, is a story of an individual. No matter how vast the subject matter or how broad the topic, it only becomes a truly powerful tale when its narrative focuses on a single person.

At its broadest, this is a book about China. But it would not have been possible without the support and cooperation of the individual who is its focus, Chairman Li Jinyuan. The Chairman has become known internationally as one of China's great entrepreneurs, a billionaire whose business success is matched only by his generosity. My thanks go to Li Jinyuan for allowing me to be his guest, for welcoming me into his business, his home and to his table, and for sharing with me his astounding tale of struggle and success.

Mr Yan Yupeng, Chairman Li's trusted and long-time lieutenant, has also offered enormous support and insight. He is the detail to the Chairman's big picture, the manager who has turned many a grand plan into reality. Thank you, Mr Yan, for your patience, your professionalism, your time, and your calming nature.

Special thanks also go to my constant China companion, cultural advisor, and friend, Professor Kevin McConkey. For offering invaluable support, management, coordination, navigation, and advice (and a whole lot of early-morning exercise sessions) throughout an unforgettable journey, thank you.

From Tiens Group there are so many individuals I want to thank for kindly sharing their knowledge and time, in particular Zhang Ke, Lucie Lu, and Carter Yue, all of whom went above and beyond, and who taught me plenty about China along the way. Also, my gratitude goes to Antonio Albano, Stephen Beddoe, Chukwuka Raphael Chibueze, Cui Huan, Chloe Demai, Dr Frank Deng, Paolo Frana, Sam Fuentes, Gao Weiwei, Geng Jia, David Guo, Dr Han Liansheng, Woody He, Joshua Hiller, Kevin Hou, Carol Huang, Mariel Kuitunen, Li Zhibin, Professor Lin Jiayang, Liu Peng, Professor Liu Shuhan, Yana

Liu, Rick Nelson, Ren Dong, Jose Antonio Sanchez, Richard Shaw, Shi Jingli, Song Xiang, Tang Wei, Tan Shean Yang, David Thevanon, Jason Wang, Leo Wang, Mike Xing, Derek Xue, Jerry Xue, Jane Yang, Yang Xuezhe, Liu Ying, Liang Yong, Jia Yongqing, Michael Yu, Vera Yu, Flora Zhang, Professor Jack Zhang, Jason Zhang, and Jeff Zhou.

Thank you to academics and China experts Bill Banks, Professor Paul Gillis, Professor Robert Grafstein, Professor Ian Kerr, Professor Liu Yingqiu, David Martin, and Professor Sara McGaughey for sharing your valuable time and insight. And special thanks to Associate Professor Will Felps from UNSW Business School, who introduced me to this project.

Thank you to my publishing team at Nicholas Brealey for their assistance in preparing the book for publication, particularly Holly Bennion, Iain Campbell, and Jonathan Shipley.

For reading early drafts of this book and offering invaluable publishing feedback, thank you to Christine Beddoe, Dr Louisa Connors, Liu Yan, and Susan Muldowney.

For sharing knowledge and acumen – and often food, drink, company, and adventures, in Beijing, Tianjin, and Wuqing – thank you to Nancy Cao, Marco Frigatti, Gao Di, Gao Fengwu, Edward Hong, Cecily Huang, Paul Kenny, Leven Liang, Liu Pei, Liu Yuan, Pang Zhiyao, Gaetano Piccirillo, Qiao An, Anne Ruisi, Jenny Sun, Mary-Kate White, Rebecca Zhang, and Zhen Lingyu. And for teaching me to make dumplings, thank you to Sophia Li.

Finally, to my wife and dearest friend Jenny Bond, whose books will always be far more beautiful than mine, and my beloved boys Sam and Ben (and you too, Mick … woof!), thank you for your love and support, for many joyful FaceTime chats, for putting up with my endless absences, and for always inspiring in me a powerful urge to return home. If there's one thing China has taught me, it's that family belongs at the center of one's world. That's where you reside in mine.

I

Courtesy and control

The rhythm of life in a Chinese corporate is governed by strict rules of interaction. These rules are in the way new staff are trained and in the positions in which attendees are seated during meetings. They are in the order that people of varying seniority step into and out of lifts and through doorways and in the way glasses are clinked during drinks. These many rules of interaction are rituals of sorts. Having been cultivated and nurtured for thousands of years they are one of the most important ingredients in Chinese society. Rituals also make up the essence of Confucianism, a traditional philosophy that has had substantial influence on modern-day Chinese thinking and behavior.

At the Tiens Group headquarters, a sprawling, landscaped industrial park at least as large as an average suburb in a typical Western city, a ritual kicks off the beginning of each working week. Every Monday morning at 8am thousands of staff congregate on the steps outside the main office building – an imposing, eight-storey, crescent-shaped structure – and gaze across the expansive grassed gardens with their life-sized sculpture of eight galloping horses, to the fountains and ponds presided over by a grand, three-storey tall, winged-lion statue coated in gold.

Flanking the right and left of the gardens is a phalanx of 110 flags, representing many of the countries in which Tiens does business. Connecting those two parallel and symmetrically perfect lines of flagpoles is a series of five larger ones. The pole in the center, taller than the rest, carries the Chinese national flag. The two either side of the Chinese flag fly the Tiens emblem. The final two, at the same height as the Tiens standards, are those of the United Nations.

It's an important piece of symbolism for the staff who organize themselves in perfectly formed lines down the steps. They gather according to the department in which they work. They stand respect-fully, straight and still, watching as uniformed guards march to each of the central poles to raise flags. As the Chinese flag is raised, the Chinese

Chairman Li Jinyuan

Image courtesy of Tiens Group

national anthem is broadcast from speakers placed around the property. When the Tiens flags ascend the poles either side of the national flag, the Tiens anthem plays and fountains around the lion statue pulse water jets timed to the music. One's country comes first, the imagery in front of them says. Then the company, which exists to serve one's country, is as important as the UN. The rest of the world follows and also deserves respect.

Earlier in the morning of the first day that I witnessed this organizational ritual, large groups of trainees and others had been marching in formation along the streets of the Tiens property. They wore the same colored shirts and their group leaders, playing the role of staff sergeants, marched alongside each "platoon," variously shouting orders and joking with their colleagues. At the outdoor athletics arena, built for the use of employees and visitors with its all-weather, rubberized artificial running track surrounding three basketball/tennis courts, the groups stopped and exercised together, in unison. There was no sitting out of this exercise and, indeed, it appeared everybody was happy to take part. The entire process was quite clearly about the group and not about any specific individual.

I'd been in China – my very first visit – for less than 24 hours when I watched these staff members marching around the streets of the Tiens Park in the cool of an early spring morning. I was out for a run and to my eyes the entire exercise appeared foreign and forced, exactly the type of treatment that would have Westerners falling about laughing, refusing to take part, or perhaps even making an official complaint to the HR department. But it's behavior that I would gradually grow to understand as I developed an appreciation of the history, culture, and philosophies that have combined to forge a nation that, in three short decades, has made an astounding leap from third-world laggard to global economic and political powerhouse.

"Stop thinking like a Westerner," I've been told over and over by Professor Kevin McConkey (let's call him "the Professor") along the way to my development of this appreciation. The Professor is my manager on this project and, more importantly, my cultural advisor. He is a retired professor of psychology, a small, strong, wiry sixty-something international consultant to Tiens, whose physical stature is boosted by his quiet sense of purpose and power.

The Professor, who has worked in universities in various countries including China, listens and observes when other Westerners would instead choose to speak their mind. When asked a question he pauses to think, spending as much time as he needs to formulate a correct and concise response, rather than filling silence by blurting whatever first comes to mind. Because his words are not wasted and his thoughts are well-considered, those around him value what he has to say. The Professor's silence offers great gravitas. I'm not sure whether he was always this way or if he has perhaps picked up such traits from the Chinese people around whom he has spent a large portion of the previous few decades. This silent thoughtfulness or modest wisdom, I will discover, is not uncommon in Chinese people. Indeed, once or twice I hear the Professor referred to as "a Chinese Westerner."

"Stop thinking like a Westerner," he says to me during that first week of an 18-month immersion in the world of Chinese business, when I ask why the staff members on the sports field don't just go off and do their own exercise rather than doing everything in a group. "Stop thinking like a Westerner," the Professor orders when I suggest that I make direct contact with each of the Tiens Group's senior managers, to hurriedly request interviews within the next day or two.

"Stop thinking like a Westerner," he warns, most disconcertingly, as we're crossing a busy road and he realizes I'm considering darting through a gap between a truck and a taxi to safety.

What does any of this have to do with business in China? Originally I wasn't quite sure but now, 18 months later, it has become clear. In this book I will share the vital insights that I have picked up throughout the journey.

Success in business in China, you see, is about so much more than business. It is about relationships and respect, about awareness, about an understanding of history, philosophy, politics, and power. It is about knowing how the collective Chinese mind works, what it desires and what it takes for granted, and how that collective mind is changing with new generations.

Let me begin with a brief illustration, a simple moment in daily life that comes to represent so much more. This is intended only as an illustration, not a rule, and not a representation of the way things always work in China. It was a small experience that helped me to comprehend a different way of thinking.

We're crossing a road in Wuqing (pronounced "Woo-ching"), a thriving, industrial, satellite suburb of the visually stunning city of Tianjin. Wuqing is what is known as a "special economic zone," a potent tool of the Chinese government in its introduction of open-market principles to an ostensibly socialist society.

On the road there are cars, three-wheeled vehicles, bicycles, trucks and dangerously quiet but fast electric motorcycles. There seems to me to be no order amongst the vehicles and their movements. Taxi drivers appear to rely on their horns more than their steering wheels to get where they are going and vehicle speeds vary from Mr Bean to Fangio. The road we're crossing is six lanes wide.

After a rare break in the traffic we make it to the halfway point and that's when I spot the upcoming gap. If I run, I think, I can make it to the footpath on the other side. The Professor sees me making mental calculations and puts his hand on my arm.

"Just walk at a constant pace. Don't change speed," he says.

"Walk? Don't change speed? We'll be killed," I reply.

"Stop thinking like a Westerner," he says, as we wander into the path of two motorcycles. Then the traffic envelops us, digests us and delivers us safely out the other side.

The significance of the moment, which I originally put down to having gotten very lucky, was lost on me for quite a while. It wouldn't reveal itself until several weeks later when I was a passenger in a taxi. I was watching and smiling as the driver leaned on his horn every few seconds. This type of behavior in the West would likely lead to road rage. Beeping one's horn regularly in traffic is perceived in the West as selfish, aggressive, and annoying. But here nobody was perturbed. In fact, those who were honked at would often wave at the taxi driver once he passed.

It made no sense at all until I consciously decided to stop thinking like a Westerner.

In the West, where actions and reactions are most often driven by individualistic thoughts, a beeped horn is angry and hostile. It is saying "Get out of my way" or "Stop driving like a fool, I need to get past" or "Move it, I'm in a hurry." It is about the individual.

Change the focus to a collective society and a beeping horn means something very different. It says, "Look out, here I come," or "I'm over-taking on your left and I don't want to hit you," or "Wait a moment before moving into this lane or we'll have an accident." That's what the taxi driver was saying with his horn, which is why his beeps were being responded to with an appreciative wave rather than a furiously clenched fist.

And what about crossing the road? What do we see in this situation when we stop thinking like Westerners?

A collective society looks after its own. Individuals within a col-lective society naturally and unconsciously feel it is their duty to look after those around them. This is a trait I witnessed time and time again in China, a selflessness and a level of genuine respect for others that is often difficult to find in the West.

So as I'm crossing the road, as long as I am behaving reasonably (don't step in front of a vehicle that has no chance of stopping) and predictably (walk at a constant pace), then drivers will generally look after me. In the West, drivers are looking after themselves, but in China, they are looking after those around them.

In the Western environment, sudden lane changes, unpredictable braking and various angry and dangerous maneuvers are the norm. But the Chinese setting is more forgiving and interconnected, one in which drivers naturally look out for each other and understand that others will look out for them.

This is all extremely simplified and generalized. Even the term "collective" to describe a society is sweeping, indiscriminate, and lacking any real value apart from lazy explanation and assumed understanding. The intention behind the telling of these stories is to demonstrate the importance of trying not to think like a Westerner when beginning to develop an understanding of how China works and the way its people think.

I recently used these stories to help explain the cultural and philosophical difference to a friend who had made a disparaging remark about a young Asian woman who was wearing a nurse's facemask on a Tube train in London. He thought she was foolish to believe that a flimsy facemask could stop her from picking up an illness from fellow commuters. I explained that perhaps she wasn't hoping to protect herself. It was instead likely that she was already ill, perhaps she had a cold. She wore the facemask to stop her sickness spreading to others. There is an individualistic (Western) and a collective (Eastern) understanding of every interaction. In China, society comes first.

Even Western politeness can have an unintentionally negative effect in China. For example, early on in my China immersion, when I was still in full Western mode, I was in a lift with a wonderful young lady whose desk was not far from mine in the Tiens headquarters building. When the lift doors opened I stood back to allow her to alight, but she also stood back for me. I gestured for her to step out, and she did the same for me. I wasn't quite sure what was going on, but I didn't want to be rude so I stood my ground until she eventually exited the lift.

What was going on? In a society where respect and "face" are very important, junior people must always give way to senior people. I was a senior, middle-aged, Western writer who had been brought in to work with the company's Chairman. This meant I was to be respected. The moment I made her step out of the lift ahead of myself, anybody witnessing the situation would have considered her extremely rude. So my own Western politeness could inadvertently lead to her losing face.

Societies are wonderfully complex puzzles that can never be completely solved by an outsider. Even after forty years of China experience, the Professor still considers himself an amateur. But in a society that at its heart is exceptionally forgiving, the outsider can survive comfortably on the basics as they develop a deeper understanding of how the local people think and behave.

Ritual and rhythm. Courtesy and control. In a nation of 1.4 billion people a small issue can get out of hand very quickly. Respectful but unapologetically strong leadership in government and in society is not just desirable, it is an absolute necessity.

This courteous control seeps down through society and it reveals itself at Tiens in several ways. One is in the time management of staff during the working week of Monday to Friday. After the Monday morning flag raising, at 8.30am music is piped through the speakers of the offices, factories and other buildings, indicating to staff that it's time to begin work. At midday and again at 1pm the music signals the start and end of lunch and at 5.30pm it says it's time to stop work and head home. Many staff catch the free company buses to various destinations in Tianjin and Beijing, where they began their journey to work that morning.

This idea may not play so well with the Western notion of lunch being a time that you choose fairly freely, and of flexible working hours. But how many of us work in an office that ensures we take a full hour for lunch? And who can say they would complain if they were told to go home every day at 5.30pm rather than stay late, night after night?

It is a system that has worked admirably for this and other Chinese businesses as they have grown and evolved into internationally respected organizations. It is a way that Chinese companies have remained Chinese after the nation opened its doors economically in the late 1980s, having spent the previous decade decollectivizing agriculture and experimenting with foreign investment and local entrepreneurship.

What is Tiens Group? It is a multinational and ever expanding conglomerate that was begun and built from the ground up by Chairman Li Jinyuan. It is a company that has done business in more than 190 countries. Tiens headquarters office, several of its manufacturing plants, and its R&D facility are in the Tiens International Health Industrial Park in Wuqing, a campus that also contains three international hotel brands, a 7,000-seat, 27,800 square meter convention center, a 3,000-seat banquet hall containing ten luxurious, multifunctional spaces, a hospital, a museum and a zoo – all owned and managed by Tiens – amidst hectares of landscaped gardens, canals, bridges, and fountains.

Broad offerings from Tiens include neutraceuticals, skin and beauty products, e-commerce, hotels and tourism, health management, conventions, luxury furniture, financial and industrial capital, and tertiary education. The company's products are roughly grouped into health products, wellness equipment, beauty, skincare and household products, and are found in over 40 million homes around the world. Tiens has recently leapfrogged many global leaders in the technology and sales arenas by using and developing truly innovative and exciting solutions in the fields of big data, artificial intelligence, and blockchain technology.

For Li Jinyuan, typically referred to by staff as "the Chairman," the road to success has been anything but smooth. Now one of China's most respected billionaires, his is not a rags-to-riches tale, although it's not far off. He grew up in a poor, rural village but his father at least had a reliable income. Li left school at 14 and learned how business operates by working in a state-owned oil enterprise, but was forced to leave this company when he and his father fell out with authorities.

Years later, after launching Tiens and developing the brand's first product, a calcium powder intended to strengthen bones, Chairman Li lost everything. But rather than give up and retreat, he pivoted the company away from the path everybody expected him to take and moved in a surprising and new direction, choosing a business model unheard of in China at the time.

"There are two ways to go. One is to give up. The other is to get stronger, to fight," one of the Chairman's longest serving and most loyal staff members told me. Li, it turned out, was a fighter.

In the next 12 months, around 1995–96, Tiens achieved two billion renminbi (yuan) in sales, and that's when many of the real challenges began.

In this book, Tiens and Chairman Li form our central case study and in doing so create a powerful business context for the reader seeking a greater understanding of Chinese opportunities and challenges. This rich case study, combined with reporting on what has been going on around the business in China and the rest of the world, helps to illustrate the thinking of Chinese businesspeople and companies. It also illustrates the ways in which China is positioning for the future in the context of its continued rise in the world.

Interestingly, the Tiens narrative is also the story of modern China. Tiens is not only part of China and a reflective result of the way the nation has shaped itself into a world power, but the company's development and growth, its foreign policies and attitudes, are a perfect match, in sync with the moves that have been made by the nation that it serves.

I will discover that none of this is by accident or coincidence, it is all by design and all for the long term. The private business, although it has no direct government connections, has been driven by its founder in unison with the directions being taken by the country's leadership, and this is not unusual in a Chinese company. The organization itself, like China, has developed into a powerful empire. Both a business and a nation require strong, long-range and visionary leadership.

Information and insight for this book come from multiple visits over 18 months as a guest of Chairman Li and Tiens. It was important that I spent an extended period rather than attempt a point-in-time snapshot. Over the 18 months I was able to develop deep professional relationships, to see business changes work and not work, to understand important cultural issues, and to achieve an authentic sense of the present and the future for the company, and for China.

In this time I was able to observe, meet, and interview many people throughout China, including business people, industry leaders, students, journalists, academics, and people on the street, as well as many international experts from other countries.

Who am I? I'm a business journalist and author who has run a professional writing company for two decades. I'm fascinated by the intricacies of business around the globe, by the sometimes inexplicable success of gutsy entrepreneurs and the equally confounding failures of major corporates. Over the last decade I have watched as the entire Western world has turned its focus towards China.

Why was I selected to pen this book? That's a fine question, and it's one I asked before the project began. When one discusses China with an expert, a certain level of knowledge about the nation's history, politics, culture, etiquette, and business practices is assumed. Despite a mountain of reading and other research prior to my flying in for the first time, I often found myself lacking some of this knowledge. During my immersion it became necessary for me to ask a lot of questions or risk not truly understanding a situation.

Why was a Chinese professional writer not commissioned for this project? After all, they would be able to speak the language rather than requiring an interpreter. They would also develop a relationship of trust more quickly with the main players in the organization. Finally, they'd be far less inclined to embarrass themselves in a professional or social situation as a result of their etiquette ignorance.

I was told by the Professor that this was exactly why the Chairman had decided not to bring on board a Chinese, or China expert, writer. This project required a person who would ask the sometimes stupid questions that any Westerner would ask, who would experience cultural confusion and seek answers as a result, and who could be thrown into social situations where they would make endless faux pas. Only then would that person be able to write a book that offered true value to a non-Chinese audience.

I was the ultimate guinea pig – a perfect mix of ignorance, insensitivity, and journalistic meddlesomeness.

Ultimately, when I was offered an opportunity to spend time with one of the Middle Kingdom's greatest business leaders, a man who has amassed untold wealth whilst taking the idea of collective thinking to entirely new levels (he has given away over 1.6 billion yuan and wholly or partly funded the building of over 100 schools around the globe), I jumped at the chance to see what was on the other side of the emperor's door.

Now it's your turn. Let's meet the Chairman.

2

Etiquette in a Chinese workplace

"Tradition evolves with social progress. When society improves, then tradition follows too. Traditions must be respected, but they also must change to match the time and the people of that time."

Li Jinyuan

Entering Chairman Li's inner sanctum for the first time is a nerve-wracking experience. He is respectfully and variously adored, revered, and feared amongst staff members on the company's extensive, landscaped property. When they're called to his office, employees quickly don ties and suit jackets then check themselves in the mirror before making their way to the eighth floor. (In the lift the Chairman's floor is actually marked "9A" – there is no eighth floor because a Chinese proverb about fluctuation and uncertainty describes "seven ups and eight downs." Just as Westerners have an issue with the number 13, the "downs" connected to the number eight can give it some negative meaning.) They walk silently through several high-ceilinged chambers containing security guards, artworks, and administrative staff, until they enter the gloriously lavish space in which the Chairman spends his days. The Tiens International Health Industrial Park is the center of the empire that Li Jinyuan built, and he is the leader at its center.

While Western business leaders consider that there is great value in making themselves approachable and available, and in walking the floor as often as possible, in traditional Chinese businesses the opposite is true. A strict sense of structure and knowledge of rank and place is essential. Meetings involving the Chairman only rarely occur in the office of a lesser-ranking attendee, for instance, and the senior member of the meeting has absolute control. Other attendees do not speak until asked to do so and are rarely invited to share opinions, only to listen and receive their orders.

Author Chris Sheedy and Chairman Li Jinyuan in the Chairman's office

Image courtesy of Tiens Group

In a conversation with Frank Deng, I discussed this particular quirk of Chinese business meetings. Deng, who originally trained as a chemist and has worked in research and development with numerous American and Chinese businesses, at the time of our interview managed R&D at Tiens. A self-described "serial inventor" (he has around 30 patents to his name), he grew up in China but has spent most of his career working for American companies in the USA. After earning his PhD at an American university, he spent 20 years with such businesses as GE, GlaxoSmithKline, and Bayer.

Deng laughed when he told me he is referred to by Chinese business people as a "banana" – yellow on the outside and white on the inside. "It means I am Americanized," he explained. "And it's true." Thanks to his time in the West, he doesn't completely understand some of the logic of the Chinese way of business.

"In America we'd have seven different people come to a meeting with seven different ideas, and that can be very valuable," he said. "In traditional China it is an authoritative environment, so people are very unlikely to give their opinion. When people come to a meeting in a Chinese business, everybody sits quietly and whoever is the highest ranking in the room talks. Everybody else listens."

Can that be a good thing for a business, I asked. Does it translate to strong leadership and clear direction?

"Many would say that with this model, you're not using the brainpower of the other employees, you're only using the brainpower of whoever is the highest ranking person in that room," he said.

Surely there must be some benefits, I suggested. After all, military organizations have traditionally thrived on this type of leadership.

"You do tend to end up with fast execution, rather than so many opinions and no decision. The highest-ranking person tells the others which way to go, and they go that way. Here, everyone goes the way the Chairman tells them to," Deng explained. "Sometimes in America, when we had seven different people with seven different opinions, after a three-hour meeting those people would still have seven different opinions."

The Professor agrees. He has had similar experiences in Chinese companies.

"A few years ago when I was doing some work in Shanghai, one young woman was full of ideas," he recalls. "I would say to her, 'Why don't you tell your boss?' She would say, 'I can't do that. I'm not allowed to do that.'"

"I told her I would take some of her ideas to meetings we both were attending and see what got picked up. Of course, some of her excellent ideas were picked up. Even then she wouldn't let me say she had come up with the ideas because that might have caused loss of face for her manager. But she was still pleased."

"As a senior Western person, I was able to speak more than others. Culturally, you often have to wait until you're senior enough to offer opinions. It is about respect, but it is also an inhibiting factor in the business world."

Then there are the naming conventions. No matter how senior an executive in a Western business, I would expect to be on a first-name basis soon after we've been introduced. But that is rarely, if ever, the case in the Chinese business world.

Let's take a step back and talk about people's names in China. Family name comes first and the person's individual name, which Westerners typically refer to as the "Christian" or "given" name, comes second. So for Li Jinyuan, his family name is "Li" and his individual name is "Jinyuan." I am often referred to as "Mr Chris," as Chris is sometimes

Chairman Li Jinyuan and Professor Kevin McConkey

Image courtesy of Tiens Group

assumed to be my surname, and sometimes it is a mixture of respect (Mr) and of my saying it is okay to call me by my given name.

In most social situations in China one is safest to stick with surname, referring to the person as "Mr Li" or as "Miss Zhang," etc. A senior person in an organization is also often referred to, by an English speaker, with their title before their family name, such as "Chairman Li" or "Vice President Yan." Do not ever jump directly to their given name, as one would in a Western environment. It indicates disrespect and is overly familiar.

Sometimes a person will, after a while, ask you to refer to them by their Western or their Pinyin (which is Romanized Mandarin) name. This is a name often bestowed upon the individual by the person who was responsible for teaching them English or another foreign language, and it will sometimes, and only sometimes, sound a little like their Chinese name. For instance, a woman by the name of Lu Xi (in Pinyin) might have the name "Lucie" (French), meaning in a Western environment their name becomes "Lucie Lu" – a merging of their Westernized first name and their Chinese surname. Other times, they may choose a Western name that they like. So a woman by the name of Zhang Xiaoye may choose the English name "Rebecca" and introduce herself to Westerners as Rebecca Zhang. Once you have permission to refer to a person by a specific name then that is okay in informal situations, but you should always go back to the more formal naming convention when in meetings or other more formal environments. Once again, social success in China is always about a show of respect.

While we're close to the topic, it's worth mentioning the importance of familiarizing oneself with basic pronunciation. Don't be the one who speaks to the waiter and orders a Tsingtao beer by saying "Sing-tayo." It is pronounced "Ching-dow." Visit YouTube and watch some of the excellent instructional videos on the basics of Chinese pronunciation. "ZH," for instance, is similar to the English "J," and an "A" can often be pronounced as an "O." So "Mr Zhang" is pronounced "Mr Tsong" and "Mr Wang" is pronounced "Mr Wong". An "E" can be pronounced various ways, so the male name "Peng" is pronounced "Pung" and the name "Ke" is pronounced "Ker." You won't always get everything right, but at the very least you'll be respected for trying.

One further complication in Chinese business meetings is seating, which follows a highly structured pattern. The highest-ranking person sits at the head of the table. When the table is round, the highest-ranking person will sit in the seat that faces the door. Their colleagues then sit down the table in order of rank, with the higher ranks, or the more trusted lieutenants, closer to the head of the table. Western visitors should not be too concerned about all of this, however, because they will almost always be gently guided to the appropriate seat. Just be sure not to walk in and sit wherever you feel like sitting.

In the case of two groups coming together, perhaps from two different departments or businesses, the highest-ranking staff members from each group will sit opposite each other in the center seats of the table. Still here there is an indication of power – although both high-ranking people are opposite each other in the middle, the most senior or most important person typically faces the door.

Then there are other markers of rank in a meeting. The order in which tea is served – and tea is always served! – is the order of seniority, although the most senior person will sometimes indicate to staff to first serve the most senior guest. The order in which people are expected to speak is the same. And sometimes the more senior people will sit on seats that are physically higher than others at the table.

During an interview with one of Tiens Group's managers, which took place in a long, luxuriously decorated stateroom in which it was only practical to use two single lounge chairs at its very end (facing the entrance, of course), our young interpreter squatted (but did not sit) on the floor between and slightly behind us. She could not be offered an office chair as she then would have been physically above her manager. The interview ran for 90 minutes and I can't imagine the discomfort she must have felt, but it was important to her that she did not stand as it would have demonstrated a lack of respect. In traditional Chinese businesses, lower ranking people are rarely offered the same consideration as their more senior colleagues.

Finally, the lower ranked people in a meeting may be expected to speak more quietly than the senior staff. This became a problem for me sometimes as I was less able to hear what my interpreter was saying. I soon learned to ask permission, on the interpreter's behalf, for them to speak up.

But don't assume that every business in China operates this way, that etiquette doesn't vary by region, or that things aren't changing with new generations, especially those who have been Westernized through study and work outside China. A legal professional at Tiens tells me of an experience that neatly demonstrates this multitude of cultures and behaviors in China. At a previous place of employment an American manager, who had worked in China for over a decade, complained light-heartedly to the HR Director that he still couldn't get his head around the cultural idiosyncrasies.

The American said, "I've been here for ten years and it's still a mystery to me!"

The Chinese HR Director replied, "Don't worry, we've been here for 5,000 years and it's a mystery to us, too."

Accordingly, a former colleague of mine from London, now living and working in Beijing and managing the Chinese office of a well-known Western brand, was surprised when I discussed my experience of Chinese meeting etiquette. In his office things are completely different, he said. The young, junior-level Chinese staff, he claimed, are brash and sometimes border on being arrogant. They are completely unafraid to let their opinions be known, even if it makes somebody else look bad. They yell and cry in the office, he said, and they happily cut each other down, whether behind backs or to each other's faces.

I discussed this incongruity with the Professor and he was quick to point out a specific difference.

"They're young Chinese people who have intentionally chosen to work for a foreign brand and they may have already spent a few years studying and/or working in the USA, Europe or the UK," he said. "That takes a specific type of person. They're going to have different drivers of behavior and different experience of the workplace from the very beginning of their careers."

The Professor agrees that China contains many different variations of Chinese culture and many different ways of thinking, especially across generations. These differences can also often be linked to the various levels, or "tiers," of economic, educational, and social change and development occurring across China.

"Think of the way things happen in the tier one cities – Beijing, Shanghai, Guangzhou, and Shenzhen – compared to the tier two cities, then the tier three and four cities," he said. "The way that business is done and the flexibility and rapidity of business differ across the tiers. Then you have a range of types of organizations. Some are effectively government departments. Others are semi-autonomous government departments. Others are almost independent but have government representatives on their Board. Still others are private companies that operate in a traditionally Chinese fashion, and finally there are those that look very much like Western companies."

Where does Tiens fall? It is a private company based on a Western model but operating, in its head office at least, in a traditional Chinese fashion. Although, as we'll discuss, the Chairman is working hard to modernize the business practices, without losing traditional Chinese cultural values. This type of simple understanding is essential for anybody to develop when they're doing business with a Chinese company or brand.

No matter where in China you are or what type of business you're dealing with, the Professor believes it's the little things that matter. He recalls one meeting some time ago that was organized to agree final contract details between a Chinese company and the Western company he was then assisting. In the room were the Chinese company chairman, several of his staff, and his seven-year-old granddaughter.

The young girl was learning English at school and her grandfather thought it would be a good experience for her to attend the meeting. The Professor spent most of his time speaking directly to her, helping her practise what she'd been learning at school, and almost no time discussing the final contract details. "The very next morning the signed contract arrived and it contained all of the terms we'd requested," he says. "The little things really do count for a lot."

"Cultural mistakes happen all the time and every time, unless you are extremely observant of how people respond to you. It starts from very little things and builds up to offending a person at the dinner table by rushing and sitting at the wrong seat, or by saying something the wrong way. Even with a lot of leniency, the Chinese culture is a minefield."

And so I, a beginner with exactly 24 hours of on-the-ground experience in China, entered the Chairman's cavernous office on day one with some trepidation. The Professor had briefed me thoroughly. Sit where you are told to sit. Speak when you are spoken to. Drink whatever is put in front of you. Lose the beard (my wife is still highly amused about the fact that I shaved for another man, speaking of losing face…) because some Chinese people are initially wary of those with facial hair – ancient philosophers get a pass on this. The Professor had told me what he expected would happen in the meeting, but indicated that the content and direction of the meeting would be "up to the Chairman."

Chairman Li was already seated at the head of a hand-made, intricately carved, sandalwood conference table when the tall, heavy doors to his office were drawn aside. The heavily decorated ceiling hovered nine meters above as the Chairman rose from his replica Ming dynasty emperor's chair to shake my hand and indicated that I should take my place at the first chair on his left for our discussion.

The Chairman is a tall man, broad, solid, and triangular, like an ageing professional swimmer, with a handsome, oval-shaped face that suits his heavy brow and receding hairline. His skin glows as if it is scrubbed and buffed on a daily basis. His dark eyes are kind and his smile welcoming, although over the next 18 months on this very same face I will see fierce fury, unrestrained pride, terrible sadness, sour frustration, and more. With a wave of his perfectly manicured hands, the Chairman gestured to the other senior and junior people to sit in specific chairs before turning his attention back to me.

This meeting was about a judgement, of sorts. Would the Chairman be happy allowing me to be a guest within his business for various intervals over an extended period of time and sharing his story with me? Did he sense that there could be a suitable level of trust between us? Was I the right person for the job? I'd been warned that if this meeting didn't go well I'd likely be politely shown around, and then taken to Beijing Capital Airport to catch the next flight out of China.

So I expected a grilling, but what I experienced instead was a wondrous storytelling. The Chairman, through the interpreter, began sharing tales of the business's early days, of intense and almost crippling struggles, of immense achievement and of new challenges brought on by success, of bad guys in bomb vests threatening to blow up Tiens manufacturing plants, of people in other countries trying to "kidnap" his brand, and of government officials, in the early days at least, making every step infinitely more difficult than it should have been. His voice was resonant with color and passion, and despite my complete lack of Chinese, the general direction of each account was clear before the interpreter had even begun to translate.

The Chairman spoke of health and happiness, of disaster and famine. His smile warmed the room and his anger was raw and fierce. When he discussed young children he had met along the way – in his old hometown in north-east China, in the far western region of China, in African nations – and the poverty he had witnessed, his eyes glistened with genuine sadness. I realized I wasn't being sold to him but instead he was selling his story to me and, from a writer's point of view, it was a brilliant one. And by my attention and reaction, he was forming an opinion of me. He was giving to me and, importantly, observing my reaction in ways that I wouldn't come to understand until much later.

He ended by making a reference that was lost for a few moments on many of us, including myself and the interpreter – something about the business, a duck, and flames. Then I realized what he was referring to. Some business people and entrepreneurs say they went through hell before experiencing success, but a private business this size, one that had international aspirations from the beginning, one that was being created during a period in which China was struggling with the idea of allowing entrepreneurs and privately owned businesses to even exist, would naturally have suffered challenges on an entirely new level. The Chairman was saying that he often felt like a duck being barbecued on a spit.

Since the business began, and even to this day, Tiens has been attacked with flames from all directions. The business had suffered a genuine baptism of fire, and from the look of satisfaction in the Chairman's expressive eyes when he brought his stories to a close, it's clear he wouldn't have had it any other way.

3
About Mao: understanding history and perception

"The ancient culture has formed my background and the background
of my country. The influence of the ancient culture can be seen
everywhere, even though not everyone will recognize the roots of the
influence ... We are all part of the river of history. The river flowed
before us and will flow after us."

Li Jinyuan

It's impossible to appreciate the achievements of Chairman Li, the reasons he has made specific decisions and the challenges he has faced, without first becoming familiar with China's history over at least the last 60 years. Such an understanding is also vital if one wishes to fully comprehend the framework in which the contemporary Chinese economy has been shaped, the purpose and drive behind China's political leaders and their practices and policies, and the values and considerations of Chinese people in general.

For instance, early on in my time in China and during the research process for this book I asked several Chinese people a seemingly simple question – why do they, and their nation, idolize Mao Zedong? I was relatively ignorant of the nation's history. I was also influenced by a general view held by many in the West that Mao's leadership, and the social experiments throughout that leadership, were not entirely positive experiences.

Most simply responded with a shrug, indicating less a lack of knowledge and more a lack of interest in politics or history. Others said it was "because he was a great leader," which of course didn't help at all. The closest I came to a meaningful response was when a Chinese university student told me, "Mao made a lot of terrible mistakes, but he did what was necessary to create what would become the new China. He made difficult decisions and created a foundation on which China could be built. He gave us a reason to be proud, again."

That final point – a sense of proud direction – is an important one to understand. Mao, it seems, was an emphatic punctuation point at the end of a long and ugly sentence. He ended a terrible period of suffering and in-fighting, and created a new nation that was united and focused. When Mao died, the nation was in a position from which it could move forward and escape what many now refer to as the "century of humiliation."

So let's take a very quick and selective trip through the mainly modern history of the nation that only in 1949 was declared the People's Republic of China, in order to find out what went wrong and what went right. And please stick with me here – this history lesson will be short and sharp, but filled with vital backstory to help understand the narrative of modern China.

For over 2,000 years, the region we now know as China had been under Imperial rule. As dynasties came and went, borders changed, alliances were formed and broken, and the region, for many understandable reasons, had very little to do with the rest of the world. It didn't need the rest of the world. It was its own empire and enjoyed many luxuries that other societies never even knew existed. Leadership was often good and was sometimes terrible. The influence of specific dynasties ebbed and flowed like tides.

During the Tang Dynasty (618 to 907) a system now known as "Imperial Examination" became widely used across the region. It was a series of tests carried out to identify the best and the brightest young people across the kingdom, so they could be trained in State ideology and become Imperial officials. Essentially it was a nationwide search for China's best public servants, and today it still shapes the nation's attitudes towards the power of education and the importance of excellent people serving in government and State administration.

"This is a society that is insane about education," says Robert Grafstein, Professor of Political Science at the University of Georgia. He and I meet in Beijing between summer classes he is teaching at a leading Chinese university. "Education is a religion, here. Families invest everything they can into their child's education – it is the marker of everything that creates success.

"That is not a recent thing, it goes back a very long time. If you read the Marxist scholars who studied Chinese history you'll see they refer to Chinese feudalism and say that for a long time China did not have a feudal period. Why? Because centuries ago they basically got rid of their hereditary aristocracy. To run the government they installed a bureaucracy that was put in place roughly on merit. That created a tradition where a series of exams was conducted. People would come to the capital and would take excruciatingly difficult exams. This launched the notion of peasants' kids being recognized as potential scholars and being picked out and trained for the bureaucracy. So that created this educational tradition as a source of achievement. Through the bureaucracy, education became an enormous source of opportunity."

In the mid-1800s, during the late stages of the Qing Dynasty (1644–1911), China had been defeated by Britain in the First Opium War and as a result Hong Kong had been ceded to the victors. This loss of independence and the resulting lack of satisfaction with the Imperial leadership caused a series of massive internal rebellions leading to the deaths of millions. Although the government was successful in quelling each uprising, treaties that had been signed with various Western powers after the Opium War defeat heightened the general feeling of loss of sovereignty.

A strong sense of nationalism began to develop amongst the people as the Imperial system and its resistance to reform and lack of societal advancement began to look very old indeed. Answering to an Emperor who considered himself the son of heaven and the divine ruler of the entire world was beginning to wear thin, particularly once it became clear that the Emperor could not defend his home turf from marauding foreigners, such as the British with their advanced weaponry and the Japanese, the traditional enemy of China. Importantly, in 1905 the aforementioned Imperial Examination system ended, which meant for the first time in centuries scholars began to look elsewhere for political inspiration, rather than being schooled in State ideology.

In October 1911 a revolutionary military uprising began, led by Sun Yat-sen, which ultimately resulted in the formation of the Republic of China in 1912. In February of that year, when the child Manchu Emperor Pu Yi suffered a forced abdication, over 2,000 years of Imperial rule came to an end. A provisional government of the Republic of China was formed, but it had no experience, no history of governing, and was weakened by various power struggles. Sun Yat-sen, for example, was quickly forced to hand over the leadership position to army commander Yuan Shikai, who became Prime Minister and would eventually declare himself the new Emperor. Ultimately those around Yuan resisted his power play and he, too, was forced to abdicate just a few months later, in 1916.

Power vacuums and power struggles characterized this period. In the meantime those in public service who were looking to the future were scouring the globe for the finest examples of government. After all, as senior Harvard University scholar William Kirby, Professor of China Studies, pointed out during the outstanding HarvardX course *ChinaX*, the best definition of a republic is "any political order that is not a monarchy." That left a whole lot of political options open for the new republic.

As public servants searched for an answer to the question of the best political system for the new nation, a period of warlords ensued. Old rivalries and border skirmishes from Imperial times began to resurface. In 1919, a protest known as the May Fourth Movement began at universities, then spread nationally in response to the Treaty of Versailles, which awarded Japan increased power over China. The protest succeeded in its aims of ensuring the government did not sign the treaty.

Here it begins to become clearer as to why this period, from mid-1800s to mid-1900s, was considered a century of humiliation. A previously great empire was not only unable to manage itself but was also finding itself increasingly influenced by foreign powers. The Treaty of Nanking in 1842, for instance, saw the British imposing extraterritoriality — exempting their own people, embassies, military bases, etc. from the rule of local law — upon China after the First Opium War. The Americans did the same with the Treaty of Wanghia in 1844 and the Treaty of Tianjin in 1858. All of these were considered by the Chinese to be "unequal treaties." Western powers were seen to be betraying the Chinese by handing ever-higher levels of power to Japan, which began occupying parts of China from 1930.

So it should not have been a surprise to anybody when China looked towards the Soviet Union for governmental inspiration. Western democratic systems increasingly appeared to be life support systems for wealthy titans of industry, set up to produce workers whose role was to provide and protect the wealth and power of the upper class. A true people's republic would require a different approach. The Communist Party of China (CPC) was formed in 1921, but it would be a long, painful, and bloody few decades before it held power.

The fledgling CPC allied with Chiang Kai-shek's Nationalist party, which had taken power in 1927 after several military campaigns finally tamed the regional warlords, and helped the party to form a national government. Chiang quickly turned against his Communist allies, however, sending his army after their leaders and destroying their military bases. The CPC survivors had to retreat to a new guerrilla base in the mountains and caves in the north-west of China, far from the cities and modernity of the coast, where they re-grouped under a new leader, a well-read, one-time library assistant who had been born into a peasant's life on a farm in Hunan Province. His name was Mao Zedong.

Mao's upbringing had offered him an understanding of the life of the common person, the worker, and the peasant. Several times throughout his life he had witnessed, and experienced himself, the cruelty of society as it looked down upon those from rural areas. Those from lowly positions in society were expected to remember their place and to remain in those positions. Those with the wrong type of accent or who suffered an unfortunate family lineage were not offered promising opportunities. Just like Chairman Li did when he was young, Mao had seen, experienced, and understood the gaping chasm between urban and rural, upper and lower. When he became the leader of the CPC during what became known as the party's 1934–35 "Long March" across China to the bleak north-west, he was launched onto a pathway that would eventually lead him to a position to do something about the entrenched inequalities.

Having decimated the CPC, Chiang Kai-shek set about a series of reforms, but his plans were interrupted in 1937 as the Japanese began a series of incursions into China. In facing a common enemy the nation found itself united internally as well as allied with the USA (after the Pearl Harbor attack) in its battle against Japan. By 1945 the Japanese were defeated – not before inflicting terrible suffering upon China in attacks on civilian populations, such as the mass rapes and murders during the "Nanking Massacre" in 1937. The Communist Army played a significant role in the defeat of the Japanese. This helped Mao and his CPC comrades to consolidate power and earn international recognition as a legitimate party.

At the end of this period, as the rest of the world began mopping up after World War II, China could have begun to rebuild. The nation could have begun the process that it eventually put in place in the 1980s to encourage modernization, to open up its economy, to develop industry, and to improve standards of living. But instead it fell back into civil war between the Nationalists and the Communists. As much of the rest of Asia leapt forward, and as even the defeated Japanese began to re-shape their future and work towards becoming an economic powerhouse, China missed an opportunity to become Asia's leader at that time.

That civil war, which caused the deaths of millions of non-combatants, ended in 1949 when Chiang and his Nationalists were forced to retreat to Taiwan. Mainland China was under the power of the Communist Party of China. Mao was the leader of the new People's Republic of China, which was founded in October 1949.

Symbolically, the announcement of the People's Republic of China looms large in the minds of most Chinese. This was the birth of their new nation, the moment they dragged themselves out of the past and began to face the future. This was when the fighting ended and the hard work began. The birth of modern China was not with Sun Yat-sen's 1912 formation of the Republic of China, but instead with Mao's leadership of the people after so many decades spent, quite literally, in the wilderness.

So, by ending the seemingly continuous fighting and bringing the country under the rule of a single, powerful party, Mao was able to achieve what nobody else had done for a century. He had restored a sense of control and direction, given the people a reason to believe that life would finally improve, and created a base on which the future China could be built, with the help of the Soviet Union.

Of course, the Mao period was itself characterized by loss of life, starvation, and attacks on groups that threatened the power of the CPC. The "Great Leap Forward" was good in some ways, but not in others. Collectivized agriculture, where farmers worked together to provide particular quotas of crops to feed the burgeoning masses in the cities, did not always work well. And as public servants sometimes exaggerated crop production figures to earn political favor, the authorities demanded higher percentages of that exaggerated amount, leaving not enough food for the villagers. But during this time the Great Leap Forward also breathed life into certain sectors of industry. The economy, many academics agree, grew during Mao's leadership, if more slowly than was hoped.

It was into this period that Chairman Li was born, and his village was one of those producing food for the cities. Although many villages were managed by corrupt public servants, his was not. In the village in which Li grew up, people were very poor and families went without, but they did not starve.

In 1966 Mao launched the Cultural Revolution, intended to remove bourgeois elements that had begun to reassert themselves after the socialist efforts of the previous two decades. At this time Chairman Li was eight years old and had already recognized the rural/urban divide. The Red Guard groups that sprang up during the Cultural Revolution took over schools such as Li's and promoted party loyalty – and protest against the bourgeoisie and capitalists – over actual education.

This period is seen as a negative one by the West. Internally, the government's management systems were paralyzed as factions formed. Anybody in a position of power could find themselves the focus of the Red Guards. Externally, as other Asian nations such as Japan were fast moving forward, the world watched as Chinese society seemingly turned on itself. And so today's China experts say that the nation's modernization and reform could have begun four decades earlier, in the 1940s, but instead were delayed for half a human lifetime.

Although the West has a different point of view, in China those who lived through the period, through stories they share with their children, generally argue that Mao tamed a wild and dangerous beast that for an entire century had run free. He restored rule to the previously uncontrollable, they argue. Nothing less than an iron fist was required for such a challenge, and Mao had what it took.

A young Tiens staff member, educated in China and in the West, tells me one day that his parents, and many more like them, idolize Mao and often wish they could return to the days when he ran the nation. This makes little sense to me, particularly considering the much-improved lifestyles that Chinese are typically enjoying today compared with just a few decades ago. I ask him to explain.

"During that period, people may lack food and other materials to live but their happiness is very high," he says. "So if I have ten dollars then you also have ten dollars, or maybe even twelve dollars. That was how life was. But today, I may have ten dollars, you may have two hundred dollars and someone else might have two million dollars.

There is a huge gap between the rich people and the poor people. In Mao's time, things were more even and fair."

Grafstein says the reasons for the nation's recent outstanding successes are many and varied. "There are several reasons China has risen to such great heights over the last several decades," he tells me. "One is that they were basically flat on their back by the time Chairman Mao died. That was a tragedy for the country but also a great opportunity. It forced them to look for alternative policies. They looked around and the Asian tiger was eating their lunch. There were countries that they should dominate – South Korea, Japan, Singapore, and so on – and it was embarrassing for them. There was a tremendous impetus to try something new."

What China did well, he explains, was begin to experiment, and this has not been fully appreciated by historians and academics, Grafstein believes. "What is also not appreciated is China's real innovation and change in the agricultural sector," he continues. "That is pretty standard for these economic take-offs. The country was not particularly well industrialized. It had industry but by world standards it was backwards and it could not compete. But the agricultural sector is what essentially funds the investment and the growth. So in the agricultural sector the authorities introduced simple ideas like making people responsible for their own plot of land and giving them the incentive to farm. This led to a huge increase in productivity. The very same people and the very same tools and the very same resources somehow magically produced a lot more."

And the timing was perfect – enormous growth and great leaps forward often come very quickly to nations that have suffered societal destruction, as if a perfect picture can be achieved only when it is drawn on a blank slate. In a book called *The Rise and Decline of Nations* (Yale University Press, 1984), American economist Mancur Olson argued that one of the preconditions for countries with strong economic growth is the extent to which institutions – government and regulatory institutions – are destroyed immediately prior to the start of the growth period.

"Look at the Japanese take-off after World War II. The old interest groups that previously had a lock on society were blown out of the water and only then could massive growth occur. The German miracle, too, is not an accident, according to Olson. It came not despite the destruction of World War II but rather because of it. Under Chairman Mao that destruction took place on a massive scale, cultural and otherwise, and it created the foundation for the nation to take off," Grafstein says.

Knowing all of this, the comment from the extremely bright, young university student – "Mao made a lot of terrible mistakes, but he did what was necessary to create what would become the new China. He made difficult decisions and created a foundation on which China could be built. He gave us a reason to be proud, again" – makes absolute sense. Mao ended the century of humiliation, took strong and permanent control of the world's largest population, and set a nation's people on a new path.

After many "terrible mistakes" Mao put into power a people's political party that still rules and which has turned China into one of the economic leaders of not only Asia but the world. And China seems well positioned to expand this role as this century unfolds, through leadership, and the efforts of its people.

4
Cultural Revolution:
Chairman Li's boyhood

"For most things in life a clear pathway does not exist before you move forward. As you move forward, you create the pathway."

Li Jinyuan

During the years leading to China opening up to external investment there was a harmony in Chinese society that brought out the best cultural values in its people, Chairman Li says. After the opening, things changed. There were greater opportunities for those willing to take risks, but in such uncertain and uncharted waters those risks sometimes had terrible consequences. Li experienced this first-hand when, early in his career, one of his own actions caused his father to lose his job.

Li was born in 1958, at the beginning of Mao's Great Leap Forward. As a period it was characterized by the collectivization of farming and various movements intended to remove any social stratification and create a truly socialist society. As discussed, although some of Mao's policies resulted in difficulties across China, he is a hero of the people as his actions ultimately united the nation, restoring pride and a sense of hope and direction after a century of mismanagement.

The village in which Li's family lived, outside the city of Cangzhou (pronounced "Chong-zho") in Hebei Province, was called Li Long Tun. It had been named around 600 years earlier after one of Li's ancestors.

When Li was a young boy all consumables, from rice to water to cooking oil, were supplied to families on a quota system. The number of members of a household and their ages were taken into account to figure out that household's share. But as collective ownership of farming land, melting down of farming equipment for scrap metal, and various agricultural experiments had decreased crop production, many rural towns and villages ran out of food. Also, as previously mentioned, although each rural collective had a specific amount of food to provide to the cities, some officials exaggerated their production figures, meaning their quota of food bound for the cities rose while villagers went without.

Towns that were well managed by honest officials came through the period in better shape than others and in Li Long Tun, the Ministry of Food official was Li's father.

"My father's duties were very important because they concerned every family's food," Chairman Li says. "Everything that could be consumed was planned. My father was known to be a good person. Each time somebody made a request to him, my father would try to meet that request, try to help people. Even if it was a difficult request he would try to meet it. Therefore in the village and in the surrounding area he was very well known.

"When my father learned someone from the village was sick he would always try to send food or equipment to them and often he would visit them. In China that is what we call 'being heartful' to people. It is helping people proactively without the people even asking. That is how my father was."

The young boy had been allowed to visit, with his father, the city of Cangzhou several times. Most rural villagers did not have the right to stay in the city. Their role was to work on farms and provide sustenance to those in the metropolis, not to create more mouths to feed.

The visits to the city filled the young Li with unease stemming from a deep sense of unfairness. Even in this Communist society rifts were developing between the haves and the have-nots, the urban and the rural.

In his own village Li witnessed varying levels of wealth, including his own. He understood that he already had more than most around him simply by the fact that he wore leather shoes that were laced, comfortable, and free of holes, as well as pants that were clean, well-fitting, and held up by a belt.

Nowhere was the social difference between urban and rural more profound, in the eyes of a young boy, than in the schools. The city schools he had visited were based in modern buildings boasting clean tiled or hardwood floors. They contained modern teaching equipment he had never seen before. Furthermore, each class had its own room and a dedicated teacher, as well as a desk and chair for each student.

In Li's school on the edge of the village in a rickety, decaying building with holes in the roof, cracks in the wall, and a dirt floor, students spent much of their time being taught the art of street protest by the Red Guards. Rather than becoming knowledgeable in mathematics, languages, the arts, and history, school students particularly in rural areas instead learned to protest and to criticize wealthy people. They were told their job was to be part of a social movement. Students at his school, Li realized, were victims of the time.

"The time" was the start of the Cultural Revolution, a period of intense socialist nationalism, beginning in 1966, intended as a purge of bourgeois and capitalist elements from society. Violence was encouraged and Red Guard factions led the charge across the nation.

If he had not seen the conditions in the city, Li says, he likely would never have realized that his own life in the village was anything less than normal. He would instead have observed the people around him, the hardened farm families in their ragged clothing and with holes in their shoes, and seen a nation doing what it needed to do to develop.

But he did recognize the gulf between city and country and even as a young boy, Li recalls, he knew that a lack of education would damage the chances of the rural people for generations to come.

"I saw the wealth and the way people lived in the cities," he says. "I saw the good food they ate in the cities and the clean water they drank and the lives they led. The difference between the city and the village was like the sky and the earth.

"I told myself that one day, if I had the capacity, I would try to give a better life to people living in the village, to improve their living conditions. Because there is only a dirt road, when it rained people could not get out of the village. The drinking water was not clean. Education was crucial to the future of the children, so the school needed to be as good as those in the city."

Those born in the Cangzhou region were famously resilient. An almost six-meter tall iron statue of a lion, known as Tie Shizi, represents their toughness. It was cast in 953 and is considered a key cultural relic. Legend says that after a decade of natural disasters, including constant flooding, the town of Cangzhou had been brought to its knees. A local sculptor spent three years creating the iron lion to protect the town. The day it was completed, so the story went, the disasters ended and the town was able to thrive again.

Cangzhou's iron lion – Tie Shizi

All children born in the region were taught the legend of the iron lion. They were told its courage ran in their blood. Li says he regularly thought of Tie Shizi as he planned his future. There is no coincidence in the fact that statues very similar to Tie Shizi exist in key places around the Tiens headquarters, and the modern symbol of Tiens is a winged lion flying skywards.

Li left school at the age of 14 for a job with a state-owned enterprise called Hebei Oil. His first few years were spent traveling around Hebei Province with a survey team, conducting exploratory drilling to discover new oil fields.

"I was 14 years old when I began this work," Li smiles, warmly. "Can you believe it? Today it would be considered child exploitation!

"This is how I met a lot of people and had new experiences and learned and saw new things. I am a very social person and I like meeting people. At the time I was able to meet people from mainstream high society of the time, including leaders. I was able to meet them and become friends with them. I learned a lot from them."

The main lesson from this period, the Chairman says, was around communication. "You learn how to behave with people and how to interact with people," he says. "It is very important to learn how to behave and how to be a good person. It is important to learn how to feel other people's feelings."

Actually, it was this idea of "feeling other people's feelings" that landed him in hot water. After seven years Li was transferred to administrative departments within the oil business, one of which was HR. Many of the workers who had been brought in to work for the company were far from their families and Li could see they were suffering as a result. He also knew that happy workers were productive workers, so Li decided to do something about it. He would provide them with special foods and other products that would help to brighten their lives.

Li began trading the organization's oil for other products such as seafood, bicycles, beer, chocolate, or meat. Sometimes he'd do several trades, first traveling to the seaside to trade oil for fish, then to another area to trade the fish for something else the workers desired.

"If you traded the right products at the right time, the more you exchanged, the more good things you got," he says. "You got to make more value with each trade.

"During that time my life was defined by one word, 'swapping.' I swapped from one place to another place, traveled here and there, and used the resources I had to get hold of the goods that I needed. All the time I was thinking about how to maximize what I had, in terms of quality and quantity. Often I would exchange something for another product that I did not need, but I would swap that somewhere else for something that I needed. The thing I was always looking for was food – sugar, salt, cooking oil, and tea – the things that are important in daily life. So I would travel a lot and all the while I was thinking about how to maximize the quality and quantity of what I was receiving.

"This taught me very basic business strategy and spirit. It gave me business skills and was my teacher around negotiation and how you interact with business partners and how you need to sense the feelings of others and know what they are thinking in order to negotiate. You need to touch people's hearts when you negotiate."

I'm interested in what he learned about negotiation, and whether the idea of negotiation differs in Chinese society compared to how it might be considered in the West.

"Negotiation, in the end, is between people. For success you must know how the other person is feeling, know what is in their heart," he explains. "Their desires are a precious source of your success. What is in the heart is a motivation for you and for them. So spend some time to find out what they want out of it, rather than only concentrating on what you want."

As Tiens has so far conducted business in around 190 countries (it is aiming to reach 220 within the next few years), the Chairman has negotiated with people from all types of companies and cultures. Do people in the West negotiate differently, I enquire.

"All humankind shares this similarity," he says. "Whether you are dealing with Chinese or Africans or Westerners, we're all sharing the same similarities. The skill and the method will be the same. Human nature is the same.

"Negotiation is not a battle. The lesson I have learned and use today is that courtesy and manners and personality are very important. So it's about how you identify one person's personality and character and what kind of courtesy or manners you should use when you're dealing with them. This is a lesson I learned and I still use it today. I use this knowledge and experience in dealing with people to get the right outcomes and benefits."

In what areas of the business does he use these lessons in negotiation, I ask. Hiring of staff, he tells me, has a lot to do with negotiation.

"It helps a lot in choosing great people for the business," he explains. "I have to choose people to work with, people I can trust. I have to figure out what is in their heart to find out what sort of person they are.

"If people do not respect their parents or are not obedient to their parents, for instance, I would not choose them. If they don't know how to interact with others then they cannot have trust from others. They can be effective but in the long term these people will not be reliable because they are selfish. They will try to be smart in a bad way. If you don't know from a broad perspective how to treat people well, you don't have life value. You cannot have a long-term perspective and vision and you cannot be grateful. Once again, it's important to know what is in their heart."

Finally, I wonder whether he negotiates less now he's at the top? Does he personally still need to negotiate, or does he simply tell people what he desires? I imagine that anybody in his position would make their wishes clear and expect them to be actioned, as opposed to entering a negotiation.

"Actually it is the other way around," he corrects me, gently. "When you're at the top the chances to utilize such skills and knowledge are greater. When you're at the top you utilize and learn more, and I would extend it to another level by saying the lessons in negotiation that you learned previously are not as important compared to when you are the executor. Learning is an endless process. In order to keep developing and keep innovating you have to keep your learning up to date. If you stop learning and stop practising what you're learning, then you no longer innovate and therefore you no longer lead."

And so as a young man Li traveled the length and breadth of China, negotiating and trading. But there were strict rules around what could be sold and what could be traded. The government's trade and customs office in Cangzhou developed an interest in what Li was doing and began accusing him of being a speculator. Instead of fighting the accusation, Li approached the officials to explain to them exactly what he was doing, how it worked, and who it benefited.

The approach worked. A grudging respect developed between Li and the officials. Eventually Li and the then chief of the trade and customs office became friends.

In fact, Li was making a lot of friends in government and the business world. The trading work introduced him to various business owners, managers, and officials all over China. It also demonstrated to him once again the chasm between opportunities for people in rural areas and people in cities.

"I saw that in villages many people had skills that could take them to the city but most were not allowed to move to the city unless they were brought in by an organization for a specific job," he explains. "Even then, it was only the one person allowed to move, and not their family.

"Rural people could not improve their lives even though they had good skills. In the cities it was easier to have a normal lifestyle but in the villages it was difficult. I very much noticed this difference. People from the villages wanted to be in the city but it was so difficult, it was like trying to reach the sky."

Li could never change the rules, but he thought he could do his bit to bring families together with the workers who had moved to the city. He began bringing relatives of the company's staff to Cangzhou by changing the residential registrations (known as the "Hukou," or the formal location of residence) of those families from rural to urban, on behalf of the business.

"These workers were suffering because they were far from their families. If their families were able to join them they would feel happy and calm, so they could focus on working and contributing to society. So I found a way to bring them together," he says. "That was a mistake.

"The *People's Daily* published news about it. In Hebei Province I was criticized by the media. My father was also criticized. At the time there was a political struggle going on between the Left and the Right. So when this happened his political enemies used it as an excuse to put him down. He was fired by the Communist Party."

Because of this event, Li was forced to leave Hebei Oil. Apart from the loss of face, this was not an entirely bad thing, he says. It was liberating, motivating, and it presented an excellent opportunity for a young man with the courage of an iron lion.

5
Saving face

"If you give respect, then you are given respect. If you expect respect, but do not do things in a way that is fair to or that respects others, then you will not be given respect. Very simple really, to be honored with respect you need to be fair and show respect to others."

Li Jinyuan

Having already touched a few times on the topic of saving and losing face, let's now dive a little deeper into why it's important and what it actually means, particularly in the Chinese business environment.

"Face," in China, can be simple or complicated. Starting from the simple end, face denotes respect. It is about treating others the way you prefer to be treated and protecting others from any form of embarrassment, ill will, conflict, shame, negative perceptions, or unease. In doing so, you're also protecting yourself from being seen as a person who does not respect others.

From the complicated end, it is about an entire sense of social scale and social prestige. It relates to a person's sense of their own place in society, and one's sense of the place, or social rank, of others. Face involves never over-estimating or strongly stating one's own importance, particularly in the presence of those who are senior to you in age or experience. It is about having the expected level of knowledge and behavior, respecting a person's modesty, and always being polite. It is about not speaking negatively behind another person's back or appearing as if you believe you have more worth than you do.

Some have described face to me as being a little like a credit card – the more value you have on the card, the more you can afford to spend. But you must always be sure that you don't overdraw your funds. You must keep your account in balance and you must always ensure nobody attempts to steal your funds.

At Tiens I see the idea of face revealing itself in many ways. It is in the order of things at meetings with the greatest respect shown, for better or for worse, to the most experienced or senior people. It is in the respect that staff members show to each other. Sometimes within Tiens I enter into conversations with junior staff about somebody who has clearly made an error, or who is not performing well in their job. The person I'm speaking with never lets on that the individual we're discussing is anything but a fine, upstanding employee.

Most surprising for me, though, is the careful and almost choreographed way the business lets people go. Nobody is ever "sacked," at least not according to the way the business chooses to present it. The ex-employee instead had to leave to take care of their sick partner ... they discovered a new opportunity and decided to see what comes of it ... they are enrolling in full-time education to further their career. Once the person leaves, they are not discussed in a derogatory fashion and nor are they referred to fondly, they are simply not spoken of at all. This protection of the person's reputation goes all the way from the Chairman to the lowest staff members. Nobody steps out of line in the upholding of that person's face and everybody understands their duty.

"It is important to appreciate that the Chinese are incredibly tolerant of foreigners who breach these rules around face," the Professor tells me. "Chinese people will guide foreigners, particularly when they know that they are new to a culture. However, if it is a foreigner who has been around long enough to know things, the Chinese will be a little less tolerant and will see it as a loss of face by that person if she or he breaches the rules. It is an important aspect of the culture that you tend not to do things that cause anyone else to be embarrassed or to lose face. There tends to be a modesty and a politeness and that can even get tricky when you're paying compliments."

If you pay a compliment to somebody in China, the Professor explains, even if you just say "That was a very good discussion we had," they will likely say, "No, no, I was just doing my job." They won't say it was a bad discussion, they are simply being naturally modest. In the same way, if you tell a clearly intelligent person that they are very smart, they will typically say they are very ordinary.

"Certain reactions are just about modesty," he says. "But on the flip side, if you do something that causes somebody to lose face then it actually damages you, the person who engages in that action."

The Professor tells me of when he was in a meeting between an American business and a Chinese business. After the meeting, and based on the discussion notes, the Professor wrote a draft agreement on behalf of the Chinese business and emailed it to the senior American executive. The executive responded to all who had attended the meeting with "a blistering email that basically said I had gotten it all wrong.

"The email was incredibly aggressive, which is possibly acceptable in American business culture," the Professor says. "I knew that I did not have to respond. I didn't have to do anything at all and I did not have to say anything to my Chinese colleagues. The next time I spoke with the senior Chinese about dealing with the American company, all they said to me was, 'Kevin, he is not a good friend.' That meant the deal was not going to happen. The American thought he was showing his power and his prestige by going on the attack. But my Chinese colleagues knew that what I put in the draft agreement was exactly what we had all discussed and agreed to. When he attacked me for getting things wrong, he should have realized that he was attacking those senior Chinese people. He thought he was getting the upper hand by going on the offensive. What he did was screw up any chance that he had."

Of course, the Chinese did not respond in an openly impolite manner and nor did they do anything that might damage the American's face. They allowed the already scheduled next meeting to occur. But at that meeting, when the Americans showed up, there was not a single senior Chinese person in the room. There was only the Professor and a junior Chinese assistant. The senior Chinese people had become unavailable because of other "urgent business," and the potential business deal did not proceed beyond that meeting.

Face is not just about rudeness, though. Humour can be difficult, particularly for those from Western cultures where putting oneself and others down humorously is an important part of the bonding process. Walking into an office, slapping a colleague on the back, and saying with a smile, "How's it going, you ugly bastard?" might elicit laughs and friendly banter in a business based in Sydney, London, or New York, but use the same approach in Beijing or Shanghai and you're likely to experience a very different response.

Clearly nobody in their right mind would ever employ such an approach in a stranger's office, no matter where they are in the world.

But the important point is that the natural inclination toward the use of a certain type of humor tends to be a reflex action, as I discovered one day.

As I was returning from lunch, I walked toward a group of young men I had come to know well over the previous few months. They were having a relaxed conversation, laughing and enjoying themselves. One separated from the group, pointed to my striped shirt, and said, "Mr Chris, you look handsome today." Before I even knew what I was saying, I blurted, "I know! That's why I'm thinking of becoming a supermodel!"

I laughed. They didn't. I tried to backtrack by attempting to explain sarcasm and Australian, self-deprecating humor, but the damage was already done. He had offered a small and therefore acceptable compliment on my choice of shirt and I had responded by blowing the budget on my "face credit card." And it all happened in a split second.

"The most important thing for every Westerner to remember is that we're not and will never be Chinese. In my observation it is frowned upon to brag or to appear overly immodest," the Professor says, offering no comfort whatsoever. "If you big-note yourself then that will not end well. The loudmouth is more accepted, up to a point, in Western companies. But in China, the loudmouth will be frowned upon."

Cultural signals and indicators exist during every moment of every day in Chinese business and social life, even when it seems time to relax. Soon after I first met the Chairman, the Professor and I were invited to his 59th (Western tradition) or 60th (Chinese tradition) birthday party. As you'd expect, it was a lavish affair for which many people had traveled some distance. The entire party of over 100 selected guests sat together around a single, colossal, circular table. Minutes before people began to arrive, women in stockinged feet were walking upon the table, liberally layering the vast tablecloth with fresh flower petals. After arriving, the Chairman, of course, sat in the tallest chair, facing the door.

He made a speech, thanking his guests and introducing me as the person who was writing this book. I didn't realize at the time, but this mention in the Chairman's speech meant I was a very important party guest. Somewhere between the twelfth and fifteenth courses of fine Chinese cuisine I spotted a friendly face across the table, a young man from the Chairman's office whom I'd met on several occasions. I wandered around with my drink, to say hello. The junior staffer from the

Chairman's inner office stood quite tall, but when we went to clink our glasses he purposely dropped his glass below the level of mine. I thought I must be doing something wrong, so I quickly moved my glass below his … and so began a race to the bottom. When we finally clinked it felt as if the glasses were somewhere around knee level. I knew I'd done something wrong, but was not sure what. So I asked the question.

When clinking glasses after a toast or simply in greeting, it was explained, the junior or less important person in the relationship always holds their glass below the level of the more senior person. It's a small but important sign of respect and deference, and I enjoyed utilizing it for the rest of that evening – holding my glass in a neutral position and letting others tell me where I stood.

Indeed, subtle culture issues are present in every interaction and relationship you can imagine. Many say this is why Chinese people are good listeners rather than big talkers. They would rather ask a seemingly gentle question than make a statement, because there is so much risk in what is elsewhere regarded as a simple relationship. I see this when I stand in front of 30 students at a highly selective university in Beijing and ask various questions about their country's history, future, politics, and more. Although they have all volunteered to be there to answer questions, the long silences followed by very quiet – but exceptionally well-shaped – responses are unexpected for somebody used to the brash openness of young Westerners.

I have mentioned several moments when the Professor told me to stop thinking like a Westerner. One in particular was his response to my request for the email addresses of several senior executives within Tiens. My intention was to contact them directly and ask them to meet with me so I could conduct interviews for this book, as I do on a daily basis in my career as a business journalist. That approach, the Professor warned, could damage face. The way communications typically happen in a Chinese business is through junior people, via assistants of assistants, to eventually (and not always quickly) get a message through to their boss. Intermediaries are used as tools of communication throughout typical traditional Chinese businesses. Direct communication is rare. I am told that intermediaries do a lot of the communication in personal relationships in China, too.

During another conversation the Professor told me that "Yes" in a Chinese meeting does not necessarily mean yes. "It means, I'm not saying 'yes' or 'no',", the Professor said. "It means, 'I am being polite and I do not wish to offend you.' People from Western companies are often confused when, after a meeting, nothing comes back from the Chinese business. But the explanation is simple. The Chinese are saying 'no' through not responding, but they are doing so in a way that does not cause you any loss of face."

I experience this several times during interviews when, for instance, I am shown a PowerPoint slide or document as a senior manager explains a particular strategic decision. When I ask if I can have a copy of the slide, as any journalist would do, I am never told "no." The manager simply says "yes" and moves on. I never receive a single document, and I come to realize that "yes" is the manager's way of saying, "Sorry, but this document is confidential within our business. You can see it for the purposes of this discussion, but I will not send it to you."

That's not all that is different between the Western and Chinese business consciousness. In order to illustrate a point, several people tell me that if you hold up two fingers and ask a Western person how many fingers you're holding up, they will immediately say, "Two." Do the same with a Chinese person and they will not answer – they will typically ask questions. Considering this more deeply, it possibly reflects the Chinese importance of genuinely understanding a situation, rather than responding immediately based on an assumed understanding.

In his book *The Way in Chinese Business* (Tuttle Publishing, 2013), author and adventurer Boye Lafayette De Mente said this type of behavior is absolutely connected with face. The concern that Chinese have about losing face, or causing others loss of face, he explained, created a deeply ingrained habit of responding in an indirect manner, rather than committing more directly in their responses. The challenge is instead to find ways to work with and around it, he recommended. Be patient, persistent, and approach the problem from various angles, but always gently and with respect.

I can't begin to imagine the loss of face suffered by Li and his family when, during his younger days, he caused the loss of his father's job by attempting to reunite rural families with their urban fathers and husbands. The incident was reported in newspapers, undoubtedly as a crime against the State. However, it does explain a little of the motivation behind the persistence, creativity, and tenacity that saw him take risks in business rather than fail, and push onward rather than admit defeat.

How does a Westerner navigate the complicated issue of face in Chinese business and society? Go back to the simplified version mentioned at the beginning of this chapter and simply treat everybody with great respect, particularly those senior to you.

6

The fall: Tiens' darkest days

"When you really have a true goal to which you are committed, and
you know how to be grateful, then you know how to be confident. The
dream, the gratitude, the responsibility and the sense of mission keep
fear away."

Li Jinyuan

In May 2015, Chairman Li and the Tiens Group took around 6,400
of their highest performing staff members and distributors, from all
around the world, to France. The four-day vacation cost US$14.6 mil-
lion and broke several world records.

To accommodate the Tiens party, 140 hotels in Paris were booked
for their stay as well as 4,700 rooms in 79 hotels in Cannes and Monaco.
Transport required 84 aircraft, 146 chartered buses and a series of trains.
Luxury Parisian shopping mall Galeries Lafayette opened exclusively for
the Tiens visitors, as did the Louvre Museum and the Moulin Rouge.
In Nice, a busy beach-side boulevard was shut down so the group could
set a new Guinness World Record for the largest human sentence – it
read "TIENS' DREAM IS NICE IN THE CÔTE D'AZUR" and
involved 6,262 people dressed in blue and white.

This was all in celebration of the 20th anniversary of the Tiens
Group, but actually it was the 20th anniversary of the re-birth of Tiens,
which came after the company's near-death experience.

But first, how did a young man who started his career with a relatively
lowly job in an oil business come to have the knowledge and resources
to launch his own company? Actually, it began with his unemployment.

After the scandal involving the reuniting of rural families in the
early 1980s, Li was forced to leave Hebei Oil. By then he had learned
all he needed to know about several specific aspects of business, particularly negotiation and trading, to launch out on his own. He made

In 2015, a total of 6,262 Tiens Group staff set a new world record in Nice, France, for the largest human sentence

Image courtesy of Tiens Group

the decision to go into business for himself and was soon trading goods across many provinces of northern and eastern China. He was on his own, a freelancer spending most days on the road behind the wheel of a truck.

Each region of China that he entered, Li realized, was at a completely different stage of social and economic reform. Only a few years earlier, in 1978, the then leader of China, Deng Xiaoping, had introduced the first of two stages of reform. But rolling out a program of change across a nation of such geographic and social breadth was a massive undertaking for the government and success would take many years. This first stage involved the decollectivization of agriculture, the tentative welcoming of foreign investment into the People's Republic of China, and the go-ahead for entrepreneurs to develop their own businesses. Li was one of those early entrepreneurs.

"Thanks to Deng Xiaoping's changes, my father was able to take back his public position," the Chairman says. "During many years my father had suffered a lot, but in the end he was a very optimistic person. He was very resilient and strong.

"My own business grew as the south of China was more open but the north was quite closed. Everything was still very highly controlled by government in the north of China. The whole country was under the same government but people in the south did not have the same mentality as those in the north. In Hebei Province they were very conservative. So there was a real difference between the north and the south.

"When Deng Xiaoping opened China, what he was doing was well accepted by those in the south. But in places like Hebei and Tianjin, even when the government tried to open China, being an entrepreneur was still considered 'speculation.' It was still forbidden in some places."

In fact, Li had to be very shrewd in his trading. Although the government had given the go-ahead for entrepreneurial activity, one could still face crippling financial penalties for running a business in certain parts of China. Entrepreneurship was not for the faint-hearted. It required nerves of steel and relationships of absolute trust in every business activity. It also needed perfect timing. Li says he lost money on several deals, but that "business is like a war zone, so you have to accept some defeats."

In a rented van, Li would take beans and rice from Cangzhou to the south, where he would trade them for other produce and products, sometimes agricultural tools that he would trade back to the north. Other times he would carry raw materials in one direction and return with processed products. Most of his deals, the Chairman says, were related to food because that was what people most needed.

The Chinese agricultural system of that time was still finding its feet so, as with every market in which demand outstrips supply, there were enormous price differences for specific products between regions. If you could make exchanges that undercut the general market, the Chairman explains to me, and if you could time those exchanges to perfection, then there was money to be made.

"In order to do this sort of business you needed very good connections and you needed courage," he says. "If you were afraid of potential outcomes then you would not have the courage to do what I was doing. You also needed to know which products in each region to buy. I had the knowledge and the experience and the connections. That is how I traded and that was the beginning of the huge business that is Tiens today."

But there were quite a few twists and turns in between the trading entrepreneur of then and the billionaire of now. After a few years on the road Li had amassed a small fortune, which he spent on the development of several small factories in his hometown. One was a flour mill that employed just under 20 people. Another created protein-based products, mainly fish food, and required around 80 staff. A third produced small plastic goods and had a workforce of around 35. In these factories he employed local people from his hometown as well as several family members.

So in his first entrepreneurial role Li was trading other people's goods. In his second, he was producing his own goods, but relying on others to distribute and sell them. This introduced entirely new problems.

"Most entrepreneurs like myself were relying on another party for success," he says. "For instance, I produced products, but I relied on another party to distribute those products, and they relied on another party to retail them. Often I didn't even get my money back. If you rely on others then you're passive. I wanted to change passive to active. I wanted to be in a position to control the market."

In 1993, while the factories were still in operation, Li traveled to Tianjin with the intention of becoming a real estate developer. But the more he researched this real estate plan, he says, the less passion he had for it. It offered little of the independence he was seeking.

"I discovered that if you want to work in real estate you had to be very close to the government," he says. "You needed an interdependence with the government and it is very complicated. I saw that issue and did not feel it was a good fit."

Instead Li began developing an idea he'd been mulling over for several years.

In the field of Chinese health products, which was closely connected with Traditional Chinese Medicine dating back many thousands of years, there were several product lines focusing on the health of the heart. Others claimed to boost brain function. But there was very little in the market that assisted the strengthening of bones.

"As soon as you're born you need calcium," the Chairman says. "When you are a young child you need calcium and when you're old you need it. When you fall pregnant you need calcium. It is something that everybody needs throughout their lives."

There was a gap in the health market that Li intended to fill. All he needed was a technical, high-end product that, thanks to China's strict pharmaceutical production and marketing laws, would absolutely have to do what it claimed to do.

The Chinese Academy of Sciences had around that time made a patent application for a method of producing calcium powder for human use. Li purchased that patent, as well as a piece of land in the Wuqing Special Economic Zone, to begin the process of ensuring the calcium powder could be manufactured in a mass production environment.

Eight months were spent building the factory and office space, and it was all hands on deck for the construction. To keep money coming in, Li had begun trading building materials. Everything needed to construct that original building was purchased and managed by the few staff he had brought on board so far. Some of these original employees, such as the Chairman's right-hand man, Mr Yan Yupeng, camped on the site during the building process.

"When I first met the Chairman I saw he had a great vision to create new things, and I was attracted by that," says Yan, a gentle and softly spoken executive and one-time electrical engineer who seems the very embodiment of inner peace – he appears to float rather than walk, and settle like mist rather than sit.

"In that period and before that period, all the Chinese people working in national, government-owned companies worked in those companies for their whole life. Nobody changed their work or their workplace. I wanted to get out of that national kind of company, but it was still a very big decision to jump to the Chairman's company. Everybody thought it was a big risk. Nobody did things like he was doing."

During the construction period, Yan says, the Tiens team hired people to do most of the building work but bought all of the materials themselves, from the earth-moving machines to the smallest things, such as pencils.

"It was a very hard time," he recalls. "I did a lot of physical work on the site to move products and materials around."

Early in 1994, when the building was finished, Li and his team purchased the various machinery required to produce the calcium powder. In total, for the building, machinery, and raw materials, around 20 million yuan was spent. Li sold his flour factory to help bankroll the venture, but the production process would ultimately fail.

Mr Yan Yupeng, Chairman Li's trusted and long-time lieutenant

Image courtesy of Tiens Group

It began with crushing the bones of cows in a refrigerated environment. A cool temperature was vital to the process as heat broke down the proteins that were vital to the final result.

"After we crushed the bones we had to create a biochemical reaction," Yan continues. "Then we used a vacuum function to dry the crushed bone, also at a low temperature. The process was very inefficient and required the addition of salt, which created an awful taste in the product that had to be stirred into water and drunk. It also left dregs in the bottom."

So although the patent-pending process had been reported a success in the laboratory, real-world, large-quantity testing was a failure. This failure was only the beginning.

The team went back to consult with the researcher who had sold them the patent, but he had disappeared. The Tiens staff also discovered the researcher had sold the same patent to another company working in the same field, which likely explains why he went to ground.

"Actually, the patent was sold to three or four businesses," Yan says. "One was in Inner Mongolia, one in Hebei, and another elsewhere.

The contract was limited to certain criteria and conditions including duration – it was only valid from 1993 to 2002. Plus there was a restriction for the area where we could use the patent and ours was for the northern part of China. We were restricted to just a few provinces. But the patent holder sold it to a company in the same area as Tiens, in Hebei. That was a conflict."

Without a working patent or a patent holder, Li was on his own and back to square one. Too much had been invested to give up at this point, so international experts were invited in. Another 4.8 million yuan was spent on consulting fees, new machinery, and R&D until a high-quality calcium powder was finally produced in September 1994.

Then came the truly challenging part – getting the product to market.

The Chinese retail scene at the time contained no chain stores and no big-brand pharmacies or supermarkets with integrated distribution networks. There was no single retailer to target to cover various regions, no brochure that went out to households that offered space in which consumers could be educated about a new product, and no single deal to be made to ensure the product was on the right shelf at the right time in front of the right customer across a number of stores. Once again, Li was at the mercy of others, particularly distributors and small, often unreliable, retailers.

Li had no money left for advertising, but without a marketing campaign a new product stood no chance. Li and Yan went to a Commerce Bank for a loan but were refused. They then went to an Agricultural Bank and were offered 600,000 yuan. "This was not enough for real advertising," Yan smiles. "For that we needed perhaps six million yuan."

To this day, Yan says, Tiens still repays the kindness of that particular bank manager who took a risk by lending Tiens an amount of marketing money. "To pay him back for giving us a helping hand during those very critical moments, we put all of our daily transactions, to a total of about 100 million yuan, through his bank," he says. "Today we are distributed among several banks, but we still collaborate closely with that particular bank."

In retail outlets, the products that were heavily advertised were put on shelves at the eye level of the customers, a pattern seen around the globe. Those that were not supported by expensive advertising campaigns had their products relatively hidden on lower shelves, and often in an unexpected part of the store.

Tiens had seven million yuan of product distributed into stores in ten cities, then spent the 600,000 yuan marketing budget in one month. Yan was right – it was not even close to enough. That month, after the advertising spend and after the 25 million yuan cost of the R&D process, Tiens took in revenue of just 19,000 yuan.

The silver lining of this menacing cloud was the anecdotal evidence coming from certain retailers that the product was developing traction within its still tiny market. Few customers were buying the calcium powder, but many of those who had made the purchase were returning for more. It was an encouraging sign, a single ray of light in an otherwise dark and dire environment. And things were about to get worse.

For nine months the Tiens product sat on shelves and trickled out to new and returning customers. As sales slowly grew to a still unacceptably low level (the business couldn't even afford to pay its energy bills, Yan says), Tiens' revenue actually decreased as a result of a disastrous policy in the Chinese financial world known at the time as "triangle debt."

In the triangle debt system, a default to one business could be caused by another company's default that is completely unrelated to them or to their own performance. Imagine that a retailer owes money to a distributor but cannot honor that obligation. The distributor is then allowed to default on their payment to the manufacturer to recoup their loss, potentially sending the manufacturer bankrupt.

At the time, the Chinese business world was filled with triangles. Defaults were being passed on to unsuspecting parties and some of the main perpetrators were large, state-owned enterprises. In some of these organizations, irresponsible management, lack of skills, and an attitude that the government would always back them up no matter their results had led to serious performance issues. The triangle debt environment meant their pain was passed on to other, better-managed businesses. The problems rippled out through the economy and Tiens was not immune to their effects.

"So there is a supplier of raw materials, there is Tiens, and there is the shop," the Chairman explains. "Tiens takes raw materials to make the calcium powder. The calcium powder goes to the shop and is sold. But instead of paying back Tiens, the owner of the shop is in another triangle and so he uses the money to pay back his own triangle. It was like a social and economic cancer. It was very hard to resolve this vicious situation."

The triangle debt problem was solved in the late 1990s by Premier Zhu Rongji, who made the difficult but ultimately correct decision to let massive, badly managed State-owned enterprises (at the time, often referred to as "zombie firms") and other similar businesses fail. In other words, he released the State's grip and let the market take control. But this all came too late for the struggling Tiens, which after nine long months in the market had exhausted its financial means.

Everybody involved, even the most senior staff, thought the end was nigh. It had been a worthy experiment but had failed, they believed. If a great product could not sell at retail then there was no other option but to close up and move on, everyone thought. Even Yan, Li's most trusted lieutenant, felt grave doubt about the future. Everybody wavered, except Chairman Li.

"We had a product and we needed a market, and if we didn't sell in that market then we were not a success. So we had product success but we did not have market success," the Chairman says.

"Everybody surrounding me, including my staff, my friends, my family members, my parents, my uncles, everyone told me to just give up. But I never thought of giving up. They told me that it was too hard and it would affect my health. They told me to cherish my life rather than chasing this project. But the harder it became, the less I wanted to give up. The more difficult it was, the more I wanted to keep going."

There was a very positive side to it all, the Chairman says.

"Without all of the suffering I would not have elevated myself, so I should be grateful and thankful for the challenges," he explains. "I did not have a choice. I had to grow up, otherwise I would not have survived. When there is pressure, there is fight. This experience helped me to grow up and to train my spirit to fight back."

7

The phoenix: Tiens rises from the ashes

"Difficulties are just drizzle, they are not a storm. Drizzle never stopped anybody from moving forward."

Li Jinyuan

Li Jinyuan did not come to Tianjin to fail.

In order to apply for a new business permit, the business manager first had to register a projected annual turnover, because China's economy was planned. In much the same way that a publicly listed business in the West will seek projections of earnings from each of its departments before providing the market with forward estimates, the Chinese government sought similar figures from new and existing businesses to keep a finger on the nation's financial pulse.

When Li the entrepreneur first arrived in Tianjin in 1993 and applied for a business permit he registered for a company that would turn over 28 million yuan annually, after a period of incubation. A business of this size was almost unheard of in Tianjin. State-owned enterprises worked with enormous balance sheets but individual entrepreneurs claiming to have the ability to create a business on such a scale were few and far between.

"I had to make an earnings promise to the government and then they put Tiens in their plan," the Chairman explains. "If you do not meet your goal it means you do not meet your promise and it negatively affects the business of government. This planned system was so specific to China that it was difficult for any other nation to understand, but actually it was a very special page of history in China."

In requesting and receiving such a high level of business license, Li believes he was creating a new challenge for himself. "The license is a promise that in the future your business will make this much money and if you don't, the license will be taken from you," he says. "In making the application I was creating a new path.

"I wanted to create a very large company. Also, at that time it is only when you register such a huge amount that you can gain trust from society. People think that if you ask for that much money then you have something and you're confident. But you have to believe, and you have to have a good basis for your confidence."

Confidence was never an issue. As to whether he "had something," that would be for the market to decide, and considering the nine months his calcium powder languished in retail stores, that decision was not coming quickly enough.

After that nine-month period, the business ran out of money and banks refused any further loans. But there were still bills to be paid, including staff salaries. Most expected Li to admit defeat and close the business down, but in his own mind he was far from quitting. For a short while though, he admits, Li wasn't quite sure of the direction forward.

"During that period, sometimes I could not sleep," he says. "I was feeling so alone at that time. I will never forget that period. There were rumors in society surrounding me and there were great social pressures on me. It felt as if I had no way back."

Beyond midnight on one of many sleepless nights in 1995, in the early spring when the evening outdoor temperature hung below freezing, Li felt as if his mind was "burning with stress." He made a decision that has become legend within Tiens – Li took a swim.

He didn't head to a luxurious, heated, indoor pool. Instead Li stripped down and submerged himself beneath the icy, still waters of a lake, known as Swan Lake, near his then home. When I ask around (admittedly, I doubted the veracity of this account), I discover that cold-water swimming is not an uncommon thing for Chinese people to do when they feel overwhelmed, confused, or simply troubled. It represents a cleansing, a new start. He swam to the opposite shore and, in doing so, washed off the demons that had been troubling him. As he made the return lap, Li let go of his past, he says. He forgave himself for any mistakes he had made so far. He cooled the fire burning within his body, and he decided on an entirely new business plan.

"It was very cold and it was maybe two o'clock in the morning," he recalls. "I jumped in and started to swim from one side to the other. Why? I needed to cool down my mind. I was thinking about whether I should give up or not. It was an existential moment in my life."

As he swam he thought of a letter he had received a few weeks earlier from a customer. It was a seven-page missive from a mother and her adult son, both experienced in the field of direct sales. The document outlined why they believed Tiens' Nutrient Super Calcium Powder would be the perfect product for direct sales as opposed to traditional retail.

Every individual had a different need for such a product, but traditional retailers simply put the product on their shelves, the letter explained. Shop assistants had no specialist knowledge of how the calcium powder worked, of why somebody might use it, or of the scientific process behind its production. They didn't know the product's story and they were unable and typically unwilling to promote the calcium powder to individuals. From a direct selling point of view though, when a trained distributor was face-to-face with a client it was the perfect opportunity to customize and individualize the value of such a product.

"That is how I ended up choosing direct selling," the Chairman says. "I chose to give up on the traditional method of selling through shops. I chose to be free from the vicious triangle debt. We would give our products directly to our distributors, our direct salespeople."

In doing so, Li realized at the time, he would finally be rid of the other parts of the market that had let him down. He would be in control of every part of the process, from R&D and production to handing over the product to the final consumer and collecting revenue.

Now all he had to do was ensure Tiens survived for long enough to be re-shaped for the new business model.

The first issue was money, and he knew where this might come from. Despite warnings from others of impending failure, he sold the protein and plastics factories that still operated in his hometown. When this didn't provide enough to pay all debts and ensure salary security for his staff for at least a few months, Li sold his Mercedes-Benz. Once all costs were accounted for, Li had just 1,000 yuan left for his own family.

"The hardest moment for me was when I realized I could not even pay the salary of my employees," the Chairman says. "I owed them a salary. I was the boss. How can I drive my Mercedes-Benz if my staff are not being paid? I am accountable for that. I am the boss and the entrepreneur so I need to face risks, but my employees should not have to. When the company is facing risks, the creator should be responsible for those risks."

The car that the Chairman then purchased so he could attend meetings and make sales calls was a beaten-up, red A85003 Xiali, one of China's cheapest domestic cars. That automobile now sits proudly in the Tiens Museum on the company's Wuqing property, yet another famous and pivotal part of the Tiens narrative.

"I was confident about the future and knew that one day I would be able to buy a better car," Li says. "I had a bigger dream."

Once staff salaries were taken care of, Li turned his attention to convincing his senior managers of the value of his idea. Few had faith in the direct sales option. In fact, according to Yan, the Chairman was completely on his own in that regard.

The other health supplement companies in China used the traditional mode of selling through bricks and mortar stores, so why shouldn't Tiens, the managers argued. Several staff left the business, convinced there was no way the new idea could work.

"The senior people did not want to do it," Yan says. "They just saw what was on the surface level, but the Chairman had looked more deeply."

In fact, the Chairman had sought advice from international experts on direct selling. The industry was virtually non-existent in China at the time but he tracked down those who were involved to seek information and insight. He interviewed people within the industry in various other countries and read as much as he could on the topic. One major challenge was in figuring out a direct selling compensation system for the company's "distributors," the people who would be doing the actual selling.

How did Yan feel about the direct selling idea at the time? "Bad idea!" he smiles. "I was influenced by the traditional business model and I thought even if we had difficulties we could find a way around them. Everybody was against the idea. The Chairman was on his own, but the truth is always in the minority."

The Chairman remembers the situation slightly differently, claiming that "one or two managers" agreed with his point of view. "The rest did not like it," he says. "Some people left immediately and some others stayed with an attitude of wait-and-see.

"I had to communicate clearly with the team. I told them my dream. I had discussions with them and spoke very frankly. I invited them to dinner, to eat together. During dinner I discussed it with them. I spoke about the project clearly, point after point. I educated them."

This is something the Chairman, and most Chinese people, consider to be very important – the act of sitting and eating together.

In shared meals, as in all parts of Chinese society, there are rules and rituals. Several times I, along with the Professor and other individuals and groups, am invited to have lunch or dinner with the Chairman to discuss various issues, or to simply listen to his ideas. To ensure I don't make too many etiquette errors during shared meals, I learn that the easiest and safest method is to observe others.

Such banquets typically begin with numerous plates of food in the middle of a round table and empty plates and bowls in front of each person. In this situation there are several important points to note. First of all, be aware of which chopsticks or other implements are for serving and which are for eating (and know how to use chopsticks, or simply ask for a knife and fork which is quite okay for Westerners to do). Second, feel free to ask which types of food should go into or onto specific bowls or plates, or simply watch what others do. Finally, don't stack your plate with food at the beginning, but instead take small amounts of one dish and finish that before moving on to the next. In the West, diners often load up all of their meal at once, filling their plate before beginning to eat. But in the East the meal is slower and taken in small portions, meaning the person who fills their plate will appear gluttonous.

The Chairman tells me it was very important for this original discussion with his team to have occurred in a restaurant rather than a boardroom. To convince his management team to follow him in a completely new and unexpected direction, into the world of direct selling, communication was everything. A shared banquet was the perfect environment to ensure such communication.

"It was important that I took the management team to dinner because when you sit at dinner to discuss something important, it affects the way you socialize and deal with people. It comes back to courtesy and manners," he says. "When you sit at a banquet table and share your thoughts with people, it is easier to see who shares the same feelings as you and who agrees with your ideas and your proposals. It is easier to see other people you can work with and who will be speaking with the same voice and having the same ambitions and visions. You can identify the partners who will help you move forward and who will work together towards the ultimate target."

At the dinner the Chairman could see which staff members bought into his idea and truly believed and trusted the plan, and who had hesitations or doubts. "I could see that some were simply trying to figure out their own advantage from it, to get something out of it for themselves," he says.

At the table the Chairman encouraged people to voice their concerns about the idea. At the end of that first banquet, Li knew where people stood and who would back him up, as well as who was still hesitant and required more effort to convince.

"I also saw there were certain people I simply could not work with," he recalls. "That is why I went to dinner and had this discussion with the team. There were about 15 people at the banquet and after I first explained things I had perhaps four or five people on my side, so I only had one third of them. I continued to have discussions with the others. Many simply had a lack of knowledge about direct selling so I explained and communicated very clearly. That constant, clear communication was crucial.

"But I only communicated with those who had real talent for what we were doing, those who had real ability and capability. I didn't waste time communicating with anybody who would not be able to help within the business. At the end, two thirds joined into the new business and one third left."

Li continued to push ahead. He sent a small group of staff members on a journey around China to collect the company's unsold product from shops and markets.

Chairman Li Jinyuan with staff on the original site of Tiens Group

Image courtesy of Tiens Group

In mid-1995, once all of the product was collected and warehoused, Li had to apply for a direct selling franchise license. Few in China had even heard of such a thing, and when he visited the trade and customs office he was told that it did not exist in their system.

"I spoke with an official from trade and customs, a Mr Lu," the Chairman says. "I started to communicate with him, to educate him. I discussed it several times with him. In the beginning he was reluctant, but I kept trying and kept trying. Then we began to understand each other's positions. I tried to meet with him every day."

In fact the Chairman inserted himself into Lu's life until he received the license he needed. "When he was at home I knocked on his door and I even talked with his family members, in the name of advocacy," Li smiles. "I tried to gain their understanding so they would start to help me to convince him. That's why in China we always say that if you are resilient then nothing is impossible. Spirit and resilience touch hearts. In the end, Mr Lu was touched."

On 3 August 1995, Lu created a "Direct Selling" business category in the system of China's trade and customs office. The license meant Tiens was free to trade. That date is now celebrated each year as the single most important founding day of the modern business that is Tiens.

Li established branches in many cities throughout China and at the same time developed a close friendship with Lu who, the Chairman says, "is precious to the history of Tiens."

"I told Mr Lu that with his help I was able to create a franchise that exponentially developed my business and that I control the distribution commissions," the Chairman says. "So I give my product to the distributors and by the end of the month they give the profit back because they want their commissions. So I have control now. Unlike the triangle debt situation, I was in control of the commissions and the profit.

"We had developed a mutually beneficial relationship between the business and the distributors and we were all motivated to further develop the company. Business doubled, then tripled, and so on. I wanted it to happen fast, and it did."

In fact, during those first 12 months from mid-1995 to mid-1996 under the new business model, Tiens boasted receipts of 2 billion yuan, at the time equal to about US$120 million.

As the business grew furiously, expanding from region to region throughout China, Mr Lu from the trade and customs office realized he had his work cut out. Li was opening satellite offices and employing distributors at an astonishing rate and each needed their own authorization letter from the government. Lu ended up writing 1,756 authorization letters for various Tiens offices and people across China.

"He agreed to do this because I was able to help him understand and appreciate how it worked," Li says. "That is why I always insist on the fact that you need to have great interpersonal skills, communication skills, and advocacy skills in business. He made exceptions for me, which meant all of these franchises could be created in one year. Lu and I created a new industry in China. He was a very open-minded person."

In August 1996, 12 months after Lu's first authorization letter, the Chairman organized a ceremony to honor Lu. He invited senior government people from Tianjin, various officials from across the country, government leaders from Beijing, and members of the People's Congress. Around 2,000 people from across China attended.

Three years after arriving in Tianjin and 12 months after many expected him to declare bankruptcy, Li finally tasted true financial success. However, money is only one ingredient in real success, he says. Once he'd ensured his business had a future, Li's mind turned to other dreams. He thought about the beginning of this journey of achievement, when he was eight years old and walking along a rutted, dirt road to the shabby school building. Finally he had the means to make a difference.

"I wanted to keep the promise I had made to myself," he says. "I took 9 million yuan from the company to complete my childhood dream."

Li returned to his village and funded the building of a new school, as well as the proper surfacing of the road throughout the town, and upgraded the water management infrastructure. His parents still lived in the town and Li's father volunteered as a construction worker on the school building.

"When I made the choice of direct selling, many people did not agree with me," the Chairman says. "I suffered so much and was so alone, especially when some of my family members gave up on me. But my parents taught me love and openness and tolerance without asking for anything in return. My dream to improve living conditions came from their teaching."

8

What's the problem with direct selling?

"Failure begins with selfishness, jealousy and arrogance, but success always comes from wholeheartedness, comprehensiveness and social commitment. Those who concentrate on the narrow view, on themselves, are less able to achieve their dreams."

Li Jinyuan

Direct selling suffers an image issue, but I have never been sure why.

When I was first offered this immersion into a Chinese multinational I was concerned about the fact that the major part of the business was involved in direct selling. My feelings of negativity toward the industry had something to do with pyramid schemes, although that didn't seem to make sense. After all, direct selling by reputable, respected firms such as Tupperware, Avon, Jeunesse and Herbalife was just retail minus the bricks and mortar storefront, right?

Today, Tiens is launching and re-launching its brand in several territories around the globe. Some of these regions have traditionally been problematic for Tiens and some produce very little revenue. Two of the most difficult markets have been the USA and Australia. My immediate assumption was that the markets were simply not receptive to the idea of direct selling, but this is incorrect. These markets successfully support several other major direct selling brands, and the USA is the birthplace and home of direct selling.

As I looked more deeply into the industry's history and its various guises around the globe, I realized the story of the rise, then fall, then rise again of the direct selling industry provides a fascinating framework for the Chairman Li and Tiens narrative. It illustrates some of the management, policy, and international business challenges he has had to navigate as the organization grew beyond China's shores. It also offers a fine case study in brand building and brand damage in various markets, particularly the USA. Let's quickly dip into this backstory, some of which was shared by 20-year industry veteran Stephen Beddoe.

When I first met Beddoe he had just been employed as the General Manager and CEO of Tiens Australia and New Zealand. Twelve months later, he became the Chief Operating Officer of the Tiens Group's entire global direct selling business.

Over two decades ago, Beddoe began his direct selling management career with a major American direct selling brand, in South Africa. The business was setting up in that market and Beddoe, as Director of Sales and Marketing, played a central role over nine months in its successful launch. More important, though, was his next role for the business – starting from scratch in India.

Because of the regulatory environment in India, nothing but raw materials could be imported. Beddoe had to identify suitable manufacturing plants, convince those third parties to invest in new equipment, have those factories refurbished to meet the business's standards, and organize visits from the USA by technical experts to ensure everything was of the quality required. Then, of course, he had to get distributors on board. A "distributor," in direct selling talk, is a salesperson who, depending on the remuneration model, receives an income that is typically related to their volume of sales and to the number of other distributors they bring into the business. This part of the company exploded in popularity, with over 20,000 people signing up every month in India.

Somebody in the US head office decided the business would only need a single distribution hub, a warehouse in the center of India. They didn't realize that India's logistics system at the time, in 1997, was "almost stone age," Beddoe says.

"The distributors were all buying starter kits costing about US$100 each, and we had stocked up enough of these kits to take care of initial demand," he recalls. "Then we began receiving complaints from the distributors that they were not receiving their starter kits.

"The CEO of the logistics company had assured me he had a nationwide network and could deliver to anywhere in the country within seven days. I made a trip to the warehouse to find out exactly what was going on. We had convoys of trucks leaving the warehouse full of business kits. We stood at the gate waving them goodbye. Then we never saw them again."

Nobody ever found out where those kits ended up, Beddoe says. Business in an underdeveloped nation was going to be more difficult than he originally thought. He then had to set up a number of smaller distribution centers around the country.

"The business went down and the business went up and the business went down and the business went up," he recalls. "By the time I left to emigrate to Australia in 2008, almost ten years after we launched, the business would have been tracking at about US$400 million and growing at a compounded annual rate of about 23 percent."

At the time India seemed like the Wild West but, Beddoe assures me, that was nothing compared to what had happened in the USA in the preceding decades. In America, the home of direct selling, business practices had developed that eventually gave an entire industry a bad reputation.

As distributors were independent salespeople who took a cut of profits from products they sold and also earned commissions on sales by newer distributors they brought into the business, the industry came to be known as "multi-level marketing" or "network marketing."

This was a healthy model, providing motivation for the originating business to research and develop high-quality products, incentive for distributors to sell products, and increasing levels of income for those who were doing the most recruiting and who therefore had the extra responsibility of training and supplying those recruits. As long as quality products were being sold and distributors received the bulk of their income from the sales of those products, then the model was sustainable.

Word of mouth and storytelling proved to be a powerful sales tool. Rather than products sitting on shelves in shops waiting to be purchased, distributors who were trained in the art of storytelling sold the products directly.

"In the early days of Amway, for example, they had a great demonstration of a cleaning product that distributors would do with shoe polish and a handkerchief," Beddoe says. "They would rub shoe polish on their hands and then they'd put a bit of the detergent on their hand and wipe it off with a handkerchief. Their hand would be cleaner than it was before. Then there was a mess on the handkerchief, so they'd dip that into a solution of water and the detergent, and it would completely remove the stain from the handkerchief. It was like a magic trick. Voilà!"

This storytelling side of direct selling is vital for success. As Beddoe speaks, I think back to an experience in an artisanal homewares store in Wuqing just a few days earlier. As I looked for a gift for my wife, I found a shop assistant who spoke English and asked her about a specific product, where it was from, and what was behind its design. She had no idea, and I made no purchase. In a shop a few doors down another salesperson introduced me to mooncakes, telling me where in China these particular ones were from, who made them, and what their traditional purpose was in Chinese culture. Of course, I bought a box full. Bricks-and-mortar retailers could learn a great deal from the storytelling skills of direct selling distributors.

But distributors had to be trained in these skills. As the industry grew, various direct selling businesses began making tapes for new distributors to listen to, as it was impossible for businesses to organize face-to-face or group sessions for all of them. The businesses would charge a nominal amount to each recipient to cover production costs of the audiotapes.

"As the industry began to evolve, 'covering the cost' became 'making a little bit of a profit,' which was not so bad," Beddoe says. "People were prepared to pay for a quality education, to further their development. So it became a very small side business within these companies."

And you can see where this is going. A direct selling model is perfectly sustainable as long as good quality products are being sold and as long as people within the chain are receiving an income mainly from the sales of these products. But suddenly there was an entirely new profit center that began to grow. Some direct selling businesses were earning up to 30 percent of their revenue from the sales of these motivational tapes and educational seminars.

"These companies were raking in hundreds of millions of dollars in profit with very little outlay," Beddoe says. "They were charging US$10 to US$15 for a tape, and they would mass produce the tapes in commercial production units. Some also wrote and sold their own books, creating what they believed was a foolproof system of success. If you followed this system, they claimed, you would succeed. If you did not then you were unteachable. Why would they spend time on your development if you're not going to invest in yourself, they said.

"People would sign up for one-year or two-year contracts on their credit card to receive this stuff, which supposedly was going to change their life and make them rich. Well, that became a problem, because the only way these companies could sell more tapes was to recruit more people. So they were recruiting people to put bums on seats in convention halls and in stadiums, not to actually sell products."

Suddenly pyramid schemes, which relied on the recruitment of people rather than the sales of quality products, were alive and kicking.

Where did Tiens sit during this rush for easy cash? Very early in the company's push to go global, governments around the world were beginning to crack down on pyramid schemes, so even if they wanted to join in, they were not able to do so. Chairman Li and Mr Yan tell me their intention was always to control the training of the distributors, hence the enormous hotel complexes on the company's Wuqing property, and the groups of distributors from countries across the world marching around its streets early in the morning, exercising, laughing, and bonding. Tiens has always offered free training to all of its distributors, so there would be no point in anybody even attempting to charge for the same service.

How are the Tiens distributors compensated? To understand this, Beddoe says, you must understand the three major compensation models in direct selling around the world. There's the Amway and Herbalife "multi-level marketing" or "networking" model. This involves distributors receiving a cut of the profit on what they sell, then a smaller cut of the profit on what is sold by distributors they introduce to the business.

Then there is the Tupperware/Mary Kay/Nutrimetics/Thermomix "party plan" model, where a distributor organizes a party at somebody's house and a group of people are brought together, products are demonstrated, everyone has an enjoyable experience, people place orders, and the host receives a gift based on the value of orders placed. Other people see that gift and want one, too. The distributor asks them to organize a party at their house and to invite their friends, and the pattern continues.

Finally there is a hybrid of parts of both of these models, and that is where Tiens sits. "Tiens uses what I would say are the best practices of both," Beddoe explains. "The selling model is what I would call 'group sales.' It's not necessarily a party in someone's home, but it's a group of people that you bring together. It could be in an office or in another setting. It's group selling, which is a very efficient way of being able to tell your story to a lot of people at once, as opposed to just doing one-on-one selling.

"This hybrid of the best of the party plan and the best of network marketing is becoming almost the norm for new direct selling companies. The more successful companies today have found a good blend and balance of both. And the education side of it is very carefully and tightly controlled by the business, so distributors cannot go out there and charge whatever they want for training, because the company provides it free of charge.

"A lot of companies in direct selling now have what I would say are very good reputations. But the damage done decades ago, the way the industry was tarnished, will likely take generations to undo."

Actually, the Tiens remuneration model varies from territory to territory around the world, in accordance with the laws of the countries in which it is operating, and continues to evolve as regulations, technology, and business practices in the industry change. In China, for instance, direct selling is strictly regulated to allow only one level below each distributor, to protect against businesses creating an endless pyramid scheme. Other territories allow three levels. Social media and globalization are changing the landscape and introducing new challenges for regulators, but responsible direct sales businesses that hope to exist for longer than a few years put effort into ensuring their business model and remuneration schemes are sustainable for all involved, no matter the platform or territory.

Yan says the direct selling business model actually made absolute sense once the senior managers thought deeply about it and how it would make Tiens a success. Health products, after all, should be promoted person-to-person to meet the specific needs of the consumer, rather than left to sell themselves off a shop shelf. The business model boasts low operation costs and requires little advertising. Most important, it allows a business to control every step of the process, from design and production through to handing over the final product to the consumer.

Of course, once the company's products gained massive popularity through the direct sales networks, bricks-and-mortar retailers suddenly came knocking on Tiens' doors. But nobody answered.

9

How the Chinese do business differently

"In these times we should all take a worldview and try to understand our place in and contribution to the world."

Li Jinyuan

There are three important reasons that business is carried out differently in China, compared with the West, Chairman Li tells me. These three overarching themes are simple and unavoidable, and they set the tone for the way businesses behave in the Middle Kingdom.

The first reason, Chairman Li says, is the fact that China offers greater business opportunity than many other major markets. Commerce in general is mature in the West. This means markets tend to respond quickly and efficiently to change. Competition is common and fierce. Markets are saturated and consumers are well served, no matter their need. In other words, in the West whatever people want, they can get. The biggest opportunities for businesses, both start-ups and established organizations, come from disruption of industry. Clear business opportunities are rare and advantages tend to come mostly from unseen angles and from previously unimaginable technologies. But in China, it's a very different case.

Thanks to the economic reforms that have occurred as China's markets have opened up over the past 30 years, the Chinese business world enjoys many completely new opportunities that are magnified thanks to the size of the nation's population. China's businesses, in what is a relatively immature open market, boast many more new and visible opportunities than any market in the West, the Chairman believes.

"Because we're a large country with a huge population and we have great government support, we enjoy a lot of opportunities in our market," he says. "The future of the Chinese economy and the Chinese market is very bright. Also, in the upcoming five to ten years, the Chinese government plans to massively reduce the poverty of the

Chinese population. The result will be an increase in the market force and market capacity, which will contribute to an even more positive market situation in China in the future."

The second reason, the Chairman points out, is that entrepreneurialism is now a natural state in China. In the West, risk and innovation have been somewhat stifled by the still-recent memories of the global financial crisis, by a tendency toward protectionism in some countries, and by ongoing market fluctuations. The interconnectedness of markets – the fact that a sneeze in Portugal can cause a full-blown flu in South Africa – also means businesses are more wary and typically more risk averse than ever. Once "risk" becomes a dirty word, entrepreneurialism and innovation go out the window.

China is at the opposite end of that scale. Businesses are still learning to succeed. In this environment of experimentation, encouraged by government and sustained by responsive markets where demand typically exceeds supply, risk is simply a part of doing business and entrepreneurialism is encouraged.

"In the Chinese markets, the Chinese entrepreneur has passion and motivation to create new things and to move forward," Li says. "As of today, this passion and motivation are greater than what you would find in the West."

The third reason, the Chairman emphasizes, as is clear from his own business success, is that momentum is a powerful force.

"China used to be a very poor country with a very poor population," he says. "But look now at what we have succeeded in achieving so far, at what we have achieved over just 30 years. It may be more than what Western countries could have achieved in 300 years."

The speed at which China has been flung effectively into the elite of the economic powers has been astounding and has had a lot to do with close, constant, and consistent management by an unchanging government. That's not going to change in the future. In fact, the lessons the government has learned along the way are only going to add to China's economic management capabilities.

"Look at central government policy today," Li says. "They have a five-year strategic plan and a ten-year strategic plan. They are focusing on innovation and on the Chinese brand, to upgrade and improve the quality of the Chinese product."

The "Brand China" issue has always been a vexing one. The "Made in China" label is still, in many territories around the globe, perceived as a negative. Despite the fact that many of the finest quality products and the most advanced technological items are made in China, many brands still attempt to avoid the connection. For the perfect example, look at the extent Apple goes to in order to inform customers that its products are "Designed in California" rather than "Made in China." This notwithstanding, within China the emphasis is now on "Created in China" rather than "Made in China."

Whether they like it or not, and no matter how many "Designed in California" (or similar) labels their local brands apply to products, almost every country in the world relies on China for the vast majority of the manufactured items they consume. No other economy in the world is so important to so many other countries for their own economic survival.

"China is still a developing country but today we can say that nobody can live without China," the Chairman says. "Of course, every developing and developed country is somehow interconnected, but China is a very special example. In today's world, no developed country could live without China."

Of the many competitive advantages enjoyed by Chinese businesses over their Western counterparts, one of the most potent is their ability and willingness to come together, share knowledge, transfer skills, and become far more powerful than the sum of their parts. The Chairman often reminds Tiens staff about the importance of this Gestalt, in his saying that "one plus ten is more than eleven."

Business in the West is very much about survival of the fittest. Outside of major conferences where specific individuals might share select information with others in their industry, businesses tend to hold useful information close to their chests. Western governments do not encourage information sharing among businesses with the aim of benefiting the greater economy. Instead they count on individual organizations leading the way as others compete through innovation, through the driving of new efficiencies, through product differentiation and other means.

In the Chinese economic environment, though, what is good for one business is usually also good for the economy. Of course, competing organizations in the same industry are unlikely to swap high-level secrets, but businesses with related needs are encouraged to come together and share knowledge. Certain decisions made by senior management are expected to benefit the broader business community, too.

For instance, when those thousands of Tiens staff members made their record-breaking trip to France, part of the logic behind it was the improvement of relations between the French and Chinese governments and people. The staff were informed that it was important to be respectful wherever they went – never be too noisy, never get in people's way, always leave an area cleaner than it was when you arrived – which would help to create a positive view of Chinese people, and therefore of the China brand.

"It is beneficial for Tiens, of course," said Mr Yan, when I spoke with him about the integration of Chinese businesses with each other. "But it is also important that people around the globe trust Chinese businesses as a whole.

"Tiens is very successful in so many countries, so others want to learn from us. Government leaders visit us and so do academic teams, including professors from different universities. They come here to gather information on why Tiens is globally successful. They learn from us, then share the information with other academics, business schools, and other companies."

The day before my first conversation with Yan, a delegation of four teams visited the Tiens property. They included staff from national transport bodies, universities, and governments of various Belt and Road Initiative (previously known as "One Belt One Road") territories. We will discuss the Belt and Road Initiative of the Chinese government in more detail, but in summary it involves China, through its government and its companies, working with selected foreign governments and companies to cooperatively undertake major, large-scale infrastructure projects across much of the world.

"China is famous for its high-speed trains, so foreign governments are typically very interested in that," Yan said. "But they are also interested in how Chinese businesses expand internationally with great success. They want to learn from Tiens how to be a global company."

How to expand internationally is a very good question for Chinese businesses to be asking. Western businesses have plenty of similar cultures into which they can expand around the globe. But Chinese businesses find themselves in very foreign territory soon after leaving their own borders.

Who does Tiens learn from? Surely all of the knowledge sharing doesn't just go one way?

"We gather information from work being done in our own foreign branches, but also from some famous local companies like Huawei and Haier," Yan said. "Huawei competes with Apple, so it is interesting to find out how they take on such a very big brand.

"Just a few days ago the Chairman sent our senior managers to Huawei to learn their systems and speak with their senior managers. We will welcome the Huawei people back here, too. We learn from them about global management systems, how to be global, how to innovate and the like."

Early on in our relationship I assumed the Chairman might be sensitive about the mention of other Chinese billionaires, particularly those whose names were better known globally, such as Alibaba's Jack Ma, Dalian Wanda's Wang Jianlin, and Xiaomi's Lei Jun. But at company conferences and training sessions he hangs an image of Jack Ma on the wall, along with others from around the globe such as Warren Buffett and the late Steve Jobs, to illustrate inspirational leadership. Ma's theory around "new retail" (the idea of retail morphing into a permanent mix of online and offline, of experience and ease of ordering) is part of Li's plan for the current transformation of Tiens. Once again, I am taught that the Chinese culture is about respect and cooperation, rather than envy and self-interest.

While the Chinese business market is clearly doing well in terms of knowledge sharing, the Chairman says the clear trend for the future is around more powerful and all-encompassing alliances and partnerships, with Chinese and foreign entities.

"In the future, we will see that Chinese companies will integrate with each other much better than they do today," he says. "In the future you will see Chinese corporate alliances and also Chinese alliances with international brands. In China we say, 'One plus ten is more than eleven.' This will be the trend and you will not be able to avoid that trend."

Businesses that see their markets from such a viewpoint will hold greater power than those that do not, just as companies that encourage open discussion, innovation, and experimentation have been proven to have an advantage over those that do not. Much of the motivation and empowerment for collective thinking among companies in China comes from the government's relatively close relationship with business. It's a relationship that means the market is "open," but that the government still has levers that allow it to take control of certain situations.

How much control does the Chinese government have over the nation's commerce? A recent example demonstrates how it can wield its power to the nation's advantage. In July 2017 the Chinese government sent out a directive to the nation's big-four, state-owned banks, ordering them to stop any loans to the Chinese company Dalian Wanda. The business, run by billionaire Wang Jianlin, had been on a foreign acquisition spree that, Chinese regulators said, stepped over the line in terms of outbound investment and the government's efforts to stem capital outflow.

Dalian Wanda Group is generally agreed to be the world's largest commercial property company and world's largest cinema chain operator. If you've been to see a movie in the last five years, it's likely the movie theater you sat in was owned by Dalian Wanda.

For that company's leader, the government's order to the banks was a sharp reminder of just how free he is to do business. Soon after the action by the regulators, he openly pledged to focus on local investment in China and to pull back the business's aggressive offshore investment plan.

The event also provided a picture for those from outside China of just how much business influence the State brandishes. It's a far flight from typical Western governments, many of which find themselves in a relatively weak position when attempting to curb the excesses of powerful corporates.

In China, the level of governmental encouragement and support is a large part of the reason for the astonishing growth of the economy over the last few decades. There is still work to be done to find the optimal balance, however.

"From a macro-economic point of view the Chinese government and its policies are very well motivated and have a good level of force," says Li, who has dealt with government at several levels on almost every day of his Tiens journey. "But once it is implemented to a micro-economic level, that force is lessened. It becomes less efficient. For example, in the past when a policy has been implemented at the macro level it feels as if it has great power and intention. But once it trickles down through various levels of government it actually becomes watered down. It becomes less powerful. But, once again, it is still better than what is offered in many other countries."

Government influence over businesses has changed a great deal over the last few decades, for obvious reasons. Yan tells me that these days the government will focus mostly on large organizations, leaving small to medium entities alone to innovate and grow.

There is still an old-fashioned attitude amongst banks, he says, that they prefer to lend to public companies rather than private ones. Public companies, or what Western businesses know as "State-owned entities," clearly have greater support from the government. But the truth is that almost all medium and large businesses in China still take their lead from government policy and still shape at least some of their strategic decisions around government direction.

"Nowadays, no matter the company or the community or even the educational institution, we all think leadership by the Party is very important," Yan says. "In return, the government supports private business. Over the many conferences of the Party they have made private business more important each time. They consider private business to be vital to the economy."

It takes me a long time to realize that what exists in China is a strong, mutual respect – and perhaps even an interdependence – between business and government. They recognize each other as vital cogs in the machine that will drive the nation to its stated goals. They work as one, as a collective, and when one steps out of line, as Dalian Wanda was seen to have done, the consequences are immediate and strong.

Each inspires the other. The government is not simply giving permission and offering encouragement for Chinese businesses to spread their wings, but the global success of businesses such as Tiens, Dalian Wanda, Alibaba, Huawei, and Lenovo has reciprocal influence on the government. It emboldens and enlivens the government in its expansionism and reform agendas.

The Chairman describes the relationship between the Chinese business and the Chinese nation as one of respectful interdependence.

"The relationship between government and business is like water and fish," he says. "The fish cannot live without the water and the water needs the fish to keep the balance of the ecosystem."

The recent work of renowned economist Professor Mariana Mazzucato also sheds light on the importance of such public/private relationships in a business sense. The popular attitude has been that innovation comes only from the private sector and almost in spite of the lumbering and slovenly nature of the bureaucratic government sector. In fact, her research shows, the opposite is true. By making high-risk investments, an entrepreneurial State gives its private sector the courage to be truly innovative, to invest, to expand, and to accept risk, as she sets out in her acclaimed book *The Entrepreneurial State: Debunking Public vs. Private Sector Myths* (Anthem, 2013).

And actually, this fact makes Li's entrepreneurial exploits all the more impressive. His early business development was a rare case of entrepreneurialism and risk-taking prior to the government showing him the path or offering support. Looking back, that path is now littered with the remains of countless others who attempted to achieve similar success but didn't have the business judgement, the foresight, or the persistent courage to see it through.

The Chairman is one of just a few Chinese entrepreneurs who caught the wave early and rode it all the way to the present day. That longevity, and the fact that he started from nothing, sets him apart from most other Chinese billionaires.

Yan tells me the government also encourages private businesses to have an internal Party committee, or a Party branch. The key word here, he says, is "encourages" as opposed to "enforces."

If the organization contains a large number of Party members, then that community within the business meets regularly and is known as a "Party committee." If the member count is less, then the group that meets is known as a "Party branch." Their job is broad and flexible, ranging from the promotion of the business within government to the promotion of government policies within the business, to the setting of good behavior examples within the company, and to improving their own business behaviors and skill sets. Essentially, it's a respected body that exists to create improvements where it can and, no doubt, to warn businesses off pathways that might go against the grand plan.

"A Party committee will promote the business and develop the business, and they want their Party members to be good leaders and good examples for the other staff. Party members are expected to be excellent staff," Yan says.

The Party committee within Tiens contains several hundred people. When I ask Yan, an extremely successful, well-respected, wealthy, and quietly powerful leader in the Chinese business world, if he is a member of the Party committee, he laughs and looks (politely, of course) as if he's a little embarrassed for me that I even asked the question. "No," he responds with a genuine smile, "I am not good enough."

I can only imagine what might happen if a Tory committee started up in a British business, or if a Republican committee launched in an American firm. The very suggestion would likely be met with raucous laughter. But if we allow ourselves to remove any idea of our predisposition toward one party or another, or our lack of interest in politics in general, then we can begin to imagine the level of power and performance that could be achieved for an entire economy if all businesses and the government were in perfect alignment – or even imperfect alignment – all with the same goal in mind. That's what China has achieved, and that's just one of the ways in which it differs from the West.

In fact, the government has recently taken this idea one step further by utilizing technology to begin to align the citizens of China, not just businesses and institutions, with its thoughts and directions. An app called Xuexi Qiangguo ("Study that powerful nation") offers a daily hit of doctrine from President Xi Jinping, updates on new government initiatives domestically and internationally, and more. Upon its release it quickly became the most downloaded app on the Chinese Apple App Store, meaning it now has a user count greater than the populations of many nations. Users can also test themselves within the app, in order to earn points.

Once again, it's an idea that sounds completely over the top for a Westerner, but imagine the immense power and opportunity offered to a nation in which government, businesses, and individuals are aligned in terms of culture and objectives. It's the sort of engagement and buy-in that many small, medium, and large organizations only dream of, but in a nation of 1.4 billion people it is a reality.

Thinking about it this way, it seems Eastern business culture and organizational practices are as foreign to the West as chalk is to cheese. But in a discussion with the Professor about East vs West, and about the many cultural differences, he reminds me that there are also plenty of similarities, that the world is globalizing, and that business practices, as with everything else, are ever so slowly beginning to normalize across regions and territories.

"The Chinese way of doing business with other Chinese businesses and with Western businesses is becoming much more blended with the Western way," the Professor says. "This is for at least three reasons. One is that many successful Chinese businesses now have in them people who have earned their MBA at Stanford University or at the University of Melbourne or at University College London. They have people who have come back with Western ways of doing things.

"The second is that as Chinese companies deal more with Western companies and in Western countries, they are adapting or localizing, perhaps more so than Western companies are adapting to foreign environments they are finding themselves in.

"The third is that there has been much more reflection within Chinese companies on efficiencies, on strategy, and on performance, which perhaps was not always perceived to be part of the Chinese culture. They are looking now for the most effective and appropriate methods of contemporary governance and management for now and for the future."

Chinese businesses, then, are fast learning the ways of the world and are working with a certain level of unison with each other and with their government toward specific goals. In doing so, they are creating new ways of doing things.

What about Western businesses in China? How are they performing and, more importantly, what are they doing wrong?

IO

Mistakes Western businesses make in China

"Everybody must adapt to the local situation."

Li Jinyuan

In a society where face and not being outwardly critical of others are vital, it is all but impossible to receive a clear answer from any Chinese person when I ask them to explain what others do wrong. For the Chinese, saying anything that could be perceived as negative about somebody else causes loss of face for all parties.

When I ask Yan about what Westerners tend to do wrong when they do business in China, he responds with, "No particular country has a culture that is right or wrong, so the most important thing is strong communication. We must respect the differences and only then can we come together and experience fusion."

It is the same when I sit with Song Xiang, Manager of the Dalian office of Tiens, and ask where Westerners fail in their behavior in China. "There is just a culture gap," he says, dodging the question entirely. "The Chairman is very people oriented. When he meets with people from different countries he pays special attention to their culture. He respects all people from different countries. Respect is the first thing we need to pay attention to. You need to respect the culture and you need to respect the people. That is one of the reasons why our business has been able to spread so far around the world."

Accordingly, when I question the Chairman about the behavior of Western businesses in China, he begins with a compliment, then turns the focus to Chinese businesses.

"Many foreign companies, when they come to the Chinese market, come prepared," he says. "They are prepared in terms of government relations, legal issues, and culture. They know a lot about Chinese society before they come to the Chinese market. For those companies, usually they will develop well in China. Some others are not very well prepared and they will be affected negatively. But for most foreign companies, when they come to China, eventually they will develop well. That is what I see.

"However, many Chinese companies, when they go overseas, tend to not change their mentality. They do not adapt to the Western market's mentality and cultures, so many Chinese companies fail in overseas expansion because they cannot adapt well enough or fast enough. If you want to be successful in your development overseas, you have to be able to adapt to the local situation."

The evasion of any perceived offence is as charming as it is impressive. It is obvious that to come up with a clear answer to the question of where Westerners, and Western businesses, let themselves down in China, I have to look elsewhere.

The Professor has plenty to say on the topic, having spent a long time in the nether world between Western and Chinese businesses.

There are three big mistakes, he says, that Western businesses make when they enter the Chinese market.

The first is that the people within Western businesses often underestimate the people they are dealing with in China. Westerners underestimate Chinese businesses on a number of levels, he says, including their commercial sophistication, their business intelligence, and the amount of background work that the Chinese business has typically done in advance of each meeting, sometimes knowing more about the Western business than those who are representing the Western business do.

The second is that Westerners do not recognize that in China, thanks to various cultural quirks, things take time. "There is a level of frustration that Westerners sometimes feel about things going slowly and nothing appearing to be happening," the Professor says. "What they don't realize is that a lot is happening, but the thing that is happening that is most important is a determination of whether the relationship is appropriate."

The third mistake, the Professor says, is not appreciating the importance of trust, in a personal sense. "Your contract and my contract might contain lots of nice legal clauses but they don't mean anything if trust goes away," he says. "Westerners often think they can wrap everything in legal terms and they will sue if something goes wrong. Well, yes. But if you start from that mindset you're never going to build trust. That said, you don't want to set up an agreement where you can get screwed. I am not saying that there are not Chinese companies that will try to screw you, but I am saying that the authentic handshake and the personal trust between the main players are essential."

The Professor relates an experience from his past, one he had a few years ago and which brought home to him the differences between Chinese and Western businesses, and the mistakes Western businesses tend to make, particularly in terms of underestimating the people they are going to meet in China.

"There was a delegation coming from an Australian business to meet with a Chinese company and the Chinese asked if I could help them to find out about the Australians and their business," he recalls. "So I found out plenty of information. I knew of some of the people who were coming and conducted a great deal of research, then I sat and briefed the Chinese team on what each person would likely say. The Chinese were unbelievably well prepared, and not just because of what I had done. My input was just a small part of their preparation.

"The Australians came in and 80 percent of what they had been predicted to say, they said. The Chinese knew exactly what was going on and exactly what the next step was going to be in the negotiation. They were completely prepared, but it was clear that the Australians did not have a clue and had done very little in the way of groundwork. It all worked out reasonably well in the end, but it was an example of Westerners coming in with the attitude that perhaps the Chinese did not even know where Australia was. Some of that can be understandable, but some of that can be a little bit insulting and potentially offensive."

One of the advisors in the Chinese business had earned his MBA at the University of Melbourne Business School and spoke fluent English, the Professor says. But none of the Australians knew this fact, and the gentleman spoke only Chinese during the meeting. Just a little research would have gone a very long way for the Australians.

Another mistake made by individuals visiting China is the assumption of a level of conformity among the Chinese. I was guilty of this at first, of thinking that because the Chinese have been under fairly strict political rule, because there are certain societal mores that have similar effects on all Chinese individuals and because of "collectivist thinking," nobody would want to stand out. If society comes before the individual, surely the individual becomes less important, I assumed.

The Professor straightened me out on this thinking early on in my time in China. Afterwards I immediately recognized, as we wandered into the Tiens cafeteria for lunch and saw staff members dressed in the latest fashions and sporting unique and sometimes distinctive hairdos, that he was absolutely correct.

"I don't think conforming is everything in China," he told me. "I think in companies there is agreed, written or unwritten, dress code, but this is no different from Western companies. There is nothing, I am sure, that is written down that says you cannot go in to work at the Royal Bank of Scotland wearing a pair of shorts. But it is not part of the culture or the company code, so I think it is wrong to call it 'conformity.' We all seek to fit in and feel comfortable in our societies and situations. We also may seek to differentiate ourselves a little bit but not to differentiate ourselves to the extreme, unless there is a real reason for it. Conformity does exist, but it exists everywhere."

This is changing as younger Chinese in particular are exposed to Western influence. The one-child policy created an entire generation of children for whom parents wanted the very best in life, including an overseas education, if possible. Such exposure cannot possibly leave Chinese society unchanged.

"This is a changing society but at its heart it is a sharing society," the Professor says. "People will think about what is good for the family and the group as much, if not more, than thinking about what is good for them as individuals. In all cultures there is a balance that must be found of individual needs and group needs.

"In most Western countries individuals will do what is good for them and if there is something left over then they will help the group. The mindset in a traditional collectivist culture is to do good for the group and hope that you can also do something that is good for you. That is beginning to change with the young people who have exposure to individualistic cultures, especially with those people coming back into the Chinese culture after experiencing the Western traditions and cultures."

Another myth about China is that corruption is the way to do business. In fact, corruption has been and gone. It was a blip on the radar, now thwarted by a very vigorous clampdown by government, which recognized that an open and free market will thrive only within a framework of rules and regulations. Of course, some corrupt activity likely still takes place, but this is no different from any other market or country.

"Corruption is absolutely not the Chinese way. It is a way that emerged and that was allowed to happen by various layers of responsibility over the last few decades but it was not the Chinese way. Senior Chinese people who want others to respect the culture have been aghast about corruption," the Professor says.

Even the giving of expensive gifts among friends has slowed down in China, I am told, as people fear that the giving of a fancy or expensive gift may bring with it some sort of perceived need for reciprocity. There is now a fear that a gift may be an enticement for a reward rather than an expression of respect. The giving of simple, genuine gifts, however, remains an important part of the building and maintaining of respect and friendship.

How else do Western businesses or business people interact, for better or for worse, in China? The Chairman, once warmed up on the topic, says foreign companies in China do well when they take the time to fully understand the needs of China. The very first condition before designing a business to succeed in China, he says, is to understand the nation's needs.

"You have to understand the key points of human or social interactions in China," Li says. "It's a very complicated kind of science. You must understand what the government needs and what society and the Chinese market need. If you have a good grasp of government and society then you can expect to develop well.

"When people come to China and meet with local people, if they keep their Westernized mentality, or if they have a superiority complex, then they will not do well. This is the same for Chinese people going overseas."

Actually, this is the single greatest gripe of Chinese who come into contact with Westerners. Some visitors from the West, I am often told, think China is a backward nation and that its people are not advanced in any way. Then they arrive and see the gleaming towers of Shanghai, the bustling metropolis of Beijing, the stunning European beauty of Tianjin, the latticework of high-speed train services, the efficiency and ease of the WeChat Wallet or the Alipay payment system, the merging of technology with anything and everything, and so much more. That's when visitors begin to realize just how much catching up their own country has to do.

An anecdote related to me by Hong Yuanqi (English name Edward), a brilliantly sharp university student taking a double major of Finance and Spanish (and who speaks English flawlessly), reminded me of the Chairman's words about Western assumed superiority.

Edward has studied in Spain and in the USA, and one trip during his youth made him realize that not all cultures are considered equal. "When I stayed with a host family in the United States for two weeks during a summer program in junior high, I was in a small city in California," he said. "The host mum and dad and their children were really very nice people, but perhaps because they lived in a small city they didn't know much about foreign countries.

"They never said it directly but a judgement I made from my experiences was that they thought China was an underdeveloped country and that they had a lot to teach us. I felt strongly that the host mum was trying to educate us in a lot of ways. She thought that we were somehow ignorant. For example, one day a few Chinese students and the host mum went to a bookstore to buy some books. She picked up a book and came to me and asked if I knew how to pick a book. I said, 'Yes, sure. We read books in China.' She asked if I knew where on the book I should look in order to find out what it's about. I said, 'Yes, I turn the book over and look at the back.' She was surprised that I knew. A lot of those little experiences made me sense that she and her family were not so knowledgeable when it comes to the level of development in China."

It's absurd to consider that a Western businessperson, when meeting a Chinese entrepreneur who has built a business from scratch that has made him a billionaire and that now operates around the world, could consider themselves superior. But it is something, the Chairman says, that he often experiences.

He explains it without malice and with a surprising amount of gentle understanding, saying the feeling of superiority would stem from the fact that Western countries have traditionally been more developed compared with the rest of the world. And he says that once he explains what he has done, once he describes his journey, most people do show him respect for his achievements.

"When I meet some Western business leaders, I tell them we're different people," he explains. "Why? Because I created everything myself. Maybe they received an inheritance from their parents or perhaps were an employee of a company and ended up being its leader. But I had to be an entrepreneur. I had to start from nothing."

Mr Yan also eventually comes up with an important difference in the behavior of Chinese and Western business people. In Chinese business culture, he says, if you want to do business together, then the relationship comes first.

"You want to get to know each other and trust each other," he says. "You want to make friends and develop a good impression of each other. After that has happened, you then move to step two, which is discussing business reason and rationale, processes and ethics. Here we talk about what we could do together, how it might work, and we make sure the businesses match up and that the people will work well together. Finally, you get on to the legal discussion and eventually sign a contract."

In the West, however, things are the other way around, Yan says. The contract is usually expected to be signed well before the individuals and businesses have spent meaningful time together or come to know each other. Then the processes are discussed and finally, after contracts and processes are decided, a relationship is allowed to form, for better or for worse.

"This is a key culture shock for Chinese business people in other countries," Yan tells me. "For Chinese business people, the contract is not the most important thing. The relationship is as important as the contract."

When I first met the Chairman before being signed on to write this book, I originally believed that he was testing me. After that meeting I realized it was not so much a test as it was a spending of time together. It was the forming of a relationship. If I was not the type of person to whom the Chairman could comfortably relate, then there could be no business done between us.

Even though the Professor had taken time to form a relationship with me and even though he was introducing me with confidence to the Chairman, it was the Chairman who had to determine in his own way whether our relationship would work. The relationship was the number one consideration, as it is in businesses across China.

From my point of view, developed after 18 months embedded in the Chinese corporate culture, the secret to success in China comes down to one simple word: respect. It is about respect for what the nation has achieved in the decades since the "opening up" of China began in the late 1970s. It is about respect for the battles that Chinese entrepreneurs have fought in an environment that has likely been harsher than almost anything a Western businessperson could imagine. It is about respecting Chinese consumers enough to spend time figuring out exactly what they want from your business/brand.

Finally, it is about respect for yourself, for the fact that you have come from a completely different culture and therefore it is only right to give yourself permission to make mistakes and to learn. This final point is one the Chinese understand perfectly well, because they experience exactly the same issues in territories outside of their own.

Fail fast, succeed faster: global expansion strategies

"To start something new, to advance down a different path, you have to be daring."

Li Jinyuan

The original plan for the international expansion of Tiens was to focus on highly developed Western nations such as Australia, the UK, the USA, and some European countries. After all, America was the home of direct selling, so it made sense to be in a territory that was already comfortable with the system. This was a mistake.

Tiens, at the beginning of its direct selling journey, lacked management sophistication in the market and also lacked international business experience. Moving into territories that already boasted complex and refined business models and practices made the brand look and feel amateurish. Also, at that particular time the social and economic conditions in these territories were positive, meaning unemployment was low and jobs were plentiful. Talent was more difficult to come by and more expensive, and similar products to the ones that Tiens offered were already available and well-known to Western consumers.

The Chairman recognized these issues after a brief flirtation with the US market in 1997 and quickly changed tack, instead looking into countries that were better aligned with China. Russia became and remains a focus.

In Russia, as in many other territories at the time, "Brand China" suffered a reputational issue. But direct selling was a perfect way to overcome such a broad problem. Word of mouth was the best way to convince people to trust a health product, and direct selling was all about word of mouth.

The first few meetings in Russia, which were set up to attract local distributors, were memorable for the fact that an animal, rather than a human, contributed to the early success of the brand. One woman who attended a meeting was sceptical about the calcium product so she tested it on her small dog. After a few months she noticed an improvement in the dog's health and posture, so she began taking the product herself. Soon she was so convinced of the product's value that she became a distributor, one who eventually brought in many more distributors.

"At that time the image of Chinese product quality, and the country's image overseas, were very poor," Chairman Li says. "So even though our products came from a 5,000-year-old medical tradition and contained all of these excellent elements, when we first operated overseas many customers did not believe the quality of the product. They were suspicious. So when they would buy something they would give it to their dog or cat first. If the animal felt well then the customer would dare to eat it. That was the mentality. So we had to build confidence from scratch."

In contrast, Li points out, these days when a Western company comes to China they often already have the brand recognition and confidence of the customer and a reputation for quality, offering them a powerful sales platform that is way beyond anything Tiens ever enjoyed during its international expansion. A walk through a typical Chinese city shopping mall, with its Zegna, Gucci, New Balance, Adidas, Nike, Starbucks, and many other brands, confirms the popularity of Western brands that approach the Chinese market in the right way. New Balance, in fact, appears more successful in Chinese tier one cities than it is in many Western capitals.

After the Russian launch in 1998, Tiens moved fast into new regions – into around 37 of them in 12 months – learning lessons as it went and always failing or succeeding quickly. These territories, included those in Central Asian countries such as Kazakhstan and Uzbekistan, as well as African nations, South American countries, and many in South-East Asia. Of course, research was conducted in advance of the company entering a country, but the most valuable learnings came from experience and understanding the best way to localize business processes.

"We did, and still do, a survey or a study to find out exactly what the local market desires," Li says. "Every market has its own features and preferences and these always become apparent through our studies. But the basic demand for human health is always the same – everything begins with health. After that, we always come back to the importance of the shopping and purchase experience. People need to know how these products will benefit them as an individual."

Local cultural preferences came into play very early on, Li says. For instance, in some countries people preferred to take health supplements as an oral spray rather than a tablet or a powder. And in India there was no consumption of any product related to cows, so calcium had to be supplied instead via fish bones.

Twelve months was spent in those countries collectively as a pilot program. When feedback was positive in a specific territory, then a more aggressive approach was taken, usually involving the establishment of at least one local office.

Using this fast-failure method, within four years of establishing the 37 pilot territories, Tiens was trading in 110 nations.

Manpower from China was stretched thin during those frantic years of expansion. Yan, on his own, oversaw or managed the business in over 20 countries.

"I did not work for a long time in every country," Yan says. "I supervised, so sometimes I would just visit for a week or two. In the periods that we were moving rapidly we didn't have time to do much deep market research. But we also had periods in which we slowed down, and that was when we did more research.

"We wanted to set up many branch companies throughout Asia and in India and in other countries very quickly. Some parts of the business were successful and we gathered information from those successful experiences. Sometimes a branch company would fail and we would learn a great deal from that. We would use the good experiences to improve the bad branches and we would use experiences from the bad branches to strengthen the good ones. This allowed us to move rapidly.

"This is totally different to the way a Western business would usually enter the Chinese market. The Western way is to do the market research and to look into the economics of everything before deciding whether to move into that country or not. But if we wanted to use that kind of business model then it would have taken way too long to move into 110 countries."

One interesting problem encountered along the way was with job descriptions, which in China tended to be very general and lacking in detail, but which in many other countries listed everything an employee could possibly be expected to do. When a Chinese manager in the US office asked an American employee to drive to the airport to pick up another Tiens staff member, he was stunned when the employee refused, saying it was not in his job description. As well as infuriating the Chinese manager, this experience led to Tiens revisiting the detail in all of the business's job descriptions in Western countries.

Another culturally confusing, and amusing, experience came in the Peru office when high-performing staff members were given a bonus as thanks for their hard work.

"If you give a bonus to Chinese employees they will think that you have confirmed that they are doing their job well and they will work harder afterwards as a result," Yan smiles. "But in Peru, when we gave the bonuses to the local staff, the next day they did not show up to work! When they eventually returned we asked them why they did not come to work and they said, 'You gave us extra money, which means you want us to enjoy our lives.' So we had to explain the meaning of a bonus from our point of view."

In Malaysia and Indonesia, Yan says, Chinese staff quickly learned to be very careful about offering guidance or criticism to local staff as many would simply become upset and leave, rather than try harder. "They had lives where they were not used to much pressure," he explains. "Plus, it was easy for them to find a job as unemployment rates were not very high."

Tiens has now developed a three-step process for entering a new market. It involves sending in Chinese managers to lay the groundwork, quickly employing and training local staff, then leaving the local staff in charge. And in completely "foreign" markets, such as Australia and New Zealand, it involves employing a local professional to lead the new branch business, bringing that person to the China head office to teach them about how Tiens works, then giving them the freedom to set the business, and its strategy, for the greatest chance of success in that market. It's a new and improved version of the "fail fast" method employed by the business 20 years ago, and it has proven to be highly effective.

So for other types of businesses looking to globalize their offering, what constitutes best practice? How does international corporate entrepreneurialism work best, and is it even possible? To develop answers to these questions, I speak with Sara McGaughey, Professor of International Business at Griffith University. McGaughey, whom I met in the lobby bar of the Crowne Plaza Beijing, has spent much of her career researching corporate knowledge and innovation, international new ventures, and international corporate entrepreneurship. She has recently written deeply on the topic in the book, *Fostering Local Entrepreneurship in a Multinational Enterprise* (J. Amberg and S. McGaughey, Routledge, 2017).

In a business that places high value on process, as is the case with most corporates, the great risk is that there is no risk taken, McGaughey says. In other words, process is rewarded and therefore risk is not. The culture is about risk aversion. When that same business attempts to do anything that could be described as entrepreneurial, managers in the business don't know how to handle it. Their behavior is characterized by indecision.

McGaughey was conducting research within Siemens when the industrial manufacturing conglomerate acquired a leading fire safety business. Siemens intended to tap into the acquired company's entrepreneurial behavior to continue to grow the business. What happened instead was a paralysis, of sorts. In a culture driven by process, corporate indecision almost ran the new business into the ground.

"Their process-oriented organization was a factor that killed, or impeded, entrepreneurship," McGaughey says. "Siemens' fundamental structure is around processes. They even have a process reference house that details all of the business processes that people have to follow for all sorts of things, from R&D right through to customer service. The idea of a process organization is to make the business independent of the individual. Any person should be able to perform a process if it's documented well enough. But if you're talking about creativity and you're talking about entrepreneurial behavior and spontaneity and risk-taking, then processes tend to kill those things."

To cut its losses, Siemens had to bring in external management to the fire safety business. The consultants had managed successful start-ups in the past, and they reduced the processes that Siemens had loaded onto the business. They allowed it to breathe, to recover, to begin to thrive, and finally to be sold off. All in all, it was a distraction that Siemens could have done without.

Of course, there are many businesses that absolutely require a strict level of process and control no matter where they operate – airlines and engineering firms come to mind. But for most companies, entering into a new market is going to require something different to a well-documented process if they are to succeed.

Tiens learned early on that the processes it used in its home market could not be rolled out into other territories, and through trial and error the business learned to make the foreign offices more independent of the mothership. In other words, the Chairman allowed and encouraged greater independence by putting local people in senior roles and allowing the local branches to operate as quasi-independent structures, developing their own methods and processes to suit their own environments. In a reverse of this, in the third phase of development of Tiens, the Chairman is now bringing more and more people from around the world into the Tiens headquarters to help the Chinese head office staff know more about the practices of the foreign offices.

The immediate employment of local managers to shape and manage the foreign branch office, rather than sending a team from Tiens Group's head office to build the local business and manage the launch, McGaughey says, is excellent practice.

"I saw this in Siemens, too," she explains. "Expats travel the world and the expectations are that they will move around a lot. Their performance metrics are based on creating new businesses and new initiatives as they move around, but because they keep moving, they never have to see those initiatives through. Nobody ever tracks what happens and connects results with what the expats did during set-up.

"This process, of course, is very costly for the organization and very costly, in personal terms, for the individual. It's also demoralizing for the local staff who are left behind in the office once the expats leave. Those people are left holding the ball and typically they're not happy about it. Most importantly, for the expats the incentive is to create the business, but not necessarily to create a sustainable business. Entrepreneurship is all about creating a sustainable business."

Best practice, then, involves partitioning off the new part of the business from what McGaughey refers to as the "corporate immune system." This, she says, is the part of the corporate that sees a new idea and says, "We tried that before and it didn't work" or "That's not the way we do things here." It means creating structures where there are separate entities that are shielded from the types of corporate behavior that can suffocate a start-up.

Taking this idea one step further, McGaughey says that one way to protect a new and therefore vulnerable part of a larger organization is to actually keep its identity separate so that it doesn't even seem as if it is part of the larger organization.

An excellent corporate example of this idea in action is the Engineering Excellence Group (EEG). An in-house consultancy for engineering giant Laing O'Rourke, EEG is a body that has been set up at a different address, under its own management and operating under a completely separate set of rules to that of its parent company. The business has been a great success so far, offering internal and external consultancy, research and development, and educational services that ensure a parent company that is process-driven by necessity continues to innovate and improve.

Then success becomes about identifying "firm-specific advantages," McGaughey says. These are the things that a business does better than all of its rivals.

"A business needs to understand this because when they go overseas, they face a 'liability of foreignness,'" she explains. "They don't speak the language. They don't have the political networks. They don't have the supply networks. They don't know the cultural norms. So the liability of foreignness is the additional cost that they face when they go overseas, one that local firms do not face."

To succeed in a foreign market, then, a business must compensate for or overcome its liability of foreignness. That can be achieved only through the exploitation of firm-specific advantages that are transferable to the new market. This might be advanced technology, reputation, brand, processes, capabilities, or something else. "Whatever it is, it needs to be identified," McGaughey says.

Combine those transferable, firm-specific advantages with host-country advantages – by investing in your business's foreign-market resources and capabilities, acquiring local staff, partnering or joint venturing with a local firm, etc., in order to reduce your liability of foreignness – and chances of success are far improved. In other words, play to your strengths and develop new or relational capabilities to mitigate your weaknesses. In doing so, many challenges faced by businesses expanding internationally will be overcome.

12

Inspiring frontier markets

"When you achieve small goals, one by one, the larger goal will be achieved naturally ... People think success comes from achieving the impossible but, on the contrary, it is about modesty and efficiency."

Li Jinyuan

I've already mentioned that some markets have not yet been fully penetrated by Tiens, particularly a few very important ones, including the USA and Australia.

Over the last 12 months the Chairman has been working on a plan to re-enter such markets, but this time with a lot more experience and far greater maturity, and as a "global organization" rather than a "Chinese business." A bulletproof strategy is vital.

To understand the problem from a Western perspective, I speak with Rick Nelson, an experienced executive from the direct sales arena and an American who consulted to Tiens during the time I was embedded there. We meet in an expansive boardroom on the seventh floor of the Tiens headquarters building. He's a confident, sharply dressed, ex-Nu Skin executive from Salt Lake City.

The Nu Skin direct-sales brand from the USA, the world's most sophisticated direct selling market, has experienced great success. Now in around 56 countries and with turnover of US$2.25 billion, Nu Skin spent several decades slowly and carefully moving out into new territories. Each new market would take around 12 months of planning and procedure. The business had no intention of failing in any of its markets, so it moved slowly and methodically to ensure the greatest chances of success each time.

The company's choices of markets were important. Nu Skin would only enter countries that had economies of a specific size. The smaller and less developed markets, referred to by executives as "frontier markets," were not worth considering. For these reasons and more, it took

Nu Skin three decades to enter some 56 markets. In contrast, Chairman Li and Tiens took less than five years to launch into over 100 markets of varying sizes and market sophistication.

One difference with Chairman Li was that he was willing to fail, to learn lessons, and to move on. The successful markets provided valuable lessons for the unsuccessful ones, and vice versa. Numbers were crunched, war stories were traded, and the business continued to try again and again. As a result, it experienced massive growth. Interestingly, the frontier markets that Nu Skin did not enter were the ones in which Tiens experienced some of its greatest success.

When I spoke with Nelson he had just reached the end of a two-month period with Tiens in Wuqing. Such extended stays are not unusual. In fact, almost every new, senior employee or consultant from another territory is invited to take an extended stay as part of a process intended to allow them the time to get to know the brand and the business. A few months in the presence of the Chairman allows a foreign employee or consultant to become familiar with the Tiens philosophy.

"I think it's excellent that Tiens immerses people at the headquarters for two months," Nelson says. "The Chinese like to build relationships. It is the Chairman's way of investing in his relationships and getting to know foreign teams. It also allows him to present to newcomers, collaborate with them, and do the things that are important in Chinese culture, such as having dinner with senior managers and others. Once that time was over, I had these amazing relationships with all of the relevant and important executives."

The time he has spent in China, Nelson says, has been nothing short of astounding. Having spent several decades with Nu Skin managing the business's entry into several major markets, he now sees and appreciates a completely different business model and a unique and daring attitude to expansion.

"The Chairman should get high marks for doing what he did, for pioneering direct selling in China and creating a framework that allows such businesses to even operate," Nelson says. "He pioneered that and now the government's regulatory framework is underneath all of the rules and regulations that cover the entire industry in China, including Amway, Herbalife, and Nu Skin. I think it is a great story. I think it is truly astonishing. The Chairman achieved the impossible by building that company."

At Nu Skin, the approach to entering new territories was the opposite of what Tiens did, he says.

"We never opened dozens of countries at once, expecting to close the ones that failed. In our world every single market had to succeed, but in the Tiens model they said, 'If we try to do 100 and we end up with 40, we still have 40.' In the USA, that attitude could never fly.

"The Chairman went after the frontier markets and that was very wise. Why would he go and engage in combat against Nu Skin and Amway? Instead, he went where they were not. And it worked. And it is totally normal for him to do that. The way he came at it and the way the Americans came at it were very different."

Nelson says the Tiens Group's original tilt at the US market was problematic because it was approached in a similar fashion to the way Tiens approaches a frontier market – move in quickly and utilize market feedback to tell the business where it is going wrong. This worked in Ukraine, Kazakhstan, Peru, and Nigeria, where a small problem was very unlikely to spell the end of the business in that territory. But make a mistake in a market as competitive as the USA and word spreads in a hurry, meaning customers and distributors jump ship to one of many other similar offerings.

"Approaching that market with anything less than a perfect offering is like thinking you can get to the Super Bowl out of the Junior Leagues. It is never going to happen," Nelson says. "So the Chairman realized he had tried it one way but now needs to try a different way. He wanted a total reboot, managed very differently to the way it is done in the frontier markets."

Nu Skin, by the way, also bombed in several markets. "We totally failed," Nelson smiles. "Our product mix was not right and our compensation plan was totally incompatible with these markets. We had a major failure in the Philippines, where we were eventually told that our compensation plan is for the 'Green Berets of the industry.' It was so demanding, we were told, that if a distributor was distracted for a single moment they'd get run over. They'd have tyre tracks in their scalp!"

While sophisticated businesses and business plans are a good fit for sophisticated markets, they don't work so well in less complex markets. Even with months of planning and market research, a business as successful as Nu Skin could not crack some of the markets in which Tiens thrived.

In the early days of Tiens' international expansion, instead of throwing more money at the billion-dollar economies, the Chairman knitted together a large number of million-dollar economies, ones that bigger players ignored or simply refused to enter. Nu Skin would not enter a market where it couldn't turn over at least US$20 million each month, Nelson says. Li instead went for 20 markets that each turned over US$1 million per month, for the same financial result and in less time.

For example, one of these markets is Kyrgyzstan, which now boasts tens of thousands of Tiens distributors amongst a population of just six million. Gross monthly revenue for Tiens in Kyrgyzstan is over US$1 million.

"I can bring health to the people of Kyrgyzstan and I can offer them a means of creating wealth," Li says to me when we discuss such frontier markets. "If this business is experiencing success, then the livelihoods of tens of thousands of people who distribute our products are also experiencing success. Adding to that, the people consuming our products are experiencing greater health effects, and so it is a very positive cycle.

"I have never feared nor favoured any market. Business success is about passionately moving forward into new territories with a powerful belief in the positive effects of your offering. Every market is different and every market has its own lessons, but to let those territorial or cultural differences slow you down is admitting defeat."

Along these lines, several experts have pointed out to me the powerful global networks created almost accidentally by brands that have a broad presence in frontier markets. These territories tend to experience greater emigration as younger people move elsewhere in search of opportunity offered by larger and more sophisticated job markets. They take with them knowledge of, and respect for, the brands that they knew from home.

As a result of the diaspora of Chinese people around the globe, for example, the Australian office of Tiens included local family and friends of Tiens distributors in China as one of their recruitment groups. And when I speak to a Tiens manager from Kyrgyzstan, she mentions that she considers the huge number of Kyrgyzstani emigrants, during the past 15 years of the brand's existence in Kyrgyzstan, as a major opportunity in terms of future growth of the business. It creates a powerful network, she says, and it's one that Tiens is able to leverage.

And so in the past Tiens had succeeded in many markets where Nu Skin did not, and Nu Skin succeeded in some markets in which Tiens did not. What was Nu Skin's secret to success in a foreign market? What processes did that organization learn to follow again and again to carefully ensure maximum profit?

First of all, they ensured local managers, fully supported by the US head office, ran local offices. Those managers gave the foreign offices an interface with the government and other vital networks. Nu Skin also implemented a ten-year, long-term incentive program that locked its senior managers in. They were offered a salary and a specific level of bonus. Half of that bonus would be paid at the end of the year based on performance. The other half went into an escrow account for ten years.

"So if you looked to the left or the right, or if you screwed us, you forfeited all of it," Nelson says. "Our managers never did anything stupid because they didn't want to jeopardize that long-term asset. In markets like Korea and Japan and many other markets, that was a big reason why we succeeded. It's an absolute necessity. I see in the Malaysian business market right now general managers jumping from company to company every two years. That is ridiculous. How can you have continuity as a company when you have no continuity with your leaders? It means you can't grow."

I ask Nelson about the difference between American and Chinese companies and he's quick with a response. American businesses, at their core, are excellent at improvization, he says. They may have found themselves in an increasingly heavily regulated environment since the global financial crisis, but they are still able to think on their feet and rapidly adapt. They have the ability to quickly build a better mousetrap when they have to. Chinese companies, he believes, have great strength in process. They are enormously sophisticated in terms of the way they do things, but this has tended to result in more layers of management. The good thing about the Chinese levels of management is that they cannot do stupid things fast. "Americans can definitely do stupid things fast," Nelson smiles.

One mistake that he has seen American direct selling businesses make is to invest too heavily in one type of product, such as exotic juices or diet shakes, which boom and bust like every other fad. Such companies, he says, are simply selling the business rather than providing value to the market.

"Tiens in China and elsewhere originally delivered a lot of value to the market because the calcium supplements were needed and were useful in the types of countries in which they operated," he says. "But we don't have calcium health issues in America to the same extent as in many other countries."

Can Tiens products really improve the health, and lives, of consumers? As I do with any health claim about any product made by any company, I feel a level of doubt about whether products can do what they say on the box. Does the Tiens calcium powder, for instance, really strengthen bones? When I sit with Frank Deng, who has worked across China and the USA and is familiar with relevant regulations around the world, I question him about the veracity of such claims. His answer surprises me.

"The good side about Chinese regulation, especially for nutrition supplements, is that they are heavily regulated relative to the USA," Deng explains. I think back to nights spent in hotels in New York, Boston, and San Francisco, switching on the television only to face a relentless barrage of advertising for medicines and medical products, many of them making far bolder claims than the Tiens products do. In Australia, New Zealand, the UK, Europe, and most other territories, such blatant medical commercialism is outlawed, and in China, too, there is no such marketing allowed.

"When I worked for GSK and Bayer, I had to explain to my American colleagues a lot of the time how the regulation works," he continues. "The good side is that the product cannot be sold unless the packaging contains a symbol that means the product has been approved by China's equivalent of the US Food and Drug Administration. When we have this approved it means the product has been through clinical studies and it does what it claims."

For Tiens calcium powder, the claim is that it increases bone density. This has been officially and independently researched and verified by a government research laboratory. The company that owns the product is not allowed to do the study itself and this, of course, is the way it should be. And yet in the USA, Deng tells me, businesses that own the product are sometimes allowed to conduct the research to prove its efficacy.

"In China, the government doesn't just accept the claims of the company," he says. "So the government does the test and either approves the product or not. China is very tough."

If a product manufacturer wishes to make any medical claim in China, their product needs regulatory approval and this means it must go through stringent independent, government-supervised testing. So in fact, a medical product or supplement made in China is likely more effective, authentic, and valid (according to its claims) than one made in the USA.

This brings us to the fascinating topic of "Brand China." When Chinese manufacturers now make many of the finest and highest quality products available today, including the omnipresent iPhone, why does so much of the world still have an issue with other products carrying the "Made in China" label? And what are the Chinese doing about this brand conundrum?

13
Made in China: fixing perceptions of a brand

"Success in business, as in life, is a result of change that comes through learning and growth. Great nations are always exploring and achieving, changing and improving. Imagine where we'll be in two decades."

Li Jinyuan

One woman in Russia was so suspicious of Chinese-made products that she first tested the Tiens calcium powder on her dog. Fortunately for everybody involved, including the dog, the animal's health showed great improvement so its owner began taking the mix herself. While it's mildly entertaining, the story also exposes a greater challenge that Tiens has had to contend with along the way to global success – the brand and reputational issues attached to anything containing those three well-known words "Made in China."

When we think logically and with reason, we know that products manufactured in China are just as likely, and just as unlikely, to fall apart as those made anywhere else in the world. In Chinese manufacturing right now, it is the best of times and the worst of times. Many of the very finest products originate in Guangzhou, Shenzhen, Shanghai, and Tianjin, as do many of the world's trashiest throwaways. The simple truth is that thanks to its long history of being the manufacturing center of the world, China can today produce everything and anything perfectly and to an exceptional standard, or to a minimal standard and a minimal price.

However, it was not so long ago that most products made in China leaned towards the lower end of the quality spectrum, and at the same time the country was famous for the knock-off and counterfeit goods it produced. When other territories created something beautiful, expensive, and unique, wily Chinese manufacturers would create their own almost identical versions, meaning rip-off Louis Vuitton handbags and Rolexes flooded the underground sales markets and were sold on the streets of Paris and Rome, and out of the backs of vans in New York City. "Fake Fendi" handbags and purses were even made famous by the cult TV program *Sex and the City*, when one of the characters did all she could to hunt down an affordable replica.

All of this created a serious reputational problem for "Brand China," one that the government and business have been working hard to reverse. But people have long memories and even longer ingrained prejudices and biases. As a reminder of this fact, I spoke recently with an elderly Western gentleman who still refuses to buy a Japanese car as he remembers the days, before I was born, when Japanese manufacturers were derided for their questionable production techniques. He was also of the opinion that New Zealand vineyards produce terrible wine, and that the streets of New York City are lawless killing fields where armed gangsters roam free. Long memories and ingrained biases, indeed.

Chairman Li regularly points out the mid-term and long-term strategic plans that the Chinese government has in place to improve, across the board, the quality of all Chinese-manufactured goods. They are going to have to do so, he says, as the Chinese population itself with its increased spending power is expecting higher-quality offerings. If Chinese people are not satisfied with locally made goods, then they'll happily shop elsewhere. They already have the purchasing power and the technology to shop anywhere in the world.

"China is the largest populated country in the world with 1.4 billion people," Li says. "We have 600 million people in the cities and another 800 million in the villages. They are the farmers. Now our government is promoting transformations and urbanizations in those villages, so they are transforming those villages either into a town or combining them into a bigger city. So the living quality is changing and their spending power is changing. A lot of villages are transforming into economic towns with some sort of specialized industry and higher productivity. The living quality for the people in those towns has been enhanced and upgraded. This is happening right now, so just imagine what will happen in ten or twenty years from now. Living quality and productivity and spending power will race up to another level.

"There used to be a big gap between city and town or city and village but now, via the promotion of urbanization, the gap is fairly small. The urbanized areas have traditionally been on the east coast of China and the west has been rural and remote, but now the gap between eastern China and western China is closing."

For its own sake, then, China has an interest in increasing the quality of its own created and made goods and of ensuring the quality of any goods that enter China from overseas. In fact, this improvement has been happening for some time as manufacturing processes, practices, and standards have improved organically. But as the perceptions from the rest of the world of Chinese output have remained somewhat negative, Chinese businesses in international markets have had to think laterally to continue to grow in offshore markets.

To discover exactly how these problems appear, and how Tiens offices outside China work around them, I speak with staff in various territories. A manager from Tiens West Europe says consumers are aware that the quality of Chinese products has been improving, but the improvement has not gone far enough.

"There has been positive development but the image of Chinese product quality is still seen to be compromised," she says. "We all know that the very best products in the world and the very worst products in the world come from China. That puts us in a position where we simply need to overcome the 'very worst' situation by emphasizing the positives, and Tiens has enormous positives."

The potentially negative image can be overcome through the way one chooses to discuss the Chinese origin, she believes. In the case of Tiens, the country of origin is relevant in a very positive way thanks to the power of the story of Traditional Chinese Medicine.

"That is where we need to play," the manager says. "That is our strength and that is what we need to bring to the forefront. To Tiens' advantage, the way the Chairman has lived his life and chosen to build his business is a very powerful tale. As an individual he is a brand, he's not just the Chairman of the group.

"That means we have two stories to tell. One is about an individual who had a huge dream of bringing health and wellbeing to the world, and that is a perfect marketing tool. It is spot on. Outside of the Chairman's brand we have a very strong product message to deliver. Combining those two creates a very powerful offering. Communicating what the Chairman has done and what are his values and how he chooses to run his business and what were the dreams he had, that is powerful. Then to add the products and the business opportunity, there is our strength."

On the other hand, the team in Mexico tells me there is no issue with the fact that the Tiens product comes from China. The fact that the products are based on 5,000 years of Traditional Chinese Medicine means much more than the potential negatives of a few decades of a nation's questionable manufacturing history. In fact, to have such products manufactured anywhere but China would seem a little absurd, they say.

When Chinese industry begins manufacturing products that are just as good or better than those from elsewhere, that is when they disrupt the world, says Paul Gillis, Professor of Management at Peking University. And China is already beginning to do just that.

"China really starts to shake up world markets when they create things that are at a higher-quality level but which they can still sell at a lower price," Gillis says. "That's when they start disrupting markets elsewhere in the world. I think that day has arrived in a few industries, but it's going to be very widespread soon across very many global industries."

Chinese businesses themselves clearly recognize their own advances in quality of output. Mr Song, from the Dalian office of Tiens and for many years a staff member within the Chairman's inner office, relates an account that illustrates this point very well.

Tiens manufactures some products in countries such as Spain, Malaysia, Ethiopia, and India. For a long time many of the European country leaders for Tiens specifically sourced their products from the Spanish factory, to be able to tell consumers they were made locally. More recently, though, most of the European distributors have contacted the head office and asked for products that are made in China.

"They no longer want the products that are made in Spain or somewhere else," Song says. "They thought perhaps that some of the ingredients may be different, and that the Chinese product would be the highest quality from anywhere in the world. So we had to explain that everything made by Tiens is to the same standard, with ingredients of the same quality, no matter where it is made. It is the same everywhere. We have always been all about quality. The Chairman has always paid special attention to the quality of the products and this is why they have received so many certifications. Quality is the lifeblood of this company."

This is the realization coming to most Chinese businesses and one that is being promoted and supported by the Chinese government. Quality is everything. The Chinese government's Belt and Road Initiative will likely move some of the cheaper industries on to other developing nations as China continues its modernization program. Then "Made in China" or "Created in China" will mean something very different and, for Chinese businesses, something very special. China's leadership talks openly about "cultural self-confidence," or the fact that Chinese businesses should be proud to remain Chinese while taking on the world. This reinvigoration of Brand China will go a long way toward instilling greater cultural self-confidence.

"China is transitioning," Mr Yan tells me as he gestures softly toward the window and beyond, to the landscaped industrial surrounds of the Wuqing head office. "The nation used to be concerned primarily with the figure, the quantity, the GDP. It was all about the numbers. But now we're transitioning into an environment that is more concerned with quality management and quality output. It is no longer only about the numbers, but also about the quality and the benefits and how these changes will benefit the nation. It has changed from 'Made in China' to 'Innovated in China.' It has changed from 'China speed' to 'China quality.' This is the transition period we're in."

In Tiens and in greater China, Chairman Li sees a confidence building from the inside out. Over the past three decades, he has seen the self-image of the Chinese people improve immensely. He has witnessed a great pride replacing the self-doubt that his fellow countrymen and women felt for such a long time. And once the people feel good about themselves and about the direction in which they are moving, it is all but impossible to stop this positive sentiment from spreading around the globe.

In fact, this is the reason that I am here in China. The Chairman, this business, and the people of China have arrived in a place that brings them great pride. Theirs is a story that is worth telling and understanding across the world.

14
The Chairman's challenges: blackmail and bomb vests

"I am grateful to those who troubled us."

Li Jinyuan

Speaking of stories, during our very first meeting the Chairman promised me details about several highly challenging moments in business, experiences that would send a merely mortal entrepreneur running back into the secure arms of full-time employment. These stories told to me by the Chairman, tales of criminal challenges the business has faced over the years, were captivating in themselves, often with elements of a Hollywood blockbuster. Even more interesting and revealing, though, were the Chairman's reactions to each event.

Take, for instance, the day some years ago when one of Li's senior managers rushed into his office and told the Chairman to leave the building. A man wearing a bomb vest had just entered and was threatening to blow himself up unless he was given money. The explosion would destroy much of the manufacturing equipment. Tiens was targeted, staff tell me, because its success had earned it a reputation in the local region as a wealthy company.

"The manager told me I needed to leave," the Chairman recalls. "But I said, 'It's okay. We can handle this.'"

Police had been called and soon armed officers and several special forces soldiers from a nearby military base surrounded the intruder.

At any stage of the proceedings the man could have been shot, but Li's concern was to bring the event to a peaceful conclusion, ensuring no lives were lost and nobody was hurt, not even the man in the bomb vest. Li and some of his senior managers negotiated with the man and he left peacefully. Once he was off the property and was no longer a threat to those around him, police moved in and made an arrest.

Another challenging experience occurred early in the business, as the calcium powder product was gaining traction around China and the company was finally experiencing positive and reliable cash flow. A man whose 80-year-old father had died from cancer accused Tiens of causing the death, as his father had taken the calcium powder regularly.

"He was a man of some power and his relatives worked in the media. He tried to put pressure on the company and used his family links to influence the media coverage about the company and about me," the Chairman says. "This guy was abusing his powers. He used every connection he had to put pressure on us. Of course this included his brothers who worked in the media.

"With this guy using his family connections in the media to launch a public shaming campaign, he could have hurt us very badly. We settled this through negotiation, not because our product had any issues but we understood the emotions around the loss of the father. That was very difficult, but we negotiated in the interests of the long-term success of the company. We would likely not do that today, but that was early in the life of the company.

"Unfortunately, at that time, a lot of others tried something similar. This is how society sometimes is. There is no way to create a complete defence against this kind of thing. Some people live in the darkness but a successful business is in a visible, bright space. This is the painful aspect of human interaction. Some people do not behave like decent human beings. In China at that early time in the life of Tiens, some people were like that. It is less likely for people to do these things now."

As the Tiens star continued to rise, for instance, one individual demanded money or, he said, he'd find a way to put poison into the company's manufacturing process. Another sent a note saying he had a gun and unless the business gave him money, he would kill the Chairman's children. These events were one-offs and were quickly and quietly handled by local police.

But a longer and more painful experience was had in 2003. The owner of a local club approached the Chairman about sponsoring the club for millions of yuan. Whilst he didn't immediately refuse, Li's response was not positive.

That club owner knew the chief of China's central tax investigation bureau, as well as people within various branches of government.

If authorities believed the business was behaving incorrectly in any way, it had to be investigated. There had never been a suggestion of impropriety but this person, Li subsequently learned, began to feed spurious but damning information to his contacts in government.

A major investigation was launched into Tiens and its financial dealings. "I heard this news one day as I was arriving at the airport in Shanghai," the Chairman recalls. "I told my colleagues to cooperate as much as they could. I told them, please just cooperate with the authorities. And don't worry about anything because this company is mine and if anybody has to be accountable, it is me."

Later that day, after the Chairman had attended a press conference on a completely different topic on behalf of the business, he was approached by three of his senior managers who believed he did not yet know about the financial investigation. They sheepishly broke the news to him.

"I told them I already knew about it," he smiles. "I had found out as soon as I arrived at the airport. When they heard this, they were amazed because my emotions had not been visible, even throughout the press conference. But I knew that I had nothing to worry about because I had done nothing wrong."

The investigative groups removed masses of documents and financial reports from the Tiens Group head office to begin an inquiry that would stretch over almost two years.

"It became very difficult," Li says. "They used every means possible to demand things from the company. The investigation lasted for 23 months. Normally a company would be bankrupt under similar circumstances or maybe the leader would be imprisoned, but we went through 23 months of torture and came out the other end.

"From a corporate perspective, during that 23 months the company lost a lot of things. We were heavily affected."

The Chairman calls it "23 months of torture" not only because of the investigation but also because of the distractions, problems, and damage it caused. One serious issue that arose during that period, as a result of the business's apparent vulnerability, was a drama that unfolded in Malaysia.

Kevin Hou, who originally began working as an interpreter in the Chairman's office in 2001, was deeply involved in this drama. That year his work took him to Thailand and Russia. Travel opportunities, in fact, were a major driver for his decision to take the job.

"China was open at the time but not as much as it is today," Hou tells me during a meeting in one of the lounge areas in the Tiens headquarters building. "Today, China is fully open to the outside world. But at that time so many young people wanted to go overseas with their work. They wanted to find these types of opportunities. I felt the same. I wanted to find an international platform. I wanted to go overseas and to improve myself. Tiens was recruiting professionals, so I sent my CV.

"I was offered a job fairly quickly but at that time I had another offer. I had to make a very difficult decision because the income I was being offered at Tiens was lower than the other offer. But I looked at Tiens as an international platform, and it was the right decision."

After just one year, Hou was appointed to the position of Malaysia Branch Manager for Tiens. In 2003 he took over Singapore and Brunei. In 2007 he was asked to manage the entire southern Africa region and in 2010 Hou was awarded the role of Africa Regional President. Hou has also held the position of Tiens South Asia Regional President. It has been an impressive progression from interpreter to one of the business's most senior global managers, but that's the way of things in China for talented people. Opportunities abound in China, and in Chinese businesses, for the talented and the motivated.

Once he had launched the Malaysia branch of Tiens and was then transferred to Singapore, Hou handed over the management of the Malaysian office to a Chinese gentleman we will call Mr Shi (not his real name, for reasons that will become clear). The new manager immediately moved the business to a different office location.

Shi began spending a great deal of company money on renovations and vehicles, and he then began to make secret deals with some of the branch's local shareholders. Those shareholders elected him as their Managing Director and he immediately told staff to stop obeying directions from China, because they were now an independent business.

The new Malaysia manager even went as far as ringing Hou, in Singapore, and telling him to leave, to go back to China. Shi said he would soon be in charge of the Singapore business and all other neighboring territories, and that the Chairman had agreed to the deal.

Hou, who'd been in continuous contact with the Chairman, knew this was not true. In actual fact, Shi was making a play for ownership of the Malaysia/Singapore branch of the business via backdoor deals, by manipulating assets and changing names of legal entities. He was taking advantage of the fact that the China head office was stretched almost to breaking point by the financial investigation, and betting that they'd be too weak to respond.

But actually, the Chairman had been investigating goings-on in Malaysia. He had also heard of threats being leveled at Hou in Singapore, including from one person who, in a muffled voice on the telephone, threatened to break Hou's legs if he didn't leave Singapore immediately.

"At that time I was quite frightened," Hou says. "It was a direct threat. I made a call to the Chairman and told him. At that time, I received a similarly threatening call every day for perhaps two weeks. These calls were full of threats. They were also sending faxes to the Chairman, telling him about problems I was having in Singapore. But Chairman Li still trusted me. I still remember at that time, every day the Chairman would make a call to me to encourage me, to comfort me, because he knew I was under a lot of pressure."

As for the Chairman, he was actually fighting similar fires around the globe. When we speak about that troubled period he rattles off over 20 country names and says that in all of these countries local staff members were trying to take advantage of the crisis the Tiens head office was facing because of the investigation.

"It felt as if everybody was taking out a knife and stabbing me," he says. "But I tried to remain positive. I believe in justice and I believe that eventually justice will prevail over evil."

In the middle of 2003, the Chairman along with the company secretary and some senior staff traveled to Malaysia and contacted Malaysian police, who found evidence that Shi had taken bribes from suppliers. He had his position stripped and was flown back to China where, facing prison, he begged the Chairman for forgiveness.

And here's the most amazing part – the Chairman forgave Shi! He did not go as far as offering him employment, but he decided not to press charges and he did not provide the evidence that would send Shi to prison. Instead, the rogue manager simply left the business, saving any face that he had left at the time.

Not that it helped in the end. Mr Yan, when I ask him about the account, offers a succinct summary.

"As we developed rapidly internationally, some of our management systems were not complete. That manager, a Chinese man we'd sent to

Malaysia, changed something in the registration of one of our branch companies so the stock was registered to him. It meant that he could be the chairman of Tiens in Malaysia. So the Chairman and some others went to Malaysia to talk with other partners, who agreed it was not the right thing to do. The other partners offered evidence. The manager agreed to return the stock so the company went back into the ownership of Tiens, and then he was forgiven. But people do not change. He went to another company and did the same thing, and they took him to court."

Tigers cannot change their stripes, it seems. Unsurprisingly, the club owner who had caused all of the trouble for Tiens was also caught in a different corruption scandal and, for a small while at least, escaped punishment when he fled overseas. But he was quickly tracked down by authorities and brought back to China for sentencing.

Around the globe, country by country, Chairman Li and his team successfully put out fire after fire, learning valuable lessons in international management and corporate governance along the way. And it is the Chairman's reaction to the series of events, his lack of bitterness and, most revealingly, his gratitude for the experience, that brings me to realize the enormous influence of specific Chinese philosophers over the behavior and thought patterns of many Chinese people.

"Some moments have been catastrophic for Tiens. They have been life or death," he tells me, with a profound calmness and stillness in his voice. "But in the end we won. All this experience I am grateful for, including the people who troubled us. These people who made us suffer and tried to control us and make our life difficult, without them we would not have grown. We are grateful to them. They are our life teachers. We are more resilient as a result of their teachings."

It's a wonderfully positive point of view. Let's now have a quick but vital chat about the philosophers who have shaped the attitudes, beliefs, and behaviors not only of Li Jinyuan but of the entire Chinese population.

15
A way of thinking: Lao Tzu and Confucius

"The culture of ceremony is very important. It gives recognition, it conveys meaning, it shows achievement, its gives passage from one place to another in your life. Ceremony honors and brings happiness to all who take part."

Li Jinyuan

More than once I am told that business people visiting China should develop at least some knowledge around the teachings of philosophers Confucius, the founder of Confucianism, and Lao Tzu (aka Laozi/ Lao-Tze – pronounced lou-tser), the founder of Taoism.

"Culture, philosophy, and religion are some of the things we look at when we go into a non-Chinese market," Yan tells me. "From an understanding of faith we begin to learn how people interact with each other and what is the basis of their practices and behaviors, and of their society's culture. People should do the same when dealing with China."

When I begin to research the teachings of Confucius and Lao Tzu, I realize both philosophers have had an ongoing powerful effect on the behaviors, beliefs, and ethical frameworks of modern-day Chinese people, including today's younger generation.

Taking up most of one wall in the Chairman's cavernous office is an artwork depicting Lao Tzu riding on the back of an ox that is being gently led along a mountain path by a child. Many senior staff, and the Professor, tell me that the ancient philosopher's thoughts have a great influence over decisions made by the Chairman.

Lao Tzu's personal name is usually quoted as Li Er. This is of great significance to the Chairman.

"Lao Tzu is a great ancestor of the Li clan," Chairman Li tells me as we discuss the artwork, which was created for him by several experts within the Tsinghua University Faculty of Arts. "He wrote one of the classic pieces of Chinese literature, a moral bible of sorts, called *Tao Te Ching.*"

Influential Chinese writer Lu Xun, who lived in the late 1800s and early 1900s, went as far as claiming that anybody who has not read *Tao Te Ching* "cannot have any real understanding of Chinese culture." One excellent, contemporary translation of this work is *Tao Te Ching* by Stephen Mitchell (Harper Perennial Modern Classics, 2006).

"Lao Tzu said that originally, in the beginning, there is nothing," the Chairman says. "Then comes one and from one comes two and from two comes three, then more and more come. Eventually it is endless, it is infinity. But everything begins from nothing. His philosophy is to be a naturalist and he says what comes from nature is best if it remains the same."

Having come to be known in images as a man with long white hair, white eyebrows, and a flowing, white beard, philosopher and writer Lao Tzu is generally thought to have lived in the late sixth and early fifth centuries BCE, a time of massive political, spiritual, and social turmoil in the region we now know as China. The age was characterized by warfare.

Lao Tzu, having been well educated, was said to have lived some of his life in Luoyang in Henan, the capital during the Zhou dynasty, where he worked as a keeper of the royal archives in the court of Zhou. But after a large collection of the most valuable books was stolen by a vanquished Zhou prince, Lao Tzu gave up the life of the royal palace. The scholar earned a reputation as a master thinker and a great philosopher before he eventually left society altogether and rode an ox into the mountains (as illustrated on the Chairman's wall) to live as a hermit for his final years.

Lao Tzu Riding an Ox. Found in the collection of the National Palace Museum, Taipei

It was during this journey into the mountains that Lao Tzu was recognized by a guard, Yin Xi, at a remote post in a narrow valley on the outskirts of the kingdom. Yin Xi, legend says, convinced Lao Tzu to write down his thoughts and learnings before the great philosopher passed through into the unsettled frontier and his knowledge was lost to civilization forever. It is this work that became *Tao Te Ching*, which roughly translates as "The Book of the Way of Virtue."

Without a little background information, the *Tao Te Ching* is quite difficult to understand. An original reading, thanks to lines such as "When you need do nothing, there is nothing you cannot do," makes the work seem relatively cryptic. But boil down Lao Tzu's philosophies and the meaning soon becomes more understandable.

The philosopher was very interested in the supremacy of nature, particularly of water. He often related the power of water to the fact that it simply does what it is supposed to do – it flows and nourishes. In this way its results are effortless as the water, which can carve out entire canyons over time, is simply doing what water does. It is not trying to be something else.

"The supreme good is like water, which nourishes all things without trying to," Lao Tzu wrote.

Water is immensely powerful, he believed, but also soft and gentle. It appears weak but it has untold strength. The very plainness of water is its greatest strength.

So a "nothing" becomes a "something." In doing nothing out of the ordinary, water achieves a great deal. It shapes landscapes, becomes round in a round cup, becomes square in a square container, flows downhill, stops when it is dammed, flows again when the dam is broken, creates and supports life, and expects nothing in return. It does nothing that is out of its nature. Similarly, the nothings in other areas also hold great power. For instance, a house is only livable because of the large areas of nothing defined by its walls and ceiling. And music is made more potent by moments of silence, by pauses or "nothings" that contain so much more than stillness.

Lao Tzu's political system, known as "Wu Wei," also began by concentrating on nothings. It started with the assumption that human nature is good. If we accept that people are essentially honest then it means the non-enforcement of law, or at least a lack of meddling with the current systems of laws and regulations, is better than changing the system and having to strictly enforce those changes. Doing nothing is better than doing something. Also, political leaders who have no need to enforce laws or to punish wrongdoers are clearly so much more powerful than those who rule with an iron fist. Lao Tzu famously said that good governing of a great nation is similar to the cooking of a small fish – one should be careful not to overcook it.

Back to Lao Tzu's seemingly cryptic quote – "When you need do nothing, there is nothing you cannot do." It now makes more sense. He is saying that when a person must try desperately hard to do something, there is a good chance they will fail. But when they "need do nothing," when what they are attempting involves no effort, they will succeed just as water succeeds without effort. Accordingly, a good government presided over by a good leader will need to make little effort to create a good society, but a government whose leader is morally corrupt will naturally fail in the effort of good government as they are trying to be something they are not.

"Those who know do not speak; those who speak do not know," Lao Tzu wrote. Recall I mentioned the natural tendency of a Chinese person toward silence. In the West we say "an empty can rattles the most" to make the same point, although that does not often stop individuals in the West from spouting their opinions. For the Chinese, Lao Tzu has come at the same idea from a different angle, and his words have been digested over generations, very much affecting common behavior today.

And so Lao Tzu's ideas often speak of the power of nothing, the necessary effortlessness of success, the natural way of doing things. As Chairman Li described, Lao Tzu believed the natural way was the only way. The philosopher says that everything comes from nothing, that the more you have, the more you stand to lose, and that the only way to gain much is by having little: "Stooping, you will be preserved. Wronged, you will be righted. Hollow, you will be filled. Worn out, you will be renewed. Having little, you may gain; having much, you may be at a loss."

"A huge tree grows out of a small shoot," Lao Tzu wrote. "A nine-storey tower rises from a heap of earth. A thousand-mile journey begins with the first step."

With a deep comprehension, appreciation, and admiration of the work of Lao Tzu, it becomes easier to understand Li's great successes in business and the fact that he carried on when others would have given up, and continued to dream as others thought his plans too grand.

What of Confucius, then? Lao Tzu and Confucius had some influence over each other. The two lived in the same period and met several times. Lao Tzu, who is said to have died in 531 BCE, was the older and more senior of the two.

Lao Tzu grew up in relative wealth and enjoyed a strong education. It is broadly believed that Confucius did not. His father, a soldier who then went into the civil service, is said to have died when Confucius was just three. His mother brought him up in great hardship in a slum on the outskirts of Qufu, the capital of the area of Lu. Despite their lack of means, Confucius did gain an education. Of the six arts all children were expected to learn – reading and writing, poetry, charioteering, music, rituals, and archery – he excelled in rituals. This subject was all about the systems that were in place to regulate people's behaviors in ancient societies.

The area of Lu itself, says Xu Yuanxiang in his book *Confucius: A Philosopher for the Ages* (China Intercontinental Press, 2007), was "renowned as a land of ceremony and propriety." His upbringing within this specific environment, Xu says, had a profound influence on a young man struggling to come to terms with the cards he'd been dealt in life.

However, constant wars meant the society that young Confucius desired, one completely driven by rituals and conventions that preserved order and denoted place, would not eventuate. Even within this environment, though, Confucius would create order in his own life. When his mother died during his seventeenth year, he elected to mourn her death for three years. Word spread about this young man who was dedicated to ritual. His name and reputation travelled far.

Having recognized the importance of education after his was lacking, Confucius is said to have started up a school, the first of its kind, where any child from any background could attend and gain a strong education. Education was a fundamental right for all, he believed, regardless of class.

The next part of his life was spent traveling throughout the countryside with a band of followers, further developing his thoughts and teachings around the ritual system. He was coming up with a set of processes and guidelines around which society could operate harmoniously. One of the philosopher's most important ideas was around achieving the state of "Ren."

Ren is most easily defined as benevolence. This state of pure kindness, of compassion, is all about love and clearly demonstrated respect not only for one's relatives, but also for everybody else in society. Upon achieving this state of love for all, one would be in a state of Ren.

Propriety and benevolence were central to this philosophy. "Propriety is the exterior manifestation of benevolence, while benevolence is the interior content of propriety," Xu wrote. The external behavior, or the ritual, was as important as the belief itself.

The observance of ritual would also help to remove selfish thoughts, Confucius said, as it was based around ensuring one is behaving correctly according to rules of society, rather than rules of the individual. Now we begin to see a relationship forming with the China we know today – the one that thinks collectively rather than individually – and the philosophy developed by Confucius over 2,500 years ago.

This behavior was not only for a specific class of person. It would work only if it was recognized and performed by all. A leader must behave like a leader, Confucius taught. A father must behave like a father, a friend like a friend, and a son like a son. If everybody followed the moral code, then behavior would be regulated and society would be awash with goodwill.

Confucius hoped to influence political rulers with his teachings but was unsuccessful during his lifetime. However, in the middle of the second century CE, during the golden age of the Han Dynasty and centuries after the death of Confucius, emperors began to look to his work for guidance around building a stable society. For two millennia after that, the teachings of the philosopher were at the very center of Chinese society.

Confucian thoughts around a peaceful and stable society with an emperor at its core worked well for leaders and people alike. In a steady, constant, unchanging society, people were content and unrest was less likely. Along similar lines to Lao Tzu's teachings, Confucius said that an upright ruler who behaved like an upright ruler would be obeyed without ever having to give an order, but a ruler who was not upright would not have their orders obeyed.

The ritual and rhythm of Confucianism created a cultural stasis that worked in terms of peace and contentment, but which caused a wave of anti-Confucian sentiment during the nineteenth and twentieth centuries when it was blamed for keeping Chinese society in a holding pattern, rather than allowing it to develop and advance. The powerful continuity caused by Confucian behaviors, it was argued, kept the culture in a state of inertia and as other nations leapt forward, particularly with industrialization, China stood still.

Despite this backlash, Confucianism had embedded itself in the Chinese way of thinking and today any negative thoughts toward the philosophy have been washed away. As a guiding principle, at its very heart Confucianism says to treat others the way you would like to be treated yourself. That thought is taken very seriously in China today. In the chapter about saving face we discussed the fact that even when a staff member is sacked, not a single soul within the organization speaks openly and negatively about that person. They are treating the person the way they would like to be treated if they were in the same situation. Should an individual act in a disrespectful manner toward another, that individual would lose face for doing so.

Many scholars have since stated that the Chinese way of thinking would simply not exist without the influence of Confucius. From common rituals such as the ones mentioned earlier in this book, to the dedication to filial piety (young people treating their parents with great respect and absolutely accepting that they will look after them in their old age), to the fact that China developed a strong collective form of thinking, the teachings of Confucius have permeated every aspect of Chinese culture.

Some familiarity with the teachings of Lao Tzu and Confucius is important as those teachings help explain the way most Chinese people think and act, and how and why Chinese society has developed. The other essential area of understanding for anybody considering doing business in China, or anyone who simply has an interest in the Middle Kingdom, is communism as practised in China, which we will look at next.

16
Understanding the Communist Party of China

"China continues to rise because of the past 30 years of economic reform and because of the worldview of the government and the people. Before that, China was a sleeping lion. Now it has woken up as an economic and social power."

Li Jinyuan

Let's talk about perception and bias.

If you're a Westerner and you think of communism, what comes to mind? Evil? Repression? The enemy?

That's the way many Western political and opinion leaders have long framed it. Our popular media, mainstream commercial news outlets, entertainment producers such as Hollywood film studios, and politicians have turned a simple name for a set of political policies into something that is supposed to frighten and even repel us.

The reality, of course, is that the majority of social, political, and economic models have excellent intentions. However, every model has serious problems, mostly created when those very good intentions run into the less attractive aspects of human nature. Soon after the Brexit vote, experts and academics were lamenting the inherent weaknesses of democracy, and the fact that some things are simply too important to put to the popular vote.

And what about capitalism? Early in her first term, New Zealand's Prime Minister, Jacinda Ardern, called capitalism a "blatant failure." This was due to the fact that many families in her country, and particularly children, were without enough funds or resources to live a life above the poverty line. But in the end, each political or economic model is just that, a model.

It helps a great deal when visiting China, or managing a business in the country, to give yourself permission to brush off the imagery and bias around communism that have been bred into so many of us. I had to consciously decide that I was going to develop my own opinion, rather than letting Western politicians and media demand that I think a certain way about another nation's leadership.

Interestingly, many Chinese people are aware of the issues that Westerners have with their model of government.

"I find that from time to time some people in foreign countries do have a misunderstanding about China," says university student Hong Yuanqi (Edward, whom we met earlier). He has spent various periods of his life studying in the USA. "I'm not saying it's their fault. It's simply a fact that some people don't understand other countries."

Foreigners, he says, think that China's leadership is somehow bad. But the Communist Party of China, from a Chinese person's point of view, is a very big concept. It's not all good or all bad. It contains tens of millions of members and each and every one of them is a different individual.

"Some of the misunderstandings come from newspaper reports in Western countries," he says. "Even if people try to remain objective, they still think the Communist Party's system is an old and useless one and that democracy is the future of all mankind. People are influenced by these sorts of reports and by a sense that anything other than democracy does not work. They think that makes the Party and communism bad."

Some university students I speak with in Beijing express surprise that people in the West think their nation's government is somehow bad. Of course, they realize that a one-party system has certain drawbacks, but so do all political systems, they say. Most admit they have not lived in countries governed by systems they can compare with their own, but the massive advancement and growth China has seen over the last few decades, and the enormous improvements in lifestyle compared with what their parents and grandparents experienced, must count for something, they argue.

"Some people from the West think the Chinese government is bad and the Chinese people are in some sort of a prison type of a situation. That is kind of ridiculous," one young woman in the university group says. "We have no real choice of government, but the Party has kept the safety in this country. They balance things for us so as Chinese we are happier and wealthier. So obviously this Party is good for us.

"Like any political party in America or Australia, each has its problems," she continues. "So what do we do to stop those problems from getting worse? Our leader President Xi Jinping is currently putting a lot of programs in place, such as anti-corruption, to keep some problems from occurring. Of course, there are now some people who are rich and some people who are not very rich. People often blame these problems on the Party, but usually it results from an individual's experience and environment. If somebody is getting richer and somebody is getting happier but you are not, it mostly depends on yourself."

From a government-business interaction point of view, people I speak with, particularly entrepreneurs running businesses at the smaller end of the scale, tell me about how very simple it now is to start a new business. The government, they say, is enormously supportive and encouraging of entrepreneurship. One man I meet in Beijing who has a part-time job with a newspaper has also started up a shop that specializes in the retail of high-end tobacco pipes from around the world. His license to trade, rent a storefront, employ part-time staff, and run his business required the filling out of a form that took up just one side of a single A4 page.

Similarly, a thirty-something woman with whom I enjoy lunch in a restaurant in the Tianjin city center tells me she owns, with her husband, a chain of restaurants as well as several fashion outlets specializing in shoes. While managing those businesses will always be difficult, she says the main challenges come from typical business issues such as marketing, branding, human resources, and quality control. I ask whether the government and its red tape caused her any pain, and she says that on a top-ten list of business challenges, government would not even make an appearance. As an entrepreneur, she feels fully supported.

Chairman Li is quick to point out, when I speak with him on this topic, that Tiens is both independent and patriotic. It exists partly to serve its country, and also to benefit those nations in which it does business or shares its charity. This means working in unison with China's leadership to achieve certain goals for the business and for the nation.

And indeed, for big business in China, government can be a little more problematic (or a lot, as has been the case with the Dalian Wanda Group). Chairman Li tells me that dealing with numerous levels of government can sometimes be an extremely positive interaction and at other times can offer delay and frustrations. Once again, this is not unique to China. Governments around the globe are famous for their ability to sometimes frustrate those who require their services.

Ironically, efficiency in Chinese government is currently suffering, and various government dealings for big businesses are becoming more difficult, as the anti-corruption movement gathers pace and strength. This is not because of the removal of corrupt practices and people. Rather it's an unintended consequence of the serious punishments, including lengthy prison sentences, being handed out to government officials who appear to be acting in a manner that suggests corrupt activity. Many officials are now far more careful about what they allow through the system, meaning the process is slowed. Some prefer certain decisions, which in the past they may have confidently rubber-stamped, to be sent further up the chain. So as corruption is stamped out, some government services have become less efficient.

But for business leaders, Chairman Li tells me, that is a small price to pay when compared to the support and direction being offered by the government at its very highest levels. For example, President Xi Jinping has repeatedly stressed his support for an open and innovative economy.

"The door of China's opening-up will not close," President Xi was reported as saying by the *China Daily* in early March 2017. He called on business leaders to take the lead in the liberalization of trade and investment, furthering innovation and intensifying reform. He particularly encouraged the development of scientific innovation centers and social governance innovation, the report said, and suggested that the enormous free-trade zone set up in and around Shanghai – which is said to have been responsible for the creation of 40,000 new entities since its formation in 2013 – should "become a bridgehead for the country's Belt and Road Initiative and help market entities go global."

During the same session in Shanghai in 2017, Xi also vowed to continue to strengthen his own party's discipline and governance, which brings us to the question of how the CPC operates.

The CPC is the world's biggest political party with around 90 million active members. The Party doesn't accept just anybody into its ranks. In other nations, political parties typically welcome any and all as members, but the Party chooses its own. Members are often the most promising and academically gifted students at schools and universities across the nation. At a post-university stage, they are often those considered to have leading technical abilities in specific fields. Just as it did throughout China's long and rich imperial history, a great education can still lead to career success within government, no matter the individual's background.

But Party membership isn't guaranteed once a potential candidate is selected. There is a 12-month probationary period as well as checks, training, and examinations by local Party officials.

Party members face greater choice of employment as certain jobs at various levels are only open to members. Perhaps more importantly, young members also rub shoulders with others higher up the chain, people with real power and whose friendship and loyalty can mean a great deal to an individual's career, business, and lifestyle.

China actually contains other, smaller political parties but they are not permitted to challenge any policy put forward by the CPC, meaning they have little to no actual power.

Within the CPC, as is the case with most political parties, there are also various factions representing their own interests, all jostling for greater influence.

At the peak of the Party is a body known as the National Congress, which meets once every five years at an event also known as the National Congress, which attracts global attention.

At the National Congress more than 2,000 delegates from various Party organizations come together to elect a Central Committee of 200 members, but this is mostly theater. In reality the decisions have been made long before the Congress. That central committee then elects a smaller group, the absolute powerbrokers, into the politburo. Seen in a certain light, it is democracy without the messy and time-consuming process of having to use a series of almost-truths to convince politically ignorant members of the public to vote for a specific representative. Democracy, or at least representation, is within the Party, rather than without.

The result is a single party that can introduce cohesive and fully supported legislation and which, without the numerous distractions of opposition, can react very quickly to various issues and trends. Its ability to think long-term, as opposed to most Western governments with their four-year terms, means economic policies, social policies, and infrastructure plans can be planned, implemented, and maintained with great confidence.

There are many positives and also some negatives with such a system. With a lack of opposition can come a lack of thorough planning and detailed analysis. This then reveals itself in the form of such issues as increased pollution, workers' rights, and social support mechanisms such as health-care systems and aged-care support. Of course, these issues are not unique to China or to any other country. Indeed no political system throughout the world can be said to have addressed such issues fully, especially given the changing nature of social and economic conditions.

During my time in China, for instance, I see many cases of hospitals rejecting dying patients. They must spend the last few weeks or months of their life elsewhere, rather than in a hospital or a palliative care hospice, because of a lack of space and the terminal nature of their illness. In a country of 1.4 billion people, hospital beds are available only for those lucky enough to entertain a hope of survival.

"The one-party system is a double-edged sword," says Professor Grafstein. "The thing about the concentration of power is that you can get things done but you can also make really massive mistakes. There are issues with checks and balances, but in China they sure can organize a society. In the United States, to do anything you have to get an environmental impact statement, and everybody around you is still going to sue you because somehow your project doesn't suit their needs or interferes with their property rights, etc. None of that happens in China. They take care of those things and they get things done. But part of what they've done is absolutely useless. There are plenty of roads to nowhere and projects that are given the green light purely for economic stimulus, but which have no long-term, productive value.

"The biggest fear is instability. China seems always on the edge of chaos, so you have to have a very strong hand leading the country and an organized apparatus below that leadership."

The overarching goals of the Communist Party of China are peaceful development and modernization, according to Zheng Bijian, former permanent Vice-President of the Central Party School, in a piece published by *The Huffington Post* in 2015 (*You can't understand China unless you know how the Communist Party thinks*, December 2, 2015). He said the CPC, having come to life in 1921, has as its goal the completion of the building of a "moderately prosperous society in all aspects" by 2021 and the "modernization of China" by 2049, 100 years since the establishment of the People's Republic of China. These, he says, are the CPC's two core centennial goals.

The Party, Zheng wrote, is not driven by selfish interests and is not "undisciplined or indolent," but rather is advanced and based on strict internal discipline. It does not seek revolution, but rather "despite the differences in social systems and ideologies around the world, it endeavors to seek convergence of interests with other countries and promotes China's peaceful rise along with the peaceful rise of a vast number of other developing countries." Finally, it is not "stuck in its old ways" but is instead constantly learning and is innovation oriented. Along these same lines, Deng Xiaoping once said the Party must always remain accepting of "things our forefathers had never said" and, Zheng claims, that philosophy is still strongly respected.

When I allowed myself to make my own judgements, I realized the CPC has brought its country and its citizens a long way forward over the last four decades, and has matured enough to admit to its weaknesses and put actions in place to address them. It is cohesive and powerful, respected by its nation's people for the most part, and respectful of the fact that the people need and deserve strong leadership.

Power is closely related to longevity. In the West, parties voted into power typically only hold power for three or four years, and leaders often for even less. The absurd game of musical chairs that is the Australian Prime Ministership, a position that has had seven people in the role in the last decade, is a perfect case in point. The seeming policy paralysis that the Brexit vote brought to the UK, and the dividedness and directional ambiguity of Presidential and Congress elections in the USA, are also cases of governments getting caught up in the short-term vortex. Corporations, on the other hand, are in existence for many decades, if not centuries, and therefore potentially hold more power than governments, at least indirectly.

In Singapore, leadership and government arguably took a structured, corporate approach to the development of that country, which has been enormously successful. The CPC would likely not see itself as similar to a corporation, but it has the longevity of vision and influence, and the plan, persistence, and patience to develop the country in almost every respect. In this way, the government has been able to engineer greater success than any Western leadership over the past several decades.

Yes, there are many challenges and there have been damaging events that the Western world points to when discussions about China occur.

Issues around human rights, stifling of protests, and capital punishment, as well as the censorship of access to the internet are often raised in the West. But every country has experienced events and challenges that – without diminishing their impact – have to be understood (but not necessarily agreed with) in the context of the country in which they have occurred.

So shake off those preconceptions and make up your own mind by first comparing China's ruling party with your own nation's leadership. Which is more effective at taking the nation in the direction it needs to go, in looking after the interests of its people, in supporting business, and in keeping its promises? And by 2049, at the centenary of the establishment of the People's Republic of China, which government do you think will have achieved more?

17
One-child policy consequences

"Families are our heritage and our legacy. Families place you in the
history of human life."

Li Jinyuan

One of China's most controversial programs was the one-child policy,
implemented in 1979 and replaced by the two-child policy in 2015.
It now presents a perfect case study for those wanting to understand
how the policies of a long-term, single-party government can have
unexpected consequences, which that very same party must deal with
several decades down the track.

Those consequences begin to reveal themselves in a casual discussion
I have with a manager at Tiens a week or so before a public holiday
week begins. I ask him what he has planned for his time off. He tells
me he's doing the same thing he always does, catching a fast-train over
1,000 kilometres to his hometown to visit his ageing parents. In order
to do this he leaves behind his wife – who is busy looking after her own
mother – and their son.

This particular manager is unusual in that he lives away from his parents and only looks after them during holidays. Most Chinese children,
while they might go away for a few years for their education or for work,
often try to stay reasonably geographically close to their parents to provide ongoing support especially as their parents age. Often they also do
double duty as they look after their grandparents on weekends, giving
their parents a break. Each generation looks after those above, and the
youngest generation often bears the brunt of the caring responsibilities.

For many younger people in China, this is an all-encompassing
and sometimes exhausting responsibility as, of course, they are typically single children as a result of government policy. But family is
central to the Chinese view of life, as it is central to the Tiens view
of its workforce.

The one-child restriction applied quite strictly to around half the population, depending on the time period and the exemptions, particularly for minority ethnic groups. There were no limits on the number of children families in some remote areas could have, for instance. At various stages and in different areas, permission was given for a second child if the first was a female (in rural areas where physical labor was important, for example), or if the first child was disabled. Those who had given birth overseas were allowed a second child upon their return to China, and even those who were under the strictest rule of the one-child policy could simply pay a fine for each further child they welcomed into the world. But most families voluntarily went along with the policy as it was seen as the responsible choice to make for their society and nation. It would help to keep the population at a manageable level and would lessen demands for basic necessities such as food and water.

I ask Chairman Li why he had four children during a period when others were being told to refrain, and his response is as effusive and passionate as expected. "When these things happen, you never want to hurt a little life," he says. "We gave in to nature when my wife was pregnant. It is a gift and I will accept it. I had no plan or intention to have four children. It was not planned and there was a financial penalty to be paid for each child, but children are a gift."

Public policy in every country and by every government has unintended side effects on society and on the businesses within that society. China is no different, apart from the fact that, unlike in most other countries, the very same government that set the policies has to deal with the consequences of those policies.

So what are those consequences? Actually, they are broad and far-reaching. They have shaped an entire generation of young Chinese people and the ramifications are being felt strongly in the business world and in other parts of society.

Consider a story I'm told by Paolo Frana, an Italian-born architect who worked for several years at Tiens Group's engineering department as Senior Project Manager, and with various other Chinese businesses. Frana and his Chinese wife have a young son who, at the time of our discussion, is in pre-school. Whenever Frana visits the pre-school to drop off or pick up his son, he notices the number of parents and carers dedicating themselves to each, individual child. He sees this from the point of view of an outsider, of somebody who has spent most of his life in Europe.

"In this country there is a culture of having one child, so parents are very focused on their one baby," he says. "Chinese families are very close and it is quite common that several generations live together. So as soon as a couple has a child, that child actually has two mothers and two fathers, or in some cases three mothers and three fathers, depending on how many grandparents are living with them or nearby. All of these carers concentrate on the one child and they never let anything happen to it. That child never gets hurt and never wants for anything. They never even have to compete with a brother or sister for attention. There is a kind of selfishness in their attitude.

"My child now is four years old and he wants to play with other children. But in China as soon as one child lays a hand on another child it is considered scandalous. You'll get three parents yelling at you because your child touched another child. They are kids and they are four years old and they're just playing around as kids like to do and nobody is crying, but it is quite common to have arguments with parents because of a small touch where nobody was hurt or injured."

Children in China, in Frana's view, are too wrapped in cotton wool and too fiercely protected by all of their carers. They are not allowed to learn by falling over, and they're quickly taught that if they do fall, someone will always be there to pick them up and brush them off. They never have to fend for themselves.

"They do not experience life," Frana says. "They are never allowed to fall down and cry."

Imagine the difference across generations. Their parents lived through Mao's leadership, a time of social upheaval, a period of protest and purging. Their parents were forced to work on the land, were often separated from their own families for years, sometimes for decades, in service of a greater good. They knew pain and they knew hunger and they saw death but they learned to survive. (The Chairman laughs after I answer one of his questions about my memories from childhood – I tell him about summer days on the beach, ice creams and frolicking in the surf – "You and I had a very different upbringing," he grins.) For obvious reasons they wanted a better life for their children, but then they were told they could only have one child.

So care, love, hope, and financial investment are all focused onto a single human being.

And it's not just when the children are young. This treatment continues throughout life. Understandably, if parents have only one child, then they wish to invest as much as they can into that child. In China, the single greatest investment is education.

As a result, the younger generations in the professional offices of today's Chinese corporates – twenty-somethings and thirty-somethings – tend to be incredibly well educated, mostly to master's level and often to doctorate level. Many have earned their degrees overseas. Two of the three staff members with whom I work most closely at Tiens have an international education, for instance. One, Lu Xi (English/French name Lucie), studied in Paris to master's level and speaks fluent English and French. Another, Yue Peng (English name Carter), attended university in Manchester, studying to master's level, and speaks fluent English. The third, Liu Yuying (English name Yana), boasts a master's degree from a leading Chinese university and speaks English. The Beijing university students I meet all have fluent English, which is a requirement for entry to their prestigious university. Most have or are learning another foreign language, and about two-thirds of the undergraduate students at that university will go overseas for their master or doctoral study.

Of course, the sum of this collective international experience is an entirely new view on life, on work, and on social conventions. Businesses that are run in a traditional Chinese manner, including Tiens, are being forced to change their ways as they deal with a new type of staff member, one at odds with their older colleagues. And these new, highly educated and more Westernized Chinese youngsters are having to deal with an entirely new level of pressure and expectation, one their somewhat cosseted upbringing did little to prepare them for.

"Maybe ten years ago you could get a good job because you had an undergraduate degree. Today you need a master's," says Zhang Guangyu (English name Jason), one of a group of young, male Tiens staff members I speak with one afternoon. "Maybe ten years from now you'll need a PhD. The competition is very strong. If you want to find a job, the managers will know if you speak English and whether you also speak any other languages. They will know what degree you have. They will know the experience you have. And they will use all this information to judge you."

The Professor tells how he was asked recently to give a "professional development" talk to a group of around 200 new employees of a major Chinese corporation, with most of them under 30, and about 20 percent from outside China. To get into that group, the employees had to have graduated with excellent grades at master's level from one of the top 50 Chinese universities or from one of the top 100 universities in the world, had to be fluent in Chinese and English (and preferably in one other language), and had to demonstrate in their interview that they had ambition, a worldview, and were committed to the direction of the company and the direction of China. "The intelligence and commitment in the room were palpable," he says. He adds, however, that "from a Western perspective, the demands that are on these young people, from themselves and from others, can be seen as just too much."

The young people I meet at Tiens agree there is a lot of pressure on them to perform, and it comes from various angles. "We have huge pressure because we have many responsibilities at work and in life," Zhang says. "Pressure comes from all sides. In the Chinese culture, men our age need to be feeding families. We also have a mother and a father and we have to show filial piety. So we have parents, children, a wife, and we have to earn a lot of money to pay for that."

But they don't all have relationships or children, at least not yet. This is partly because the young men and women of China are working so long and so hard on achieving success in their careers that they often have almost no time to look for romantic partners. In fact, two of the three young men I speak with are still looking for love. There's also more pressure on that front in a society where males clearly outnumber females and women are able to take their time in choosing a future partner. The expectations, almost demands, on the young men by the young women and their families can be enormous.

"I studied abroad so I know that in Western countries, if you fall in love with a girl you just fall in love without anything. All you need are two people," says Yue, another of the young men. "But in China if you don't have a car, a house, and a good job, no marriage! It's just a society rule. This is not the case with every Chinese woman, but it is for most of them."

Interestingly, although two of the three young men still live at home with their parents, all three own an apartment of their own. Where love is concerned, it seems no chances can be taken!

And what about young Chinese women? Do they also feel mounting pressure? Of course they do, I'm told, when I discuss social issues with a group of young, female Tiens staff.

"For our generation, we got all the love we needed from our parents," says Lu Xi, a mother of one young boy. "We all have a good quality of education because our parents wanted all of that. They did not enjoy a good life so they wanted to give us good things. But for me, I feel a lot of pressure as an only child. My father is very ill so I have to take care of him and there are so many things for my husband and I to take care of. There is a lot of pressure for me – pressure to get good marks when at school, pressure to get a good job, pressure to look after our parents and take the best care of our children. I want to have another child also."

Over several months I watch Lu Xi's journey as she cares for her young son and, at the same time, nurses her ailing father. As her father's illness worsens, Lu Xi welcomes her parents into her own apartment so she can look after him more closely, and so funds can be raised from the sale of her parents' apartment to pay the medical fees. I admire the way she juggles motherhood, nursing of her seriously ill father, and a full-time job, and I feel a reserved and respectful sense of relief for her, and for her husband and son, when her father finally passes away; her mother then stays with the family to help raise the young boy.

In the office Lu Xi never exhibits a single moment of unprofessionalism. She doesn't skip a beat, even after several consecutive sleepless nights during her father's final month of life. Lu Xi's son still receives all of the attention a young boy craves, her mother is still looked after as she grieves, and her bosses at work are still overwhelmingly impressed by Lu Xi's performance, so much so that she is regularly offered more senior roles. She may not have wanted for much as she was growing up, but Lu Xi is certainly earning her responsibility stripes now she's an adult. She's also paying back her parents' valuable investment, using as her currency pride, respect, love, and effort.

A female, 21-year-old university student, Liang Yun (English name Leven), who says she has only been in love once (with a boy who didn't love her back, she groans), tells me that frustration about marriage and love is just as real for females, despite the fact that they appear to be the gender that has the greater choice. "We have much more pressure than our parents did," Liang says. "In their time, China had not developed so much, so they did not need too much like we do now. They didn't need a car or a house. When my parents got married they did not need many things at all, just love."

Moving back to the professional sphere, the Chinese business arena now boasts a richness of well-educated and worldly-wise young professionals who are all but guaranteed to remain in China as long as they have parents to look after. During my 18 months in China I do not meet a single young person who said they will not look after their parents as they age. Of course, the parents also consider it their role to keep their children close so they can continue to look after them, too.

"This is a difference between Western and Chinese cultures," Zhang says. "If you grow up in the West and you turn 18 you can just move to another place to live forever. But in China, no matter if you're 20 or 30, even once you're married, your parents will be taking care of you until they die. And you'll be taking care of them. So we are not so independent. Foreign people seem to be more independent."

What if you do decide to move away for a great job and a happy life, I ask. Will Chinese parents be eternally disappointed or will they quietly approve? There is no answer because it would never realistically happen, I am told.

"My parents would never allow me to do that," Zhang says. "I have wanted to be that kind of person, to live and work in Australia, but my parents would never allow that. Even if I have a great ability to do that they would not let me. They think they are taking care of me and they would worry. Every day they consider that you live together in one place as a family. Even now, when you're living near them but not with them, parents will ring every day to make sure you are alright. You can go abroad to study, but never to work for the rest of your life. You must always come back."

Does he feel trapped, I ask. "I don't feel trapped," he says. "I am used to living with my parents and it's okay. Maybe I could go away and work for three months or six months, but never for longer."

The pressure being put on single children to perform at work and in society is also, I suspect, having another very powerful effect on China. It could be responsible for the undoing of China's greatest asset, the shared mindset amongst members of its community.

The young men and women I speak with, most of whom have no siblings, tell me that society in general sees them as a selfish generation.

But after their upbringing in the environment of the one-child policy, it is hardly surprising if they are slightly more self-focused than older generations. For the first time in several generations, people have permission to be concerned about how much they can earn from their work, or how much they can make from a business, rather than the good they can do for society.

"Our parents focused on community first, but now a few people think of themselves first," Zhang says. "Actually, we should balance the two. We should balance the individual and the community. A lot of people say we're a selfish generation, but they also put us under pressure to improve ourselves. That is good for everybody. If we improve ourselves then that will also be good for society."

It is important to realize that older Chinese generations have not had a mindless, robotic dedication to the community. Of course there has always been some consideration of self, of the individual. There has simply been a different level of prioritization to what we feel in the West.

One of the young men tells me a story of his father, who worked for a particular business for over a decade, then suffered a non-fatal heart attack at work. The business let him go, refused to pay any health support, and didn't offer any assistance during his recovery.

"After that experience he told me he should have been a selfish man," he says. "If he had been more selfish during the previous ten years he would have been a wealthy man, would have had a lot of money, and would have been able to help me buy a house and a car. So he had that experience and realized there was another way. He told me that I need to remember to be a little bit selfish, because sometimes the community will not be there to look after you."

18

Pollution: clearing the air

"The environment is a legacy we pass to the future generations. We must work to make that legacy a good one for them."

Li Jinyuan

Another major and pressing issue being faced by China's government, one that affects everybody living in and visiting China, is air pollution. It's important to understand the causes and effects of such pollution as the government begins to take significant steps to address it. So much of what happens in corporate China today is shaped around various ways to improve air quality.

For example, when I first visit a furniture factory belonging to Tiens I am offered a tour of an expansive showroom where finished works of beautiful hand-made wooden furniture are held before they're sent out to various homes and offices around the globe. The intricacy of the carvings and the sheer effort that goes in to each piece are almost beyond comprehension. The closer I look, the more detail I see. On one cupboard door a small, carved bird grips tightly to a branch as it reaches its beak downward toward some berries. The detail in its feathers I can only fully appreciate by taking a photo and enlarging that image on my phone screen as my naked eyes do the work no justice. Even after taking the photo, although I knew the work was carved wood, I reached out and touched the carving, my mind refusing to believe it would not feel like a soft, downy feather.

All of the work in the factory is carried out by hand in the same way that artisans have likely been working for thousands of years. Once I've had my fill of the showroom I ask to see the furniture workers plying their trade but I am told that I cannot. The factory's workroom has been closed today by government order, as has every factory in the region, as air pollution has increased above a pre-determined level. Despite the fact that in this factory staff work with small hammers and fine wood-chisels rather than heavy machinery that requires power and that produces heat, noise, and fumes, it is still a factory and therefore must follow such orders. When I visit the work floors I see the tools of the artisans as well as several pieces that are currently in various stages of completion. I wonder how often these shutdowns occur and how they affect productivity, and I marvel at the delicate balancing act being carried out by the government, which must protect the livelihoods of business owners and their staff while also tackling this serious and deadly problem.

Pollution is responsible in part for the death of around a million Chinese per year. In a population counted in billions this may not seem a lot of people. But consider that it is roughly equivalent to the entire population of Cyprus, or of Dallas, Texas, or of Birmingham, UK, or of Adelaide, South Australia, being killed every year by a preventable cause. And this figure doesn't consider the people who suffer serious illness as a result of pollution.

The government is acutely aware of the problem and the topic is openly discussed on a regular basis. In 2017, for instance, as one step toward clearer air, the government announced it would cut steel capacity by 50 million tonnes and coal output by over 150 million tonnes by the end of the year.

Before I travel to China the first time, the Professor advises me to purchase a few respirator masks, and says standard surgical masks will not do the job. His suggestion originally elicits nervous laughter. I think and hope that he is joking, but of course he's not.

Here's where I should share some practical advice. Obviously, air quality can be a serious issue in and around Chinese cities. A very useful app called Air Matters offers live, up-to-the-minute pollution readings at your location, including a general Air Quality Index (AQI) figure, PM2.5 readings, PM10 readings, and other details. This can be very useful, particularly if you fall into a sensitive group (older or with existing health problems), if you're traveling with kids, or if you just want to know when it's okay to get out for some exercise.

When the Air Matters app is telling you that the quality of the air is not so great, you'll want a good quality face mask to help keep the nasties out. But don't go for a surgical-type or plain dust mask. Instead move one step up to a particulate mask that has a PM2.5 rating, sometimes referred to as a "P2" rating. Such masks are inexpensive and so light you'll not even notice they're in your bag, but when you need them you'll be glad you've got them.

Air quality on certain days, and particularly in winter when winds are lighter and less frequent and heaters are running in offices and homes day and night, can be extremely unhealthy. And it's not just if you're unlucky – it can sometimes seem that healthy days are the exception in China's industrialized areas during certain seasons. The air sometimes has a brown tinge and some days it's possible to taste the pollution. Having said that, there are also very good periods. During a particular stay in China, I saw blue skies and a level of air quality that, while not perfect, was better than the air in Melbourne, Australia.

Each morning I'd check the Air Matters app for a reading of the local air quality. At a level of 50, I'd been told, air is beginning to become unhealthy, but it also depends on whether you're in any high-risk groups (young, old, asthmatic, etc.). When the air quality reading reaches 100 it's becoming unhealthy for everybody, but once again it can depend on which factors are driving the figures. High levels of PM2.5 particulates (airborne particles so small they can only be seen with an electron microscope), for instance, are dangerous as these can penetrate deep into the lungs and even make their way into the bloodstream. Over time, they can cause heart and lung diseases, lead to heart attack and stroke, and influence various other fatal and non-fatal health issues.

For most of my time in China the air quality rating averages low 100s to low 300s – not great. But imagine my reaction when I fired up the Air Matters app early one morning, as I was preparing for a run, and it told me the local air quality rating was 1240. The air quality description, which sometimes said "Good" in friendly green lettering or "Unhealthy" in a less confidence-inspiring red font, instead declared "Beyond Index" in deadly, bold, black type. I launched into a minor panic and messaged the Professor, who was in another country at the time. (And here's another tip – don't go to China without the WeChat app. In Chinese business and personal life WeChat is more important than email, more heavily used than traditional telephone or mobile voice services, always works, and is never blocked by the "Great Firewall of China.") "What do I do?" I asked. He replied immediately. "Don't go for a run," he said. "Don't leave the apartment. Put on your mask even while you're in the apartment and don't do anything strenuous. You might suffer a nosebleed or two and your eyes might sting a little, but you'll be fine." And I was. I survived my first "airmageddon" by staying put and doing very little.

However, during my time in China I am always aware that I'm only a visitor. This is not the environment in which I am bringing up my children or building a life. It's not the place where I'm looking after my ageing parents or trying to stay fit and healthy. The people who do spend their lives here are the same people on whom the CPC relies for support, which is why the government is so interested in finding solutions.

During lunch in the Tiens headquarters canteen, where staff members queue for a partly subsidized plate piled high with rice or noodles and a choice of numerous delicious beef, lamb, chicken, seafood, or vegetarian accompaniments, I speak with some staff about their children and sports. I have two boys who are obsessed with soccer, so I ask if any of their children are also interested in playing the beautiful game. But of course my assumption, as it always is in China, is off the mark.

One mother simply points outside. "The air," she says. I immediately understand. When the air quality is so bad that it's unhealthy for children to be outside, it would be irresponsible for a parent to encourage an outdoor sporting interest. I wonder if this is why Chinese athletes excel instead at such indoor sports as badminton and table tennis.

What about at schools, kindergartens, and daycare centers, I ask. How is the health of children best managed when the air that they breathe is inherently unhealthy? In that environment, I am told, parents often come together to purchase numerous air purifiers for each room of the center or school. Air purifiers are big business in China and Tiens manufactures its own brand. On good-air days the children are encouraged to play outside as much as possible. Bad-air days are treated the same as rainy days—all of the action is indoors.

The people of China know that pollution is a very serious problem. They love their children and want only the very best for them, so they expect their government to do something about it. The government is itself highly conscious of the problem. After all, the people will only allow themselves to be governed if they feel the ruling party is doing its job. In a different political environment, an angry public may band together to vote out the problem party and vote in another. In a single-party environment the people may rise up and revolt. The single party is therefore kept honest, just in a different way.

What, then, is the CPC doing in terms of pollution control? Much more than most other major economies, actually. When the USA under President Donald Trump announced his administration's intention to pull out of the Paris Accord, an agreement that aims to prevent global warming, the world looked elsewhere for leadership. China is providing some of that leadership.

The Chinese government importantly agreed on transparency in its dealings around pollution. The Air Matters app is fed from data that comes from a national network of monitors that track the real-time levels of various types of pollution. Rather than keeping the information to themselves, the government makes this data publicly available. If readings in a certain area appear unusually high, meaning a factory might be releasing dangerous emissions, anybody with a smartphone can report the potential offenders via a social media platform.

Public office holders are also held personally responsible if polluters in their region are not reined in. The performance of entire provinces, and therefore the performance of the leaders of those provinces, are now judged on environmental as well as economic standards. In the past the measures were almost exclusively economic.

Chairman Li and Tiens, as with all of the businesses and residences in the Tianjin region, are in the process of moving away from coal-based energy and are relying far more heavily on natural gas for their energy needs. This is common across China as the nation eases away from its reliance on coal in order to reduce carbon emissions. Natural gas supply shortages are being addressed by gas pricing reform measures intended to lead to better predictability and transparency for both the supplier and the consumer. There is also a great deal of research going on into greener production processes and technologies.

"Addressing the pollution issue is very much about technology," Mr Yan tells me. "The Chinese government is trying to increase the productivity within the factories and at the same time reduce energy consumption. This requires an improvement in technology.

"This has already occurred with energy sources. In the past we used coal as our energy source but now we're using natural gas. Here at Tiens, and in the entire city area of Tianjin, we are using natural gas as our core source, as are many of the major cities. This will have the most significant effect on air pollution."

There are stringent regulations around green credentials for any new business starting up in China, Yan tells me, particularly in industries that are traditionally polluting.

"When you want to set up a company or a factory in China the approval bureau has strict rules around what kind of business you're doing and how environmentally friendly you are," he says. "They want to make sure you are using green energy sources and you are polluting very little and wasting very little."

At the same time, Yan says, residential towers in cities are being retro-fitted with better insulation materials – including within walls, ceilings, and windows – to prevent heat loss in winter. Chinese engineers, in fact, are now experimenting with the green design of entire towns, including the world's first "Forest City." Currently under construction in the mountains of the Guangxi region in southern China, the Forest City will accommodate around 30,000 people, with every building covered in greenery. The almost one million plants, including 40,000 trees, are expected to absorb 10,000 tons of carbon dioxide and 57 tons of pollutants annually whilst producing 900 tons of oxygen each year. Using only renewable energy sources such as solar and geothermal, the town will actually improve its own air quality whilst providing habitats for wildlife. Construction is expected to finish in 2020.

The general consensus is that China reached peak pollution several years ago and that things have been improving since. In March 2017, Premier Li Keqiang said officials who do a poor job enforcing the anti-pollution laws, and therefore knowingly allow environmental violations, or respond inadequately to worsening air quality, will be held accountable and prosecuted. "We will make our skies blue again," he was reported as saying.

By 2020, the government aims to cut 800 million tonnes of outdated coal capacity. The closure of 103 coal-fired power plants was also announced. And by 2020, car emissions standards similar to those in the USA and Europe will be introduced, assisted by the supply of higher-quality, less polluting fuels for vehicles.

Residents are being urged to upgrade their coal stoves and furnaces to newer heating and cooking equipment that releases little, or no, emissions. In many cities, cars can only be driven on certain days, according to odd or even registration numbers, although I'm told by several people that this has only really convinced many families to purchase a second car when previously they survived with one (yet another unintended consequence of a well-intended policy).

The pollution conundrum is being attacked on many fronts, which is better than it not being attacked at all. However, for parents of young children living in China right now, it's still not enough.

The issue highlights the many unanticipated problems that come with rapid modernization and rampant commercialization. With success comes enormous challenge. Some solutions are sophisticated and others are hammer blunt. The shutdown of the Tiens furniture factory, and all factories in that area, is as blunt as it gets.

Cities have specific annual pollution limits and the closure of factories for amounts of time is one way to ensure those quotas are not exceeded. Foreign brands with any part of their business or supply chain in China must be aware that the government has the authority to close down production plants, sometimes for weeks at a time, particularly in winter's high-pollution season. High-profile events such as international summits and major sporting tournaments are also often partnered by factory shutdowns, to clear the air for a while both before and as the event takes place. It's not perfect, but it's all part of the solution. And, over my various visits, it does appear to be working in terms of the increased number of blue sky days in at least some of the major cities.

The Air Matters app shows that China is not alone in the smog. A look at the table for the worst air-quality rankings shows parts of China in regular competition with many regions of India. Paris, London, and New York sometimes make appearances. The American city of Oxnard on the Californian coast, with its power plants, oil fields, refineries, and high use of fumigant pesticides on surrounding strawberry fields, regularly earns a spot in the top five most-polluted list. But when I compare the efforts that various nations are putting in to solving the problem, China appears to be a world leader.

At the 2017 Congress of the CPC in Beijing, President Xi Jinping said, "What we now face is the contradiction between unbalanced and inadequate development and the people's ever-growing needs for a better life." He went on to say that his leadership's priorities would be the constant and noticeable improvement of the lives of families, particularly through the reduction of pollution, as well as a focus on the improvement of schools, health care, and a fairer judicial system.

Chairman Li tells me he strongly believes in the tackling of the pollution problem as an essential ingredient in the success of China's modernization plans. He has ordered over 30,000 trees, currently being grown in various parts of China, for the campus of the new Tianyuan University, the private university he is founding close to the Tiens head office. Air conditioning systems in Tiens corporate offices are restricted to specific temperatures during eastern China's severely hot and humid summers, and Tiens' manufacturing plants are run to meet demand, never to over-supply. The Chairman insists on small things being done to help the greater whole.

A canal runs through the landscaped gardens, and under ornate bridges, in Tiens Park

© Kevin McConkey

During the mornings when I take a run or work out in the Tiens outdoor exercise area, I admire the environment that the Chairman has created. Most other properties nearby consist purely of large, brutalist factories surrounded by concrete carparks, but Tiens is different. Visitors, school groups, and tourists regularly enter the Tiens Industrial Health Park to admire and take photos of its gardens, trees, fountains, canals, sculptures, animals, and bridges. When I run past the recycling center, where all of the rubbish from the Tiens Park is hand-sorted by Tiens ground staff into types of reusables, recyclables, organics, and other waste, I marvel at the fact that the Chairman is actually spending money on staff to recycle what most industrialists simply throw away. "Think locally, act globally" used to be the catch cry of the green movement in the West, and that is exactly what the Chairman is doing. It's his part of China's clean and green war on pollution which, for the sake of the nation's children, will hopefully make a drastic difference in the near future.

19
Appetite for destruction: failure is an option

"Business is bloody. Business is war. In all wars there are casualties but it is always worth the fight because those that succeed in business then have the honor of going on to make life better for their people, for their nation, and for the world."

Li Jinyuan

"Risk," in the Western business world, became somewhat of a dirty word during the global financial crisis. Suddenly those posters that encouraged learning through failure, that said the road to success is paved with pain, and that quoted the impressively large number of baskets that Michael Jordan missed before he became a sporting superstar, were taken down from office walls.

Instead, new business buzzwords emerged around risk management and risk mitigation. Roles such as Risk Analyst and Chief Risk Officer came to the forefront as organizations looked for any and every way to avoid negative business outcomes. Strategies were rewritten to say businesses would continue to be pretty good at everything they were traditionally pretty good at, and that growth would be slow and steady and organic. Individual staff learned to keep their heads down and never make any waves, lest the redundancy axe should be swung again sometime soon.

But China didn't receive that memo.

This is one of the most important, and sometimes most confusing, realizations I make during my time embedded in the world of a Chinese corporate. Despite the sometimes autocratic nature of a company's leadership and meetings, and the lack of innovation that could be associated with that singular source of leadership, the organizations themselves are some of the world's greatest risk takers. They never seek to be average but instead typically shoot for the stars. When their grand plans fail, their businesses are then more experienced and far better placed, allowing them to try again another time.

This type of attitude only ever comes from the top. The message being sent out loud and clear by the nation's leadership is that China thinks big. One only need look as far as the Belt and Road Initiative for evidence.

The Belt and Road Initiative is President Xi Jinping's ambitious investment plan that dares to imagine the development of a new Silk Road leading to and from China through the creation of land and sea corridors. It outlines a loose directive for Chinese businesses to get out into the world, particularly along specific land and sea routes connecting Asian, African, and European continents and countries, though it is extending into Pacific Island nations and elsewhere. The initiative is most focused on the development of transport infrastructure such as roads, rail, and ports, to assist movement of goods as efficiently as possible. I spoke with several experts about the Belt and Road Initiative, what it is, and its reason for being.

"It's an attempt to increase China's soft power," says Professor Gillis. "It is well conceived in looking at how it can deploy China's strengths to develop the countries along the traditional sea routes and land routes from China. It is in part a response to a fairly long-term trend where the United States began to withdraw from international organizations such as the World Bank and the International Monetary Fund. This made the USA a less important driver at a time that China wanted to have a greater influence in these international institutions. The Belt and Road Initiative also concentrates mainly on regions that have been left out, largely ignored by the powers that be. It targets areas that are potentially ripe for growth."

Existing powers, particularly the USA, ignored Central Asia and focused instead on whether they could have a heavy influence on East Asia and in Europe, Gillis says. That way it would better contain Russia. But this strategy left a vacuum across the Belt and Road Initiative countries.

"The south Asian and old Silk Road countries, all the 'Stans' of Central Asia, India, Pakistan, Africa, etc., really weren't relevant to the world order in the twentieth century," he says. "I think China is saying those regions are the future, because they are underdeveloped and China can develop them. And they don't have a lot of competition. These areas have large populations and they have the potential for significant reform that could create a lot of demand for Chinese products.

That potential demand is a big driver behind what we're seeing here. Of course, the initiative could also significantly change the world by reordering the power structure."

China, in fact, is deploying many of the same techniques that America used to build its power structure in the twentieth century, Gillis believes. It's a mix of investments, building of infrastructure, and facilitation of trade.

We should expect to see many new trade agreements done and, as a result, special relationships forming along the Belt and Road in which China will play a greater role. The Trans-Pacific Partnership (TPP), from which the USA announced its intention to pull out, under the Trump Presidency, was designed to exclude China and to set standards the rest of the world would comply with and which would facilitate easy trade.

"I think China now steps into the role of the United States and does the same kind of thing," Gillis says. "In my opinion, one of the next stages is a TPP-like agreement that will simply integrate the economies along the Belt and Road much more closely by using common standards and labeling."

Bill Banks, Global Infrastructure Leader for Ernst & Young, said the Belt and Road Initiative is about China seeking to build economic and trade corridors to help facilitate the movement of goods from China in an efficient and orderly manner, and to increase efficiency.

"Along the way it adds value to the country that it passes through," Banks says. "So clearly there's an economic value capture for these countries that benefit from the initiative. We're looking at three types of resources, including all forms of transport, such as rail, roads, ports, and airports, as well as utilities such as power stations, water treatment plants, and anything that facilitates economic growth. We're not really looking at the social infrastructure side, such as schools and hospitals."

Because of the enormous scale and experience within its state-owned enterprises, China boasts massive technical expertise and plentiful capital, Banks points out. These enterprises are looking for new markets in which to utilize that expertise and experience and to build economic capacity. The nation has modernized its cities and transportation systems in a very short period of time and now the government is asking how it can export that know-how and earn an economic and social return for it.

The Chinese expertise and experience in particular areas truly are enormous. As I spoke in a Beijing café with a British expat now in a senior management role in China, we laughed as he recalled a recent and rare opening of a new underground station in London. It was considered such a major event that the Queen attended to officiate. Compare that, he said, to the more than 10,000 kilometres of high-speed rail the Chinese have developed over the last decade, and over 500 kilometres of new Beijing subway (much more than the entire London underground system!) being built between 2015 and 2020. Plus, according to a report by the World Bank, the cost of building high-speed rail in China has been around two-thirds of that spent in other countries.

David Martin, Director of Marketing and Communications for the China Britain Business Council, said the Belt and Road Initiative is a way of linking, through infrastructure and trade routes, Asia to Europe via the land route, known as the "Belt," and the sea route, known as the "Road." "It's about joining the dots of areas that cover two thirds of the world's population, a third of the world's GDP, and about 60 countries," he said. "It joins them for greater connectivity and to increase trade. It is not a written policy or a list of specific goals. It's an overarching theme, a commitment, a direction of travel for the Chinese government."

It's a big statement, indeed. So what does all of this have to do with risk? First, it demonstrates the type of big-picture thinking previously mentioned, and helps to explain why Chinese businesses are perfectly comfortable to follow their government's lead in shooting for the stars. Second, it clearly illustrates an expansive and risk-taking mindset that is quite the opposite of the protectionist one we saw coming out of the USA, for instance, under the Trump regime, out of the UK with its Brexit decision, and out of Australia with its musical-chairs leadership that paralyzes policy makers and means few infrastructure projects are ever green-lighted. High-speed rail has been under discussion in Australia since the 1980s. Its failure to go beyond the realm of the "feasibility study" has now made it a regular subject for local, satirical TV comedy programs.

At the University of International Business and Economics in Beijing I attend a lecture by Guenter Heiduk, Professor of Global Economics at the Warsaw School of Economics. He is discussing the Belt and Road Initiative, its scope and its weaknesses. The lecture hall offers standing room only after it fills early with students keen to see an outsider's view of their nation's grand plan.

Heiduk calls the Belt and Road Initiative "the most ambitious and complex investment initiative in modern times, namely by geographic scope, monetary volume, financial risks, and political outreach."

His criticisms of the initiative, though, include the fact that no detailed business plan or statement of clear economic goals exist. Neither does a detailed management plan that sets out how to "organize the implementation in a timely manner and within the budgetary conditions," or an institutional framework that sets values, ethics codes, or a code of conduct. The initiative also lacks scientific monitoring and a comprehensive dialogue on a "new world order," Heiduk says.

As an example he points to the Chinese ownership of Piraeus seaport in Greece, and the planned Piraeus–Belgrade–Budapest sea/land high-speed route. The European Commission is organizing a probe, he says, into the high-speed railway part of the project to ascertain whether the agreement violated any EU tender laws.

"China needs to consider the reality of European integration when advancing the Belt and Road Initiative," Heiduk says. "As the policymaking is decentralized among member governments, China needs to coordinate with the governments of these countries at all levels. Hence, when going overseas, Chinese companies cannot stick to their own wishful thinking, but need to assess all possible risks and come up with coping plans. More studies should be done on relevant countries and regions."

Heiduk's criticisms are completely consistent with the way a risk-averse Western company thinks. They are especially fitting for a Western business that is considering a major, expensive project, let alone one that will change the way the world works and will forever alter the economic balance of power. The focus is on background research, business plans, specific goals and timeframes, risk analysis and mitigation, and the like. But his comments about such matters almost entirely miss the Chinese point of view.

From the Chinese perspective, I suspect, such matters are mere details that will be worked out over time and as things progress, rather than over-analyzed before any activity has actually begun. If the Piraeus–Belgrade–Budapest rail project cops a large financial fine, or even if the entire project is closed down, then the organizers learn a new and valuable lesson. Those in the know (including the Serbian government), Heiduk says, are optimistic that differences between all parties will be sorted out during a "harmonization of procedures between EU members and Serbia and also in a much wider context of cooperation between China and the EU."

The simple fact is that China is on the playing field. They might be suffering injuries and they'll certainly lose a game or two, but if you're looking to pick a winner for the entire tournament, they are a good bet. In China, risk is there to be embraced.

Western businesses need to be prepared for the change in the global business environment that will be brought on by the development of the Belt and Road Initiative. If a business is not already facing serious competition from a Chinese company, Professor Gillis says, it's only a matter of time.

"Chinese businesses are becoming world-class organizations," Gillis says. "They are not just going to beat you in China, they're going to beat you all over the world, including on your home turf. A good example of that is Sany, a Chinese construction equipment manufacturer that is making concrete machinery and earth-moving machinery, etc. They're now competing against industry leaders like Caterpillar and Komatsu. Sany is all over the world and is competing well. They started out using the basic Chinese model, which is to provide 80 percent of the quality at 60 percent of the price. But today, they're trying to provide 100 percent of the quality at the best possible price, which is perhaps 80 percent, so they can compete all over the world. That is going to happen in many industries. Businesses will face new, sophisticated Chinese competition." Coincidentally, during one of my visits to Tiens, Sany is using the Tiens accommodation and conference facilities to hold a meeting of some thousands of people to discuss its future goals and expansion across the world.

Along similar lines to China taking its domestic infrastructure experience onto a global platform, several years ago Tiens attempted a similar feat when it announced it was making a global push into hospitality with its range of All-Legend Hotels.

On the campus of the Tiens head office in Wuqing are various All-Legend Hotels belonging to Tiens, built in part to accommodate the large number of visitors from around the globe, including trainee distributors and business managers from foreign regions, high-level government and business guests, families holding weddings and other important personal events, and other companies holding conferences in the facilities Tiens provides. The hotels were built in 2009 at a cost of 1.8 billion yuan.

There's the grand All-Legend Hot Spring Resort Hotel, a five-star hotel that often hosts lavish events and wedding ceremonies. There's the four-star All-Legend International Hotel, a series of four, five-storey buildings containing single guestrooms as well as multiple serviced apartments up to three bedrooms in size. There's also the All-Legend Business Hotel, marketed as a "boutique hotel offering customers good value for money."

The hotels on the Tiens Group head office grounds contain around 2,000 rooms, plus there's the 7,000-seat International Conference Center, the International Banquet Center that is capable of feeding up to 3,000 people at once, and the large Tiens Experience Center, which showcases many of the products and services that Tiens offers and is staffed by multilingual staff from around the world.

These hotels and associated facilities are regularly booked out. Their quality, location in resort-like grounds, proximity to both Beijing and Tianjin (about 20–25 minutes to each on the fast-train, traveling around 300 kph) make them very attractive. Companies from all over China use them for conferences, workshops, and executive retreats, and large weddings and various anniversary events occur most weekends. The Chairman also sponsors, especially for students and younger people from across China and other countries, large and often week-long events in areas such as developing leadership, science and mathematics, music, and the arts.

The experience and knowledge gained within Tiens from the operation of these hotels convinced management, in 2011, to expand the hotel business into a global brand, one that would possibly be ripe for an initial public offering (IPO) over the coming years. An editorial in the glossy China Hotel magazine, which for that edition contained an image of Chairman Li on its cover, outlined the young hotel brand's global strategy.

The All-Legend brand planned first domestic expansion, then global. The writer noted that there were already over 800 domestic hotel management companies competing within the Chinese market. Many had already hoped, and failed, to break into the international market. In fact, the writer pointed out, there had not yet been a successful case study of a Chinese hotel brand expanding far beyond the country's borders.

But the Tiens Group's business experience and presence globally, it was believed, would give it the edge it needed. The business had confidence that the company's global marketing network, although it had little to do with hospitality, would be of enormous value.

Today the hotel brands exist only within the Tiens International Health Industrial Park in the industrial zone of Wuqing Development Area, although they are a vital part of the plan for the next iteration and expansion of Tiens. As Western business managers instinctively knew prior to the global financial crisis, lessons learned from risk-taking can be immensely powerful tools and weapons in the battle to win in business.

Professor Gillis believes the economic environment in China over the last few decades, and the rampant growth and endless opportunity it presented, created an ecosystem in which the Chinese business world now encourages and supports a high level of comfort around risk.

"Many Chinese businesses have been able to take extraordinary risk, in part because capital has been so accessible to them," Gillis says. "And there seems to be an unwillingness to force failure. When we've seen problems in the shadow banking sector, the government has generally showed up to bail them out, so that basically creates a moral hazard. If you're going to get bailed out, you take higher risks than you would if you don't have anybody there to catch you in the safety net if you fall.

"But this will likely change in the very near future, as growth slows. The government is not going to be able to afford to bail everybody out. Ideologically, I think the government is going to have to come to terms with the fact that especially in the private sector, that's not the role of government. If entrepreneurs screw it up, then they're just going to have to suffer the consequences on their own."

Consequences or not, massive and detailed forward planning in the Belt and Road Initiative, or in any other major business undertaking, is not the Chinese way. Businesses in China may be sometimes heavy with bureaucracy and slow to make decisions, but they are perfectly happy to jump in and learn their lessons in the market.

Interestingly, Western businesses are re-learning how to do things the Chinese way, but ever so slowly. Not so long ago I interviewed an executive from McDonald's Australia, a gentleman who was responsible for the restaurant chain's Create Your Taste innovation.

In 2014 McDonald's began feeling the heat from smaller, classier, trendier burger businesses that offered a fancier eating experience (the industry calls it "informal eating out" as opposed to "quick service restaurant") and more customizable, higher–quality burger choices. The Australian business came up with an idea to beat the upstarts at their own game. But rather than moving at the pace of a multinational and therefore becoming bogged down in the process of years of market research and R&D, the business decided to move at the pace of a start-up.

Speed became a priority in the delivery of the new system, which would allow customers to "build" and pay for their own customized burger on large touch screens at the entrance to the restaurant, then have the meal delivered to their table.

Six high-performing staff members from various departments were selected to make up a small, crack team within McDonald's Australia. Executive support was essential, but the main role of the executives who were involved was to ensure constant communication with the rest of the organization and to smash through any barriers that got in the path of the team's work.

Previously, the brand was very good at using research, and at constantly testing and refining before going to market, the executive told me. This meant failure was almost unforgivable. But under this new, start-up model, failure was built into the process. It was expected. McDonald's would get the offering out into the real world and in front of real customers as quickly as possible. The process would involve using the actual customer to help the business make vital decisions on the run.

Over five months the Create Your Taste project was developed and tested in just a few selected restaurants. During this period the team observed what worked and what didn't and made changes as a result. They failed and succeeded in the open, as every good start-up does. In the end, the project brought new customers into the business without alienating any of the usual customers. The brand was reinvigorated.

After the Australian arm of the business had rolled out the offering to all restaurants, McDonald's then began introducing it to the rest of the world, and it hasn't worked in every market. In 2016, McDonald's restaurants in the USA ditched the Create Your Taste program and replaced it with another, called Signature Crafted Recipes, once customers complained of the customized burgers being too expensive, of the time they took to make, and after receiving feedback from franchisees who said it slowed down the rest of the kitchen.

Still, McDonald's said the project even in the USA had been a success for the business as a whole. It is still popular in the Australian market, as it showed the business a new way forward.

McDonald's Australia did, on a smaller scale, exactly what China is now doing with the Belt and Road Initiative. Professor Heiduk is correct in saying the initiative is little more than a name, a loose idea for a series of infrastructure projects whose scope and purpose change almost daily. But the Chinese government is getting out into the market and learning through success and failure, amassing knowledge and using that knowledge to fine-tune the process and to continue moving forward with its plan to re-channel the flows of world trade. At the same time it is setting an example for Chinese businesses, which are following the government's lead. And it is showing global leadership at a time that other major powers, such as the USA and the UK, are intentionally retreating from international matters.

One further example of such a mindset in China reveals itself in attitudes toward construction of any kind. Much has been made of the ghost towns and empty airports, unused railway stations and abandoned shopping malls, which have come to characterize the speed of China's relentless and furiously fast modernization.

A five-minute drive around the area of Wuqing in which the Tiens head office is based reveals skeletal structures (one, a large building with floors completed but no walls or windows, was originally intended to be a hospital before authorities confirmed that it simply wouldn't be fit for purpose – it now resembles a decrepit, multi-storey carpark), abandoned factories now overgrown with weeds and looking like a film set for an apocalyptic zombie thriller, and land cleared of vegetation but never built upon.

Paolo Frana tells me that after he left his home city of Milan many years ago to ply his architect's trade in China, where buildings are appearing at a pace never before witnessed anywhere else on Earth, he recognized a comfort level around risk that simply didn't exist elsewhere.

"I did many jobs in Italy where there was an age spent designing and planning and because of that, at the end we were not able to carry out the project," Frana says. "Here in China, they are building on the site at the same time that you are doing the design. They waste a lot of money and a lot of energy by doing that, but in the end they do things rather than just talk."

I had a conversation about this with a Chinese executive well-versed in Chinese business culture and he said something that captured the topic perfectly. He said, "If you let the water flow, there will be a lot of water lost, but at least the water is flowing." That is the important thing that the Chinese recognize. You cannot control everything, and if you try to control everything then nothing moves.

"Who dares wins," the motto of the British SAS, or "Carpe Diem," that of the US Marine Corps, come to mind when one considers the future chances of success for Chinese businesses. The message from their government is to get out there and give it a try, and as a result there will be some spectacular failures. But the lessons in those failures, the benefits of all of that risk-taking, will likely be far greater compared with the mild gains experienced by businesses that actively avoid risk. If there is any truth to such strong mottos or calls to arms, the Chinese business world is in for some very big wins indeed.

20

Economic development areas

> "Innovation is the driving force of enterprise development. Innovation means to challenge yourself constantly. It means going into a new frontier, beyond borders, beyond the existing framework."
>
> *Li Jinyuan*

Before construction began on the Tiens International Health Industrial Park (opened in October 2010), Chairman Li had a scale model of the campus built by his architects and it took pride of place in the small building in Wuqing that was the original home of Tiens. Visitors were shown the plans which included grand garden areas, a long canal around its borders which was crossed by several bridges, a small zoo, countless lakes and fountains, several large hotel buildings collectively accommodating over 4,500 guests (one hotel incorporated a hot spring into each of its luxury chalets), a conference center capable of holding 7,000 people, a banquet center able to feed 3,000 diners at one time, a modern, multi-floor hospital, a major R&D center, several manufacturing plants, a corporate museum, two supermarkets, several restaurants, and, of course, a commanding head office building.

After witnessing the scale of the Chairman's vision, many of those visitors would openly doubt its genuineness. In a region where other business leaders simply set up factories surrounded by parking lots, the Chairman was creating a place that people would be attracted to, a site where employees would want to work and others would like to visit. That vision was simply too much for most to grasp.

"I remember clearly that whenever we had guests and visitors the Chairman would show them the master plan for the Tiens headquarters," Song Xiang, of Tiens Group's Dalian office but who previously worked in the Chairman's office, told me. "He would show everybody and frankly, most of them were suspicious about it. They thought it was just a silly dream. They thought it would never happen. Nobody believed it would ever be built, except the Chairman himself.

Even people in the business did not believe it! But that is one of the essential ingredients of Chairman Li being such a successful business-man, that vision. That is a substantial part of who he is."

Of course, the Chairman's dream was realized, at a cost of around 7 billion yuan. Importantly it was built within the Wuqing Develop-ment Area, one of many special economic zones spread throughout China and particularly on the nation's east coast.

What is a special economic zone? For any business considering developing a presence in China it is valuable to understand the role these zones play in China today, and the crucial role they have played in the rapid development of China over the past 30 years.

I speak with Mr Yan about the reasons that a company might con-sider basing itself in a special economic zone. "In Tianjin we have several special zones and they are at two different levels," he says. "The first is at a national level and the other is at city or province level. Closer to the city there is the Binhai New Area and the other one is Wuqing. These are both special zones at a city level.

"Companies that set up within special economic zones enjoy special privileges. These include what we call a three-plus-three policy. That means the business can waive its first three years of income tax and then, for the next three years, the business only pays half income tax."

That is just the tip of the iceberg in terms of special treatment for companies based within a special economic zone. They run under different laws of business and trade compared with companies based elsewhere in China. Organizations in these zones operate in a far more autonomous fashion. They are heavily market-driven. These zones allowed small, geographically specific areas of truly free markets to be developed under a central communist government and these free markets quickly attracted the attention of foreign investors.

Managed by area-specific administration, special economic zones often enjoy duty-free benefits and dramatically streamlined proce-dures. Decisions around infrastructure, investment, production, mar-keting, HR, and more are made without government consultation. These zones create an environment in which foreign direct invest-ment is allowed and encouraged, but also one that foreign investors are attracted to in terms of setting up shop, whether that be by joint venture, merger or acquisition, management interest, building of new facilities, or transfers of technology/knowledge and the like.

Such an idea is not unique to China; special economic zones exist throughout the world. But in terms of foreign direct investment, they have been vital in making China one of the world's top three recipients. A report in the *China Daily* (*Top 10 countries projected to attract most FDI*, May 3, 2017) quoted Dan Starta, Partner and Head of Greater China at A.T. Kearney, as saying, "China is the third-largest recipient of FDI in the world. Beijing appears keen to continue to improve China's attractiveness to foreign investors with its continued plans to cut red tape for foreigners and its announcement to increase foreign investment in health care, education, sports and culture. If implementation of these reforms is successful and the new rules are transparently applied, then China's FDI inflows may grow even more in the coming years."

The first such zone in China was the Shenzhen Special Economic Zone, opened in 1980. As has been the pattern for much of China's success over the last 30 years, it was all about trial and error. The zone would work as a test base for various practices and policies, and successful lessons would be shared out to businesses and industrial zones around the country. As it turned out, there were a lot of successful lessons. Foreign investment came in thick and fast and new cities seemed to appear overnight as entrepreneurs, businesses, and workers were attracted from across China to exciting new ventures. Shenzhen's population exploded from around 30,000 in 1980 to one million by 2000 and to almost 12 million in 2016.

Once trade was unshackled from the regulation and intervention of the central government, growth was unstoppable. Special economic zones have contributed to China's economic success thanks to their unfettered ability to test the market economy as well as the lessons they were able to pass on to other sectors of other markets. Employment in these regions rose dramatically as labor was attracted thanks to the influx of new businesses. Exports of Chinese-produced goods skyrocketed.

Just as importantly, rather than further devolving into a market that only ever ripped off the intellectual property of businesses from other parts of the world, innovation blossomed as tens of thousands of invention patents were registered each year in each special economic zone. New technologies and modern management practices poured into China as a result of the rush of foreign investment, and as high-tech processes were developed, careers of R&D personnel in domestic businesses flourished.

The experimental nature of the special economic zones only really worked because of the government's absolute commitment to their independence. The State itself provided all that was needed in order to allow these zones to work autonomously, which was a brave move from an entity that previously kept strict and total control of everything to do with business. These zones were the opposite of the traditional Chinese model in almost every way and, as such, they were a great success.

Along the way, China's special economic zones suffered their fair share of challenges, too. Rarely mentioned in the discussion or analysis of the development of these zones is the fact that they were once land on which farming families eked out a modest living. Private land ownership does not exist in China, so those farming families had no legal claim to their properties. Although these families were given apartments in which to live, they found they had no way to make a living. Their farming skills were no longer of use. They were also in no way prepared for the culture of high-density apartment living, having spent their lives on the land. A cycle of underemployment and unemployment amongst these groups resulted.

Another much discussed issue within these zones is the proliferation of cheap labor, and the relative lack of labor laws to protect individual employees. A completely free and unfettered capitalist market with relatively weak labor protection regulations (the Labour Contract law came into effect in 2008, requiring businesses to at least have internal hiring and firing rules) combined with a massive influx of people from around the nation adds up to an environment in which workers must accept whatever they're offered and be thankful that they're in a job at all. Often it is only the insistence of Western brands that source their materials or products from these regions, and those brands' customers' increasing will to ensure ethical sourcing and manufacturing, that influences change in this area. Real change, though, will likely be a long time coming.

There is still a lot of underemployment in rural areas, from which more labor can be released. And as China is already looking at its massive and inefficient state-owned enterprises, introducing technology, modern management processes, and other productivity drivers, that will also create a sizeable release of labor.

"But the future is not so much about labor," Ian Kerr, Professor of Economics at Curtin University, says. "It is about becoming more productive with new products and processes, and getting technological processes going. In the USA and Western Europe, capital and labor are not such a big contributor to growth. It is technological progress that really gets countries moving. That is the path for China.

"The main reason for economic growth in China has been the mobilization of labor and capital. The nation has been belting along at 10 percent plus but now it's down to 6.5 percent, still mobilizing labor and investing a fair amount of capital. But the complaint has been that they are just catching up with the West and if you compare US GDP with Chinese GDP, it is still a multiple. To truly move ahead the Chinese have to get into technological progress and start innovating and developing their own products. And there are innovations coming in, in the service industry in particular, possibly thanks to time the Chinese professionals have spent in the West. There is more innovation in manufacturing and agriculture. So from that point of view there is convergence."

Conversely, while there is an overflow of unskilled laborers in China, there is also a serious talent shortage in the skilled labor markets.

The more attractive lifestyles and greater employment options in major cities mean skilled workers and managers from fields such as HR, IT, and marketing tend to shy away from the more industrial manufacturing areas. Often companies have to bus staff in, as Tiens does, or set up satellite offices in nearby cities to attract these staff. Tiens, for instance, has an IT function as well as e-commerce staff presence in an office in Beijing, as well as in Wuqing.

China has learned that the environment comes a distant second to profit in a lightly regulated business environment. China's special economic zones sometimes can lack sound urban planning and appear unattractive. That is not the case at Tiens Park, and it's no surprise that people from the local community, as well as from across China, come to the Tiens Park as tourists. Wuqing does offer a grand cultural center with an opera house, parks, a riverside walk, restaurant precincts, and a major museum, as well as several shopping malls and retail strips that boast such international shopfronts as Starbucks, KFC, Nike, and Walmart. It has golf courses and universities, waterways and botanic gardens. But there is never any escaping the fact that you are in a manufacturing zone.

Interestingly, new economic zones were not the only places in which entrepreneurship was revealing itself. Professor Grafstein says some success came outside the management of the government.

"These special economic zones were unburdened from a lot of the regulations of centralization, but some of the success also happened outside government control," he says. "There was a very poor province in the south, it was dirt poor. But they worked their way out of poverty. That province is an example of one that did not wait for permission to be told that they are now allowed to perform. They just went ahead and did it out of desperation. That starts an important cycle in which money is produced and that creates more incentive and more money. That was a big part of the take-off."

In a thought leadership piece looking at the successes and challenges of China's special economic zones, published on the World Bank website in 2011, industrial development expert Zeng Zhihua said that while China's economic clusters and special economic zones have experienced great success, their sustained success will come under challenge from such matters as moving up the global value chain, sustainability of export-led growth, institutional challenges, environmental and resource constraints, and lagging social development.

Other challenges include the diminishing of the zones' preferential policies and privileged status, and the homogeneity problem as more and larger special economic zones open up.

Given these major challenges, Zeng recommends that China moves gradually toward a more knowledge- and technology-based development model, puts greater emphasis on domestic markets and consumption as a source of growth, upgrades special economic zones through technology innovation, and implements strict environmental standards.

All of these recommendations have been confirmed as priorities for the government as President Xi Jinping's second five-year term (and the nation's 13th Five-Year Plan) begins. In his marathon 205-minute speech during the 2017 Congress of the Communist Party of China, President Xi promised containment of financial risks, boosts to consumer spending, a greater concentration on lifestyle issues, particularly as relates to pollution, and the prioritization and support of innovation in business. Thanks to President Xi's support, most business owners in the special economic zones will begin moving in the right direction. But some made that move a long time ago.

One of the many colorful events that take place in the
Tiens Park grounds

© Christopher Sheedy

One weekend, when I return to Tiens Park after a trip to Beijing, I'm thrilled to see the streets of the park bustling with color and life. What appears to be a national cucumber festival – attracting gourd growers and other agricultural experts from across the nation – has descended. Neighboring properties lay silent over the weekend but at Tiens, many thousands have gathered to mix and mingle, to network, and to discuss the latest advancements in the growing of cucumbers, tomatoes, watermelons, cabbages, broccoli, corn, and more. The conference center has standing room only and several streets are lined on both sides with hundreds of exhibitor tents. The hotel lobbies are heaving with guests and finally I see what the Chairman has likely envisioned all along – even in an industrial zone, people will always be attracted to a place of nature and beauty.

21

Trial and error: China's risk and reward

"In much of life we must be like a bullfighter. Accept challenge. Face challenge. Do not be afraid of challenge. Stand your ground, move a little when needed, but keep your eyes, your mind, and your heart on success."

Li Jinyuan

A healthy appetite for risk is beneficial for an organization, or for a nation, only if the lessons learned from failure are constantly fed back to produce better decisions and results next time. It is in this process that China has excelled over the last several decades, as a nation and within the country's organizations.

Let's talk about the way government can use trial and error to manage a way forward, from a centrally managed, closed economy to one that is open but closely monitored and controlled.

But first, the Russian experience is instructive. At the end of December 1991, the USSR came to an abrupt end. On the first day of January 1992, the Russian federation was born. The entire Russian economy, as the clock struck midnight, was expected to immediately switch from a centrally controlled economy to a market-based one. Massive changes would be required in the spheres of economics, law, politics, finance, and even culture.

Of course, the shock for Russia was overwhelming and led only to deeper problems that are still felt to this day. The legal system came close to collapse, meaning the most simple and important tasks of government became impossible. A state of near civil war was reached as health and education sectors found themselves unable to provide even the most basic services. Organized crime flourished and massive wealth was split amongst an elite few who boasted strong political connections, even as the quality of life for most Russians dropped. Corruption was widespread and the armed forces were used against selected social and political movements.

Over a decade earlier, in contrast to the experience of Russia, China under Deng Xiaoping had launched itself onto a slow, staged, and far more successful (but not without significant drama) road to an open market economy.

To discuss the way China did such an effective job of changing the way its economy worked, in Beijing I meet Professor Ian Kerr. Kerr is in demand around the world, particularly in Asia and the Middle East, for his expertise on the global economy. I begin with the absolute basics, asking him to define exactly what is an "open economy."

"In economics the definition of an open economy is an economy that has a large percentage of its economic activity involved in international trade," he says. "The closed economy is one that has little or no international trade. So the American economy, by this measure, is relatively closed. If you look at exports and imports as a percentage of GDP, in Singapore it is 95 percent. That is a very open economy."

The USA is a closed economy? Of course, the American economy is an open one in terms of title and intention, but thanks to a barrage of trade barriers and tariffs it does a surprisingly small amount of international trade. And it's not just a result of recent "Trumponomics." A 2013 study of economic openness, from the International Chamber of Commerce, listed Canada as the only G20 country that made it into the top 20 for openness. Hong Kong, Singapore, and Luxembourg took out the top three spots and the USA languished in 38th place, behind Poland, France, Ukraine, and Romania. China, at the time, was 57th.

"When China opened up it slowly started exporting and importing and engaging with the rest of the world," Kerr says. "None of it happened suddenly – there was staging. Deng Xiaoping in 1978 launched a lot of his reforms and one of the first steps for China was to apply for membership of the World Trade Organization. That membership gives you certain rights and duties. It took the Chinese about 15 years to get into the World Trade Organization, so during that process there was a gradual opening up.

"Unlike the Russians, who had a big-bang opening – 'Yesterday we were socialist and today we're capitalist' – the Chinese took one step at a time and experimented. They opened up tax-free zones as trading zones in Shanghai and Shenzhen on the coast. They took feedback from how that went and then gradually liberalized more areas."

Now, some 40 years since Deng Xiaoping began the process, the economy is still an experiment, Kerr says. The government is slowly and carefully feeling its way around what types of market forces have what types of effects, and how much in the way of pure capitalism can be allowed into the system. Stock market development has been a part of the process, as has the introduction of private ownership of real estate. Mainland Chinese people can purchase and own property, but cannot own the land on which it is built.

Earlier in that process the nation saw the decollectivization of agriculture in an undoing of Mao Zedong's experimentation with collective socialism, and a gradual release of labor and population from the rural areas. This, of course, was the very issue that landed a young Li Jinyuan in hot water near the beginning of his career.

Interestingly, Kerr believes capitalism may have always been in the Chinese way of doing things, even throughout Mao's experiments with collectivist policies.

One of the questions he asks in lectures is whether capitalism or socialism is in the Chinese approach. "Most people would say that it is capitalism in their DNA because, if you look back through Chinese history, the Chinese have been everywhere, all around the world, running businesses and making money," he says. "They are capitalists. There was just a small period when they experimented with communism proper, and they still now have features of socialism, such as state-owned enterprises and no land ownership.

"The Chinese went everywhere. It was probably to do with poverty. Maybe there was a desire to earn a bit of money and send it back home. Under the Qing Dynasty the Europeans were coming in and trading. But a series of Chinese emperors said they didn't need the rest of the world. Their empire was the center of the universe so they didn't need to trade. In that respect, the Imperial rulers in China for quite some period preferred to forget about the rest of the world. So from that perspective they certainly were not global, at least the emperors were not."

Looking at China's modern history, from the founding of the People's Republic of China in 1949, we see experiment after experiment and learning after learning. Even Mao's policies and political positions changed, beginning with a Soviet style of communism then moving to what became known as a "Chinese form of communism." Then there were experiments in agricultural practices during the Great Leap

Forward and further movements including the Cultural Revolution and, near the end of the Mao period, warming of relationships with the USA, Australia, and other Western countries.

All the while the nation was learning from its experiments and, two years after Mao's death when Deng Xiaoping took power in 1978, a new path was becoming clear. The opening of the market began.

Many experts, including the Professor, argue that China is now the single most globalized nation on Earth.

"Particularly given recent changes in Europe and North America, China is the most globalized country socially and economically, as well as through soft power," the Professor argues. "And the character of China and its global influence is a heady mix of Confucianism, capitalism with distinctive Chinese features, and communism again with distinctive and changing Chinese features. This mix can be confusing for Westerners, especially when it is wrapped in the particular cultural traditions and communication protocols of the Chinese."

In fact, China could well be the most globalized nation in history, he says. "Keeping in mind the technical definition of globalization – the exchange of products and knowledge and people – and keeping in mind the difference between globalization and imperialism, the Chinese people have possibly been the most globalized in their outlook for the longest period. Especially considering the fact that the British were imperialists, not globalists."

Kerr agrees, saying there has not been a Chinese period of globalization like the one we're seeing today.

"There was the Silk Road, which went on for quite some time, but that was individual traders; it was not official Chinese or imperial policy," Kerr says. "I don't think China has ever had a time where their government officially engaged with the rest of the world. They are doing it now and that is fantastic, because it is at a time that everyone else is pulling in their horns."

Many now describe China as an "economic superpower." The term is used so often and so loosely that, to me at least, it has little meaning. I ask Kerr for his view.

One indicator of an economic superpower, he explains, is how much of a country's trade is with another particular country. For instance, 40 percent of Australia's exports go to China, which makes China an extremely powerful trading partner for Australia.

"If one country, such as China, is up there in first, second, or third place for most countries, then that is a simple indicator of them being a superpower," Kerr says.

"The other measure is GDP per capita. In that ranking, China is still fairly low, but given the population, in overall GDP they are up there in second place behind the USA. So on those two criteria, trade and GDP, you would say in one way China is a superpower already and in another way it will be a superpower within five or ten years. They have a way to go in terms of GDP per capita."

So depending on which way you cut the numbers, China is already an economic superpower or is fast on its way to becoming one. This creates great opportunities for its own businesses as well as for those from elsewhere that are dealing with China. It also presents new challenges that have to be faced by the nation, its businesses, and its government and business leaders.

A key point here is that almost every challenge is being dealt with by China from a position of power, thanks to decades spent learning valuable lessons in the market, and comfort around certain levels of risk and experimentation. Political stability and the government's resulting capacity to plan for the long term have put China in a position where greater globalization and the further opening of its economy and its society are desirable and beneficial not only to itself but also arguably to the rest of the world. It's a stark difference to some other economically powerful nations that are, mostly as a result of political change, increasingly looking inward for solutions to economic and social challenges.

22

The power of three

"When I do something, I always try to create something that is different, that is extra to what I've done before and to what others have done before."

Li Jinyuan

Since the formation of the People's Republic of China in 1949, the nation has been through three broad stages. The first was communism. The second was a careful transition to an open market. The third, the phase we are in right now, is a confident, open, globalized nation ready, willing, and able to influence the world.

Tiens, as one of China's corporates, has followed a similar three-stage pattern and Chairman Li says that is no coincidence. As the nation has re-discovered its confidence and found its feet on the international stage, so has Tiens.

The first stage of Tiens, Li says, was all about expanding within China and establishing a base market. That was the start-up era. The second stage was shaped around looking for markets offshore, but always with a controlling hand. The Chinese business would remain "Chinese in nature and character" no matter where it existed around the globe.

The third stage is now being developed as Li rolls out his grand plan for perspective and technological transformation. The business has developed an appreciation of the fact that true success in the future will require a very different set of skills, including systems and processes built to cope with constant and massive change, full integration with local cultures, and the ability to source and sell from anywhere in the world. Today, many Chinese businesses looking to succeed in international markets send their people to Tiens to learn from the company's decades of global experience. But at the same time, Tiens is constantly looking outward for signals around the future shape of the retail world.

What do businesses learn from Tiens? It's mainly about the steps taken to ensure a smooth transition into a new territory and culture.

"The first step when we move into a new territory is to transport some of our products to the country, and at this stage we assign some Chinese managers, IT people, administrative staff, and financial staff. They move to the new territory and hire local people to carry out other roles," explains Mr Yan.

"The second step is to decide on business models. We gather successful business models from other territories with similar cultures and we translate these models so the new territory can use them. We teach the local people in the business about these models and the Chinese managers use them to develop the local managers. They teach them about IT and finance and administration. The local people begin to help us run the business.

"The third step is to actually hire the local professionals and consultants, legal people and financial people, to give us some suggestions. They help us to improve and fine-tune our business model for that particular territory. We show them how other territories have developed their markets and talk to them about giving donations and doing other things to ensure Tiens is always having a positive effect on the local society."

The business has learned how to succeed in new territories through two decades of trial and error, and it is still unafraid to make mistakes. Right now Tiens, under the guidance of Chairman Li, is not only chasing success in markets that have conventionally been difficult to crack, such as the USA and Australia, but has also spent several years experimenting with entirely new businesses and business models, patiently figuring out what works and what does not.

For instance, on the Wuqing head office property stands the Taijisun Hospital, an impressive, modern, four-storey building containing equipment that some other Chinese hospitals might only dream of owning. It's designed as a diagnostic and short-term treatment facility and it is large enough to treat hundreds of patients using both Traditional Chinese Medicine and Western medical approaches. It contains a luxurious VIP wing (primarily for celebrities and other individuals seeking a high level of privacy), and its research capabilities, thanks to the money that has been spent on equipment and personnel, are extensive and impressive.

Although Taijisun is still not making money after six years in business, the Chairman continues to invest to discover the best model of operation. Li's plan has been to eventually duplicate the successful business model, then roll it out around the country, and potentially around the globe. That strategy, though, has changed as Li has learned lessons around what gains traction in the market and what does not.

Then there's the furniture factory mentioned earlier, a business down the road from Tiens headquarters based in a nondescript, two-storey industrial building. Here, under the Tiens brand, a team of artisans creates exquisite and traditional furniture bound for offices, boardrooms, and bedrooms of the world's elite and uber-wealthy. Desks, four-poster beds, bookcases, and more are hand-carved and individually shaped from rare timbers, including sandalwood, sourced from across the globe, in a process that includes no nails, screws, or glue. This part of the Tiens business is sometimes referred to as "the Chairman's hobby," but as the unique and beautiful nature of the furniture is increasingly recognized globally, it could also become a greater focus of the business.

And on the property next to the head office, a 3.2 square kilometre piece of land also belonging to Tiens, Li has invested billions of yuan in the construction of an international university, Tianyuan University. Tiens already owns and runs the not-for-profit Tianjin Tianshi College, a full-time private college educating and accommodating around 7,000 students annually, located just a few minutes' drive from head office. That college has provided massive experience and learning for the business. This knowledge is now being put toward the larger establishment. The Chairman imagines a day when over 40,000 students from around the world will enrol in the new international university.

"Based on the national standard and taking into consideration the size of the university, it should be able to contain 80,000 students," the Chairman tells me. "But I would like to focus on quality. I want the university to create international talent. I don't want numbers, they don't matter to me, but I want to produce quality talent – specialists such as politicians, business people, scientists, or teachers – for my country and for my people."

That university, for a man singularly obsessed with quality of education, is a risk in itself but also represents reward for the risks he has taken in the past. Let's explore the Chairman's views on education, as well as its importance to the nation and to his own legacy, as we take a deeper look into the life of this billionaire.

23
Getting personal: a billionaire's life

"To do something extraordinary is to create a small miracle that brings great joy to many."

Li Jinyuan

There is a piece of wisdom passed around amongst those who write biographical books that says until you make your subject cry during an interview, you don't yet have a book worth writing.

A colleague once told me an amusing tale about his planning of the interviewing process for a book about a renowned sporting hard-man. During the preparation, before he had even written a single word, he was already quite upset about the book's slim chances of success. Its muscle-bound star, you see, was not the type of person to ever shed a tear, so how could this author possibly write a book worth reading? But then, during the very first interview, conducted on the balcony of one of the sports star's many beachside apartments, the interviewee broke down and sobbed as he discussed his latest romance break-up. This woman was "the one," the star believed, although to most onlookers she simply seemed the latest in a long line of bikini models to adorn the athlete's arm. At one stage my writer friend, who admitted with some guilt that the sportsman's tears made him quite happy about the now-improved chances of success of the book, wondered if he should take the interview indoors in case any paparazzi were lurking on the beach below, their long lenses trained upward.

The moment of emotion for the book you're reading right now came as Chairman Li was seated at the head of the intricately hand-carved sandalwood conference table (from the Tiens furniture factory) in his office. I had asked about his parents and he was telling me of his mother's death. When a few tears came the Chairman took them in his stride, neither attempting to hold them back nor hiding them away. It was a proud and respectful moment for him, I realized. Of course he would cry openly when speaking of his mother's death. Of course there is no shame in such a show of emotion. And how different, I thought for the umpteenth time since first entering this office, are the beliefs, actions, and behaviors of people from the East compared with those from the West.

Chairman Li's emotion was brought on by various memories, blending sadness for his mother's passing with regret and, perhaps, a small amount of shame.

When his mother passed away the Chairman was on a business trip in South Africa. "I feel sorry," he told me as he gently wiped away a tear. "I was not beside her when she passed away. I feel such regret. I was supposed to be beside my mother.

"There were many things I wished and wanted to do for her, but when she died I had lost my chance forever. In China, filial piety is important. You serve your parents when they grow old. Your parents brought you up and took care of you when you were young so you take care of them when they are old. I was away when she died so I did not serve my mother properly. That is why I feel regret."

When he received the news of his mother's passing the Chairman raced home and helped with funeral arrangements, and soon after his mother's death his father suffered a stroke.

"During this period I suffered a lot," he said. "My mother passed away and my father had a serious illness. I felt very sad and helpless. My mother was dead and my father was sick. The sky was collapsing. My earth was breaking down. This kind of emotion comes to everyone when their parents become ill and pass away.

"I have siblings, so we all took care of my father. We put him in the best hospital, in very good conditions. He had the best doctor and two dedicated nurses and good medicines. It helped that I had siblings, because at that time I was also very busy with the business."

His father survived for 12 years after his mother's death. The Chairman honored his mother by naming after her the landscaped park at the entrance to the Tiens property – the expansive, green space containing water features, flag poles, sculptures of eight running horses, and the golden, winged lion. A similarly grand garden in the new Tianyuan University will be named after Li's late father.

He has been able to use his business and its property to honor the memory of his parents, but the Chairman still struggles with the balance, or lack of, that he has personally achieved between work and family life. I am originally surprised to hear the Chairman discuss this issue, then I realize that I'm guilty of assuming that everything in the life of a billionaire is picture perfect.

As a father and a titan of industry, the Chairman says, he has had to make difficult choices in terms of achieving balance. While he is proud of the business he has created, he is not altogether satisfied with the amount of time it stole from his own family and particularly from his two daughters and two sons, all of whom are now adults and some of whom work within the Tiens Group.

"I have lost my balance in family and work," he admits. "Perhaps I have failed to be a good father in the family, but the children became a great motivation for me to work harder. I couldn't really bring up my children in person, like other fathers did.

"But the motivations that came from the children were for me to work harder and provide more, rather than take care of them in person. The responsibility that I felt was the biggest part of the change that came from me becoming a father. I could provide something more for them. I could work harder to provide more and provide for them better education and teach them to be useful people, to be good people. This is how I bring my children up."

In work, the Chairman tells me, he admires the late Taiwanese industrialist and billionaire Wang Yung-ching, a rare entrepreneur very much in the same class as Li. Wang founded and owned Formosa Plastics Group, a company described by *The New York Times* as "Taiwan's most profitable manufacturing conglomerate." Wang died in 2008 while he was on a business trip in New Jersey, at the age of 91.

"Wang Yung-ching is a very famous businessman in the north-east Asia region," the Chairman says. "He created his own business and built up the kingdom himself. At that time there weren't many people who could do such a thing, but he did it.

"I have met a lot of business leaders and every one of them has their own unique strengths and features. Learning is an endless process and I have learnt many things from the business leaders I have met. I blend this learning into my own experience and use it in my own style. I love innovation and I love creating something new rather than copying and duplicating. So I use the things I learn from other business leaders to strengthen and enhance the areas in which I am weaker."

Indeed, lining the walls of the Tiens Museum are hundreds of images of the Chairman with various business heavyweights from around the globe, including Warren Buffet and Bill Gates, as well as political leaders such as

George W. Bush, Jimmy Carter, and Tony Blair, as well as Secretary-Generals of the UN, such as Ban Ki-moon and António Guterres. His work has taken him far and wide and put him next to countless influential leaders.

Chairman Li Jinyuan and António Guterres, ninth Secretary-General of the UN

Image courtesy of Tiens Group

Chairman Li Jinyuan and Ban Ki-moon, eighth Secretary-General of the UN

Image courtesy of Tiens Group

What, then, do leaders learn from him? It is likely mostly lessons around persistence, the Chairman says when I put the question to him. Many of the most respected world leaders, in business and in politics, were born into money and power. Few began at the bottom and built everything on their own. When these people meet Chairman Li, he tells me, they are most interested in how he did what he did, particularly in an environment that was not originally supportive of private business.

"Things that other business leaders learn from me are perhaps about attitude and spirit," he says. "My persistence never falters and once I lock in a target I will never save myself a way back. I will never give myself the option of retreat. I will keep moving forwards until I get what I aim for. I am persistent and I never give up, so it is about attitude, spirit, making sure you know what you are aiming for and doing everything you can to get it."

I want to find out how the Chairman spends his billions. Of course, there are properties around the globe and impressive automobiles, all of the usual trappings of the wealthy. In addition he has appreciation for beautiful items that are custom made, often using traditional Chinese craftsmanship. His office, for instance, is furnished with intricately carved, handmade pieces that appear completely unique, because they are. The exquisitely crafted tables, chairs, cabinets, and other items come from the aforementioned Tiens furniture factory, which is staffed by a team of China's finest furniture artisans.

These furniture makers often begin their training at the age of 15, learning how to use a collection of hand tools to shape joints (there are no screws, nails, bolts, or glue used in these pieces) and to carve patterns and small sculptures onto the surfaces of cabinet doors, onto the arms of chairs, and onto the heads of four-poster beds. The most expensive pieces begin as sandalwood logs imported from India, and the factory also uses rosewood from Myanmar, Africa, and Laos, as well as silkwood from China.

The furniture factory is considered by some to be a hobby of the Chairman. But what are his hobbies outside the office? On what luxuries does he spend his spare cash? After several months I have only come to know a man who works seven days a week, who is always in his office no matter what time I arrive and is still there no matter how late I leave. What does a Chinese billionaire do in his spare time? The answer, it seems, is "What spare time?"

Here's how that part of our conversation goes.

Q: How many hours do you work each week?
Chairman: I usually only sleep three to five hours each night, and it has been this way since I started the business. Recently, I am having more rest, meaning I have five to six hours of sleep.

Q: Is all of your waking time about work?
Chairman: Yes, it is.

Q: Are you working less than you did 20 years ago?
Chairman: I am working just a little bit less, yes.

Q: How many meetings do you have each day?
Chairman: On average I would have more than ten meetings per day, but sometimes many more.

Q: Is it difficult to make so many decisions each day?
Chairman: Not every meeting is about decision making. Sometimes it is simply about coordination and communication. Sometimes it can be exhausting and I become very tired, but mostly I am in good form.

Q: Do you have any time off at weekends or for holidays?
Chairman: Not really, no.

Q: Do you have hobbies outside of work?
Chairman: No.

Q: Do you have a guilty spend?
Chairman: No.

Actually he does have a hobby, but not one you'd refer to as a "guilty spend."

While many executives' offices contain at least one or two framed pictures of the individual on a yacht, strolling a golf course, reeling in a big fish, or posing under the Eiffel Tower, I never once see an image of the Chairman enjoying a hobby or holiday. What I do see, in his office and around the Tiens headquarters building, are countless images of a man who is quite clearly committed to social wellbeing and to education. The Tiens Group's three-word slogan is: "Harmony, Responsibility, Prosperity."

Tiens Group principles

Image courtesy of Tiens Group

Li and Tiens try to act in these ways. The Chairman has been personally responsible for funding the building of over 100 schools around the world. He and the business have collectively given away over 1.6 billion yuan (at the time of writing, this was the equivalent of around US$250 million) to various charities and for a range of purposes. In 1997, he tells me, he donated over eight million yuan to a group of educators for the building of an elementary school and a secondary school in western China. He also set up a philanthropic body to fund the further building of primary schools and to pay for the drilling of wells in the same region.

On one memorable trip to China's western frontier he spontaneously handed over every last yuan that he and his traveling party were carrying (over 200,000 yuan, or about US$30,000), before realizing he now couldn't afford to travel home! It's best explained in his own words.

"During that trip I saw many orphans and elders," he says. "I was on a business trip and with me were several reporters. I had brought 200,000 yuan with me for the trip, and I donated it all. I even convinced all of the reporters to hand over their money for this donation.

We gave away all of our money and then had a small problem. We didn't have enough money to get home."

Of course, a billionaire always has the means to travel and on this trip he simply made a phone call and his staff organized transport. What I'm more interested in, however, is what exactly brought him to the point of literally emptying his pockets on the spot.

"When I saw those lonely elders and orphans, I realized that they had nobody to rely on and their lives were very tough, they struggle every day," he explained. "The elders had no children and lived on their own. You cannot imagine how much they struggle just to survive through a single day. Something burst out from deep within me. It was empathy and sympathy and compassion. I realized that because of all of the changes within China and because the country had developed, I had managed to create my own business and my own kingdom. Now that I was much richer than what I used to be, I could afford to help others. My role is to serve society and serve the community, to help whoever needs my help.

"If we are talking about charity then I will always focus more on education. When you help somebody it is best to help them improve themselves, rather than just give money. When you help them and rescue them just in the moment, it has no long-term, positive effect. Once you educate, you give somebody a chance to learn and afterwards that person can use that knowledge and experience to improve themselves and create something."

In China there is a simple saying that I hear several times – "It takes ten years to grow a tree." The Chairman prefers the planting of a seed and the ten-year wait over the transplanting of an entire tree. That way the sapling has a chance to adapt and thrive, to be nurtured and to become one with its environment. In the schools he builds, the types of schools he was never given the opportunity to attend, talent is nurtured. It is given the time to grow and flourish.

That's not to say he has never offered financial assistance when it has suddenly been required. In May 2008, for instance, when the Sichuan province was decimated by the Wenchuan earthquake, resulting in the death of almost 70,000 people and injuries to over 370,000, people around the world were shocked by the images of destruction and by reports that around 4.8 million people were suddenly homeless.

As soon as the reports surfaced, Chairman Li called upon the international Tiens community to give whatever they could. Three days later

Tiens staff watched as a fleet of aid vehicles, loaded with essential supplies and made possible by the staff members' 23 million yuan fundraising (around US$3.5 million at the time), left the Tiens headquarters and headed for the disaster zone.

When I ask about his very happiest moments, Li immediately describes the results of his charitable work. Most rewarding of all, he says, was when he was able to fund the building of his very first school, the one that replaced the ramshackle building that he had attended as a child in his hometown. He also created an education fund for children in the town, to ensure they could always afford an education.

"My best moment of happiness, the thing that made me most happy, was when I saw the students studying in the school that I built," he smiles. "When I see that they can grow up and study happily in the school, when I see them smile and laugh and I see that I can bring happiness to them, that makes me very happy. It means that I have wisely spent the money that I have earned through my own efforts. I have used the money to create something very meaningful.

"I see myself when I was young, and especially when I was a teenager and I should have been studying at school. There was such a big difference between the town and the city. What I have done is narrowed that gap between rural and city, providing more opportunity for the kids in the village to go to school."

So finally the Chairman admits to a hobby of sorts and, for a small moment, he is distracted from the business and awash with obvious satisfaction. From my cynical, Western point of view I look for signs of dishonesty, for indicators or tells that might give away the fact that he simply wants to be seen in a positive light, to be recorded by history as a humane, benevolent hero. Then I realize I will never see such signs because they don't exist. I've had to drag this information out of him. I am thinking like a Westerner and ignoring the fact that giving to others is at the very center of traditional Chinese society. It is completely normal, it is virtually expected, and is therefore considered by Chinese people to be relatively unremarkable.

"Every one of us, no matter what status, has inexhaustible riches – the riches of charity," he says, in a matter-of-fact tone, as if sensing my circumspection. "When you give out charity, you will feel that the world has become a more beautiful place for it."

24

What can't be bought with money?

"The more you have wealth, the more you have social responsibility. You must use that wealth for a purpose, to help others find health and to find wealth themselves."

Li Jinyuan

In 1908 John D. Rockefeller, America's first billionaire, published an essay called *The Difficult Art of Giving*. It was a tale of extreme wealth and the challenges faced by those in possession of such. Most noteworthy was the fact that it addressed the complex problem of deep satisfaction. It said that no matter how much money a person had, and particularly once an individual came to the stage where they could quite comfortably afford anything they ever wished for, they soon realized that purchases actually offered them very little in terms of what it was that their heart truly desired.

In other words, no matter how much financial wealth an individual has accrued, it is extremely difficult to use money to purchase the things they truly long for. Not impossible, mind you, just extremely difficult.

"The novelty of being able to purchase anything one wants soon passes because what people most seek cannot be bought with money," Rockefeller wrote.

"These rich men we read about in the newspapers cannot get personal returns beyond a well-defined limit for their expenditure. They cannot gratify the pleasures of the palate beyond very moderate bounds, since they cannot purchase a good digestion; they cannot lavish very much money on fine raiment for themselves or their families without suffering from public ridicule; and in their homes they cannot go much beyond the comforts of the less wealthy without involving them in more pain than pleasure. As I study wealthy men, I can see but one way in which they can secure a real equivalent for money spent, and that is to cultivate a taste for giving where the money may produce an effect which will be a lasting gratification."

Chairman Li Jinyuan provides financial support to elderly widows

Image courtesy of Tiens Group

This is completely consistent with comments from the Chairman. "When you help someone and rescue them just in the moment, it has no long-term, positive effect," he says. "Once you educate, you give somebody a chance to learn and afterwards that person can use that knowledge and experience to improve themselves and create something."

Education is the Chairman's "lasting gratification." Much of his charity has been used to build schools in areas that desperately need them. But on an expansive piece of land separated from the Tiens head office by a four-lane motorway is the big education project of Tianyuan University. This vast city of knowledge into which Chairman Li has already poured more than ten billion yuan (around US$1.5 billion) and which had a soft opening in 2017, is still in construction. The Chairman's vision for the university, illustrated splendidly in an artist's impression that takes up an entire wall within the Tiens Museum, involves lakes and sports stadiums, arenas and accommodation complexes, bridges and roads, canals and gardens, and, of course, countless modern buildings dedicated to various educational specializations – all of which will cost more billions over the coming years.

Tianyuan University has represented the Chairman's greatest pleasure and most intense pain during my times talking with him. It has elucidated the fantastic efficiencies of one-party politics as well as the colossal frustrations involved in dealing with state and local government. Every month or so I leave China to spend time at home with my wife and children and each time I return, the plan for the university has evolved, often as a result of government policy and processes that are in place to deal with the development of a large private university. The Chairman and I spend almost as much time discussing this project as we do the business itself, and for good reason. It is of vital personal importance to him. This is how he gives back to the nation that gave him so much. The university is a force for good that will continue to give back to China long after the Chairman's life has become legend. It will be part of his legacy.

During one of our many discussions, after a two-hour chat about the Chairman's various achievements and changes he is making to ensure further business success in the future, I ask whether he will ever recognize his own success. Is he locked into a forward-facing seat on his journey through life, only ever able to see how far he has to go? Or will he one day enjoy the luxury of being able to turn around and appreciate exactly how far he has come, and what he has created along the way?

"So far I don't think I've succeeded," he responds, "but I think I will know I have succeeded when I can see that I have truly contributed to the social benefit, the common good. It will be when I feel that my colleagues and my friends, the people who joined the business, really are able to improve their lifestyles and their living conditions for themselves and their future generations."

Then he pauses, distracted, before taking a different tack.

"What will contribute to my feeling of success? That will be the university," he says. "If my university is able to train talent for our country and for the international community, if it is able to truly contribute to education, I will feel success. My dream is very closely linked to the university."

Tianyuan University is in part an extension of the Chairman's creation of Tianjin Tianshi College, which was founded in July 1999. Chairman Li experienced almost as many challenges with that project as he is with the new university. "I decided back then to take

80 million yuan to launch this project, Tianshi College," the Chairman recalls. "Many people did not understand why I did that. 'You are a corporate leader, are you crazy?' they said. 'Why are you stepping into education? Your foolishness is quite weak!' Even some government leaders did not understand. They thought I was a fool. Society as a whole could not understand. Public opinion was against it."

Pressure, negativity, and restrictions came from everywhere, but this simply motivated the Chairman more. Private colleges were extremely rare in China at that time. Most educational institutions were owned and managed by government. For that reason, government did not altogether trust a leader of a private business. He represented competition and potential advancement. The Chairman was a threat to the status quo.

"When a private company wants to create a school, there is some prejudice against it," Chairman Li says. "But there were some very good people in the government. I met a gentleman who had just retired and who used to be the deputy mayor of Tianjin. I told him about my plan for Tianshi College and he was very touched. Even though he was retired, he agreed to help me."

Connections are as important in China as they are everywhere else, and the Chairman had a knack for finding friends in the right places. "There are some other people who had retired from the education area who also helped me. Some were former professors," he says. "These people created a group and figured out how to help. I told this group of good-hearted people that I wanted to create an educational institution in order to motivate educational reform in China. I told them that sometimes we think the Chinese national education system is very hard to reform, but from the private company side I would try to push this reform. The country cannot be stronger if education is not stronger, so I do it for my country and for my people. They were very touched by what I said."

Tianshi College was one of the first private, tertiary colleges in China, with ground first broken in October 1996. Building was completed two years later, in late 1998, with the first students arriving in late 1999.

"When I asked for the schooling license at the time the government had only just begun to offer a few possibilities to fund private universities in China," the Chairman says. "The public universities have subsidies from the government. But in Tianshi College's case, there was no subsidy because it was funded by a private company. All of the scholarships and funding had to be taken from the company's income. But once I showed by example that a private company could invest in education then some other people followed my example in China. I was proud to lead the movement."

Since the foundation of Tianshi College, some regional governments have decided to give subsidies to private educators in their regions while others, including in the Tianjin region, have not.

"We're all under the same leadership of the Communist Party," the Chairman explains. "Some local governments give 5000 yuan subsidies per student, others more. But Tianjin, where Tianshi College is located, never gave anything. We are not treated as equal, so the company must keep supplying funds. However, for the future of our Chinese people, no matter about the situation we're facing, I do not forget my dream. It is to contribute to education and to China."

Just as he did in the early stages of planning for Tianshi College, the Chairman gathered a small team of experts from China and around the globe to guide the development of Tianyuan University. This is how the Professor first came to Tiens. As a retired academic who had experience in the governance and management of several Western universities, he knew what was required to develop a world-class university and to attract the caliber of academics that would be needed to produce the level of graduate the Chairman desired.

The Chairman was never interested in packing the new university full of students. True success, he tells me, is about quality of output.

"I want to educate people but to do it with a good heart. That is very important for the country and for society," he says. "To then develop a good heart is each individual's responsibility. For its own development a country needs talent, and talent requires education."

When I first walk through the completed buildings on the Tianyuan University campus I catch a glimpse of the future, a dream being brought to life by cranes and concrete mixers. Around 1,700 students moved into their dormitories just a few days earlier – Chinese university students must live on site. Today they're in military dress including camouflage pants and shirts and black boots. All first-year college/university students undertake two weeks of military training, as much for bonding as for discipline. The students come from all over China and often know nobody, so the forced closeness of this serious, if short-term, military training helps to break down various barriers.

Outside every window is a seemingly endless series of buildings in various stages of construction, punctuated and separated by moonscapes, fields of dry, tan dirt that will one day be hidden under lakes or carpeted by parklands. The scene resembles a film set, a futuristic vision of creation and invention, but also of dust and decay. I've never witnessed construction on such a scale, so my imagination immediately leaps to abandoned towns and post-war cityscapes in order to digest and process what it is I'm seeing. Of course, there's no decay and no degeneration. There's just the physical almost-reality of a very big idea that has been maturing and crystalizing in the mind of Li Jinyuan since he was an eight year old, walking along a dusty road to the derelict schoolhouse for yet another day of protest practice under the strict supervision of the Red Guards.

In the first fully completed teaching and research building there are 100 classrooms and laboratories on each floor, and the building has five floors. Hallways and a cavernous central space are sleek, clean, and modern with exposed, sheet-metal conduits, chrome accents, and polished concrete floors and walls. There are numerous conference rooms and 99 offices for academic and administrative staff in this first building.

Each year from now on, new students enrolled in Tianshi College, which offers 31 undergraduate majors, will be sent to the new Tianyuan University campus.

When I visit a second time, just six months later, a total of 7,000 students are living and learning on the university campus. Hundreds of mature trees have been planted to provide shade in the grassed and landscaped common areas between the numerous completed accommodation buildings. A canal, similar to the one on the main Tiens estate, runs around part of the grounds and rings a sporting complex containing several fenced basketball courts and soccer pitches complete with synthetic turf, goals, and line markings. On these soccer pitches a teachers vs students match takes place every Monday.

The heart of the campus is well and truly beating while work continues at pace on a series of buildings and landscape features on a property that stretches almost as far as the eye can see.

Chairman Li is "getting in early and will be very well placed to meet the boom in demand from millions of families seeking quality, private education within China," an American staff member at the university tells me. China is moving in the direction of the USA, the administrator says, in terms of private institutions offering a very high quality of education.

By the time this book is published, several more of the buildings and landscapes at the new university will be completed. The university's leadership has a goal of turning the institution into China's number one private university within five years, with an emphasis on excellent teaching and applied research. Indeed, a number of senior professors, including some Nobel Prize winners, are involved in the development of various new offerings that will add extra courses and specializations. Until then, students will be able to witness the creation of a small city dedicated to learning, an educational nirvana born from the imagination, passion, and very deep pockets of Chairman Li.

25
"Washing a rental": preparing for a new world

"Those who only focus on the long-term goal often take no action at all, therefore they fail."

Li Jinyuan

As students at Tianyuan University prepare for the future, Chairman Li is also re-learning his art and readying himself and his business for an entirely new set of challenges. In this way, as the world changes sometimes quickly and dramatically, he is similar to many business leaders in Western countries who are seeking to future-proof their businesses. The shape of Tiens has required change at several stages, but never more so than now. Competition is fiercer than ever, regulations around direct sales are tightening, and the war for talent in China and around the world is raging. Staff retention and engagement are being widely accepted as a priority by Chinese businesses, having been proven time and time again to offer organizations an edge over their competitors. The Chairman is telling all who listen that now is the time for everyone in the Tiens family (and yes, he uses that term) to develop and act from a global point of view.

The importance of staff perspective, empowerment, and engagement was made crystal clear to me several years ago during an interview I was conducting with an organizational psychologist in the UK. We were discussing employee behavior, particularly around the topic of motivation, when he turned the questions on me. This conversation always stuck with me as it so efficiently explained the importance of the drive and enthusiasm of staff.

"Have you ever hired a car?" he asked.

"Yes," I said.

"Before you return a rental car, do you wash it?" he asked.

"Of course I don't," I replied. "What does that have to do with anything?"

"Why don't you wash it?" he continued.

"Why would I?" I retorted.

"Seriously," he said. "Why don't you wash it?"

"Because it's not mine," I said. "I have paid to rent it for a certain amount of time. Why would I waste my own time and energy washing a car when it has nothing to do with me and doesn't benefit me?"

"Exactly," he said. "That is what employee motivation is all about!"

He'd hit the nail on the head. Most employees do what they do for the money. They do no more than they have to, and why would they? It's not as if they will benefit in any material way if their longer hours or greater effort result in more success for the company.

Why would a staff member go over and above if there's nothing in it for them, if they are going to be paid the same either way, if there is no clear pathway for professional advancement, and if they feel no ownership of the business? Why would they waste time and energy washing a rental?

We have discussed that businesses in China are working in loose synchronization with the nation's government toward a greater goal. At the same time that China has been unifying toward a singular plan for development and further growth, Chairman Li has been developing a similar strategy on an organizational level.

The period of my immersion in Tiens has been a time of dramatic change within the organization. I'm sure the timing of my invitation was not planned around such change as some of it was out of anybody's control. But the Chairman, the entire time I have known him, has been hinting at a major restructure, a ground-breaking new plan that will kick off what he calls the "third wave of Tiens."

"At Tiens we are going into the third generation of our entrepreneurship," he explains. "The first generation was our growth in China. The second was our expansion internationally. The third, which we have now launched, is our true globalization."

During my final visits to Wuqing these changes are officially announced and a change program, the main driver of which is a series of five four-day training conferences for senior staff from around the globe, is implemented. I am offered extra time with the Chairman, as well as access to managers and consultants who have worked with Li to turn his vision into reality. What follows in this and the next chapter is the new Tiens strategy, one that demonstrates a willingness to shape-shift and a high level of comfort with dramatic change, within the business and within the Chairman's management style. There are lessons here not only about the Chinese way of thinking but also things that Western business leaders could usefully reflect upon. But first, some background.

From day one on this project it became clear to me that Tiens was run as a series of silos and was top-heavy with management. Fourteen Vice-Presidents overlooking 13 departments reported directly to the Chairman. Many department staff had up to seven levels of management above them. Certain directives that were clearly and passionately communicated by the Chairman to the Vice-Presidents were simply not being actioned at the required levels. Unsurprisingly, as is often the case in a large organization, several blockages had developed.

This was a concern for a number of reasons. It indicated that staff in some areas were working in different directions (and sometimes, knowingly or unknowingly, against each other) rather than toward a certain goal. It meant the sum of the business's parts was less than its whole. And perhaps most importantly, just as messages did not make it all the way down the line, vital market information was also not making its way up the long chain of command. This meant strategic decisions were being made without all necessary data, putting the health of the entire enterprise at risk. The fact that market intelligence wasn't able to travel up to the decision-making level made the business slow to react and inflexible to changing market scenarios.

It is easy to assume that this is a problem unique to Chinese businesses as a result of their management-heavy structures and the command-and-control nature of their leadership. But, of course, it is a typical issue in businesses around the globe. Almost every large and mid-sized organization that has been around for a decade or more suffers from middle-management bloat. Most recognize the problem only when the massive inefficiencies created by such a structure become a serious problem, and only then do they do something about it.

The Chairman had this realization a few years ago. But when you're at the helm of a ship the size of Tiens, or more correctly a global armada of ships the size of Tiens, you can't just stop and change course. Instead, he began charting a new course that could be embarked upon once the conditions allowed. It involved a new organizational structure, greater autonomy for senior managers and for geographic regions around the world, and a more holistic coming together of all of the enterprise's various businesses. A technologically driven big data, membership, and incentive scheme would be developed to make staff, distributors (or business partners, as they tend to now be called), and customers feel more like owners of the business.

"I wanted to reform the structure because when it comes to a certain time in business, the entire structure becomes too heavy. It becomes too complex. This is not efficient, and also it is not inviting to the young people I want to attract into the company. The company very much needs more young people who see the world as their stage," Chairman Li says.

Chairman Li Jinyuan speaks with the staff during an outdoor meeting

Image courtesy of Tiens Group

"Within an overly heavy structure there are many people who are not responsible. They sign papers just to get things through but somehow they are not responsible for the results. There are many bad habits and bad actions by some of the personnel and they create negative impacts on the organization. So I had this idea to make changes both in individual roles and organizational form and function. We needed first to clarify what are the necessary roles and functions. We needed to make sure everything would still run smoothly and efficiently. Efficiency and responsibility had to be emphasized."

On top of the problem of the company becoming too bureaucratic in its behavior, the Chairman had another specific concern, which once again was not unique to Chinese businesses. Rather it is a problem that occurs when a company begins to transfer power from its founder to new generations of leaders and managers. The founder of a large and well-known British business once described it to me this way – "The first generation creates the business, the second generation grows the business, the third generation destroys the business."

In China there is a similar belief, but the Chairman expresses it in a different way. "We say that the rich will never cross three generations," he explains.

Chairman Li is making plans to protect his business from the forces that can come with second- and third-generation management. He is looking to future-proof the organization.

"We need to make sure we've got the right people on board, to attract all the right talent, and to make all of the Tiens family feel that they own part of the business. This is a platform that I have created to make sure everything is run the right way. Starting a business is a lot easier than maintaining and running a business. To maintain it is more difficult. We require strong plans to ensure everything is on the right track. And we need talented and educated young people who perhaps understand the direction of the world more than some of those who are older."

His plan, the Chairman says, will offer the company the greatest chance of longevity in a market that is more challenging than ever thanks to greater competition, ever-increasing expectations from customers, and always-changing regulations.

"Business was much easier 20 years ago," he says. "Looking back to the establishment of the business, nothing has become easier since then. Everything is much tougher. To thrive in this environment we must transform and integrate all parts of the business into one, to have all of the various brands and platforms performing as one, supporting each other and making the body stronger."

How exactly is such integration achieved? How do you create a single, coherent whole from a business that has traded in 190 countries and that is involved to varying extents in at least six different industry sectors?

Before the Chairman introduced his grand plan, he simplified the organizational structure, as well as improved and made more transparent the lines of communication. A talent audit was run by a management consultancy and some departments were merged. Headcount was reduced and many work areas now contain fewer, but higher-quality and more professional, teams.

"Even though we have fewer headcount, the efficiency has been increasing," Chairman Li tells me. "And the actions are still ongoing. We are continuing to reduce manpower but increase the efficiency of our work."

Another reason I'm seeing fewer people on some floors of the building is because more staff are being despatched into the field. "If you want to grow a business it's pointless having all of your staff sitting in the head office," Li says. "Staff need to understand the reality in the field so they need to be on the frontline, thinking like the people on the frontline, and making decisions on the frontline."

I think of the shrinking staff levels in this spacious and beautifully landscaped Chinese head office campus and ask the Chairman what he imagines when he pictures the Tiens International Health Park ten years from now. With fewer staff on-site and more being sent into the field, won't a precinct containing buildings with some unused areas risk becoming a ghost town?

He smiles warmly, clearly glad for the chance to describe the images and ideas that have long resided in his imagination and driven his strategic thinking.

"With the industrial park and the university, this will become a spot to which all the Tiens family, including staff and distributors and consumers, will be attracted. Also, friends from other companies and from schools across China will continue to come here, and large groups of visitors from various countries will increasingly come, too," he says. "The only word they will say upon arrival is, 'Wow.' The entire area will become one. And it won't be just the park and the university, there will be more coming soon. This will become a place that makes people feel proud to be part of the Tiens brand."

What exactly is "coming soon?" At the first of five global conferences, the Chairman begins to unveil his master plan. It is a plan of such scope and intended rapidity that it would make many Western companies both envious and sceptical. But this is China, and things are often writ large and fast.

26

One Body Multiple Wings

"It is very precious to have opportunity available to you."

Li Jinyuan

The Chairman's strategy, one that transforms the business from a direct selling organization into a "big health" player, is one he refers to as "One Body Multiple Wings." I discover early on that Chinese business is full of slogans. Every idea must be boiled down to a few words that vividly illustrate its shape or purpose.

He explains the strategy as "a system project across regions, countries, and industries, involving relatively complete and integrated business segments."

My immediate understanding of the new plan is one of massive technological transformation. It is a particularly clever and unique combination of the finest motivational ingredients of direct selling around the world with the best components of new retail. The intention is to create a recipe that is easily replicated by Tiens in various markets but difficult for competitors to duplicate, and at the same time it brings together the various Tiens business units into a meaningful whole.

It is about re-organization of the company structure, followed by the integration of all of the business units under common and mutually beneficial systems. This is where the total technological transformation comes in – it is technology that will link the various industry sectors and brands of Tiens Group.

"The key for successfully implementing this strategy is the linkage among the 'body' and 'wings,' integrating and interacting with each other, exchanging customers and supporting each other, effectively consolidating social resources and keeping the benefits within the Tiens realm," he tells me.

Success with such a strategy will ensure that "one plus ten equals more than eleven" or, as we say in the West, it will create a situation such that the whole will be greater than the sum of its parts.

So what exactly does all of this mean? Let's explore the "integration" part of the strategy, because there are lessons here about company transformation, irrespective of the particularities of the Chinese context. There are also interesting and sometimes surprising insights into how a business that has built two decades of success on word-of-mouth marketing utilizes technology to further enhance trust and loyalty.

The "body" in One Body Multiple Wings, depending on geographic location, can be any part of the business. In China, where the government is increasingly regulating the direct selling industry, the body is a new e-commerce platform that will sell everything that Tiens currently produces as well as products from other brands around the globe. Blockchain technology has been employed to ensure the provenance of purchases. If a person in Russia orders a special item from Peru, then the blockchain keeps a record of that product from its production in Peru to its delivery in Russia.

Tiens' retail offering will move increasingly toward higher-quality and more aspirational, but always affordable, products in order to attract a younger and higher-spending demographic, especially in the health and beauty brands of Tiens. The platform will also sell services from Tiens' range of brands, such as the All-Legend Hotels, All-Legend Travel, and Tai-jisun Hospital. So it will begin as a mini Amazon and will grow quickly as individual consumers can also open their own shop spaces on the platform.

The wings are the other business units such as the hotels, hospital, travel service, educational offerings, and new, bricks-and-mortar "experience centers." Those wings continue to operate and grow, but they always support the body, helping it to fly higher. In return, the body provides further life to the wings in the form of new customers and new markets.

However, there is great flexibility and cross-border opportunity in the One Body Multiple Wings model. For instance, in another part of the world where online selling has not yet gained traction, the body might be direct selling. Or in a particular segment of a market, amongst students for example, the body might be Tianyuan University.

The Chairman describes the model as a "Transformer," able to alter its shape and purpose for different environments and able to adapt to cope with potential disruptions within long supply chains.

So in any single region the "body" and "wings" can change but all the while the business thrives, as long as systems within the various parts of the business work in synchronicity.

For customers and business partners to recognize and value the links between the various Tiens businesses, some form of glue to bind them together is required, something more than the sharing of back-office processes. For this purpose, Li's staff have developed several technological platforms, including the e-commerce system that makes purchases simple and drives customers to each of the Tiens brands and services.

Another is a Tiens e-wallet app, which customers can use to buy products using funds or points that reside in the app itself. They can use the app to pay for products or services within Tiens partner businesses. The e-wallet also offers access to financial products such as high-interest savings accounts and insurance services – in some territories Tiens has already partnered with financial institutions to make such services a reality.

The third is PointsWin, a loyalty system partly secured by blockchain technology and presented as a smartphone app that uses points to reward registered members of the app for purchases and more. So, for example, when Tiens sends electronic marketing out to its network customers, those customers will earn points for sharing the marketing with friends on social media platforms. If a purchase is made by someone else as a result of an individual's sharing of a promotion, then that individual will earn even more points. This means every user of the system is incentivized at every stage to become a part of the marketing, sales, and recruitment process, rather than a simple, one-time purchaser of a Tiens product or service.

At the same time, Tiens collects valuable purchaser and product data, bringing an immediacy and transparency to the business, one that the organization has never previously enjoyed. Customers, who have more touchpoints than ever with the business and its various brands, have a direct line through the app to customer service and are served advertising and special offers that are of interest. Importantly, they will feel much more a part of something, the Tiens family, as they sense the business understands, appreciates, and rewards them.

The points earned, much like points earned in a frequent flyer program, can be spent on products or services from businesses across the group and with other organizations that partner with Tiens. For example, if a customer attends a sales training course via the company's internal training body Innoviera (earning 10 points, let's say) and, during that course, they stay at one of the All-Legend Hotels (20 points) or another hotel partner, and go for a check-up or health treatment at the Taijisun Hospital (10 points) or another health provider partner, they then have 40 points to spend. By spending money within the Tiens environment, they are rewarded.

Loyalty programs are nothing new. But injecting the DNA of the direct selling approach into the process brings the performnce of, and loyalty toward, such systems to an entirely new level.

At this stage it is important to explain that within the One Body Multiple Wings model, customers are not just customers. Each can become what was once known as a "distributor" (in direct selling jargon) and is now known as a "partner."

They can open their own shopfront online, just as individuals and businesses can do on Amazon and eBay. The difference with the online approach of Tiens is that the reward and loyalty system is far more powerful. When partners enlist their personal or social media networks to sell products, or to encourage others to become Tiens partners, they earn reward points. When they introduce new product retailers or service providers into the Tiens e-commerce system, they are rewarded. And if they recommend customers on to other offerings, such as the All-Legend Hotels, the All-Legend Travel service, or the Taijisun health service, they are similarly rewarded. Suddenly, the power of social connection is able to bring benefit to all of the business units.

Previously, business units operated relatively independently of one another. Tiens had been set up like many conglomerates with multiple brands sharing a few back-office services. When such conglomerates, whether in China or in the West, go through transformation programs they tend to concentrate on one brand at a time, developing new, individual strategies, one by one. Often during such programs, certain non-core brands are sold off in order to free up management bandwidth to focus on core profit centers.

The difference with Tiens, however, is that the Chairman chose to see his business as a single whole, with all parts working together to create a strong and dynamic entity. In doing so, he has formulated a way for customers to be encouraged from one brand within Tiens to another within that whole, for them to be rewarded at each step along the consumer path, and for them to then become valued business partners.

They begin to feel ownership and, as they profit from the relationship, they finally have a reason to wash the rental car!

27
Real-time data from a retail store

"If your innovation does not meet the demand of the market or if it does not meet a social need, then it is not meaningful. Innovation must be connected to its setting and context to succeed."

Li Jinyuan

One of the newest Tiens attractions in Tianjin is a showcase Tiens Experience Center. It sprawls across 2,000 square metres of shop space and sets a precedent for what new Tiens physical spaces – including smaller shops and other showrooms around the globe – should look like. Tiens Experience Centers have opened in Shenzhen, in Moscow, Russia (facing onto Red Square), in Almaty, Kazakhstan, and in Osaka, Japan. Others are in various stages of development in numerous locations around the world.

Michael Yu, Deputy General Manager of Innoviera, the Tiens training and education business, helped me to understand the importance of the experience centers. Having worked with high-end, European fashion houses, run his own sales and leadership training business, and managed a manufacturing facility producing handbags for the European market, Yu has developed a fine eye for sophisticated design. The new experience centers, he says, are about as good as it gets.

"The design is very modern and very fashionable. It is a very clear statement," he says. "Most of our distributors, when they visit the showrooms, say they never thought it would look like that. In their eyes, this company is very traditional. Designed by the person who designed shop spaces for major French labels, the new showrooms are very fashionable. This is the new Tiens, and it will attract a new and younger market."

The experience centers are a place where partners can invite customers, and potential new partners, to touch and feel the products. It's so much easier to go fishing in a pool than in the ocean, Chairman Li says. In other words, if somebody is happy to come along to the shop, half the sales job is already done. And as members of the public can visit the shops, they also act as brand-building tools.

The experience centers don't just contain Tiens health, beauty, household, and other products. They also boast a café, a mini Taijisun Hospital where people can have basic aspects of their health and wellbeing tested, information and booking systems for Tiens-owned and partner hotels, a high-end beauty parlour called Faith Channe, an All-Legend Travel agency, a kitchen area where Tiens food and kitchen products can be used to create meals, and a meeting room for distributor sales sessions and training.

Scenes from the opening of the Tiens Experience Center in
Red Square, Moscow

Images courtesy of Tiens Group

Just as partners can open their own shopfronts online on the global, cross-border platform, segments of this offline experience center can also be taken and recreated in various markets as free-standing, bricks-and-mortar stores. A partner might decide to open their own Faith Channe beauty parlour, for example, or an All-Legend Travel agency. Online and offline, the segments of the Tiens offering can be split and utilized by Tiens partners.

Experience centers and shops are part of a "new retail" strategy that involves the modernization, fusion, data synthesis, and transformation of all the brands of Tiens Group. In terms of technology, it is a strategy that clearly demonstrates how some Chinese businesses have not just caught up but are leapfrogging their competitors around the globe. And it demonstrates a heady mix of globalization and localization facilitated by the technology of social media, big data, and artificial intelligence.

Let me share with you a technological development that offers an example of such leapfrogging.

I'm in the office of Jason Wang, an IT veteran from Shanghai who left JP Morgan to help launch Tiens into the future. At JP Morgan, he says, the IT budget was US$10 billion. The firm employed around 40,000 technical systems experts around the globe. When he arrived at Tiens, a business that had traditionally been more concerned with human relationships than data, the IT system "seemed old fashioned," he says, with typical Chinese politeness.

"When I arrived there were a lot of systems without connections, which means that data was isolated in systems, or lost," he explains. "When a business grows to a certain level it needs to invest in financial and technological factors that support its various parts. This business did not do that.

"We realized there were a lot of opportunities both within Tiens and externally. The hotel and travel businesses are very much involved in travel, for example. This opens itself up for travel insurance products. Product selling also has a natural connection to personal and business loans. So the business is actually quite connected to finance. We don't have a license for financial services, but through an aggregated platform we can connect our members to such products at the same time that we connect them to the various brands within our own business, all on the one platform."

Wang is keen to show me a little of what he and his team have achieved so far. He opens a screen on his laptop, which is mirrored, for my sake, on a larger monitor on his desk. He talks me through a dash-board that offers information around what is going on right now – at this very moment – in the Shenzhen Experience Center, which, as the crow flies, is around 2,200 kilometres from our Wuqing office.

As we watch, we see in real time that there are 29 customers in the center. Yesterday at this exact time there were 18. Yesterday a total of 92 people visited but today the store is already up to 125 with most of the day still to go. Of today's customers, 49 have never been to the shop before – they are "unique visitors," in online parlance. The rest are return clients. Sixty percent are female.

How can Wang know all of this? Facial recognition cameras have been installed above monitors around the store, he explains. Such technology was originally mass developed for use in smartphones but is now being utilized by Tiens to develop strong data feeds from the experience centers. And what he has told me so far is only the tip of the data iceberg in terms of information coming from the store.

On another section of the dashboard is a floor map of the expe-rience center. Various sections glow as hot spots, showing where cus-tomers are gathered right now, as well as which sections of the store customers are most attracted to throughout each day, or at various specific times of each day.

Not only does Tiens know who is male and who is female, the business also knows each individual's age group, level of education, income, disposable income, marital status, and, after a few visits, their product preferences. It's here that I openly doubt what I am being told. How can such information come from a face scan, I ask.

"Right now, of the people in the store, 46 percent did not study beyond high school," Wang teases, before revealing the secrets behind his technological witchcraft. "This does not come from their face. We also installed another technology called 'Wi-fi Detector.' Everybody always has their phone with them. Your phone has your device ID. We can match up your device ID, your face ID, and your WeChat ID [almost everyone in China uses WeChat] with data from such services as Baidu [a Chinese company specializing in internet searching ser-vices] to develop a good picture of the individual."

Wang quickly identifies my look of concern and relates my worry, quite correctly, to privacy issues. "This is all group data, not individual data," he says. "We do not know your name. But we have a very accurate picture of the type of group that you fit into. For example, in the store right now we can see that most of the people are aged 25 to 34. Most are in technical jobs and their income is a certain level. Half of them have a car and half do not."

It's spooky, but brilliant in terms of optimizing product positioning and marketing. It doesn't come close to the sometimes creepy insight that major technology companies such as Google and Facebook have into our lives, but it is an elegant and effective solution to a problem Western retailers and other businesses have struggled with ever since the power of data was realized. How does a company gather useful, real-time data in a bricks-and-mortar environment? And how does a brand bridge that gap between online and offline without any noticeable loss in data quality or customer experience?

The data being collected in the Shenzhen Experience Center, once it has been sliced and diced by analysts, will help Tiens with targeted marketing, such as emailing or messaging particular customer groups with news and product offers they will likely be interested in. It will also greatly improve customer service, allowing all parts of the organization to know exactly where on the customer journey an individual might be, or allowing shop staff to know, as soon as a customer enters the store, what they are interested in or what was their last purchase.

And remember, like many Western companies, Tiens is interested in attracting the image- and fashion-conscious twenty-somethings and thirty-somethings who are willing to invest in their health and their beauty. Finding the way into that technologically savvy demographic, whether in China or in the West, not only taps into their spend but also helps to future-proof the business. Loyalty to the brand continues with that group as they and their families have needs for other products and services that Tiens Group can offer across the world, even if people move countries.

This technological innovation in the experience centers also offers Tiens the ability to identify new 'potential' customer groups, giving the business the power to create accurate images of lookalikes of the various customer demographics and to identify where those lookalikes can be found, for marketing purposes.

Finally, the data can be used for highly practical day-to-day purposes. It will influence store layout and in-store product and service placement for specific times of day. It will inform new product and service development. And it will link the previously disconnected brands and services of the Tiens business for the benefit of the customer, and therefore for the benefit of the business.

This horizontal and vertical integration of products and services is something that multinational conglomerates often struggle to achieve. Tiens is seeking to do this through business innovation, technological advances, and investment in people, especially those who are younger and wish to grow themselves with the company.

It's big data developments such as this one within the experience centers that hint at the real power behind technological projects going on within Tiens. This is also entirely consistent with the strategy of China, as stated by President Xi Jinping, to become the leading future force in the development and use of artificial intelligence in all aspects of government, business, education, and social activity.

Technology, the glue that holds the Tiens business units together, will create stronger and more meaningful links between other Chinese businesses, their partners, and the Chinese government as it drives its economy onward and outward. And yes, there are downsides to this in terms of privacy and in terms of potential or actual control of behavior. But neither Tiens nor China is alone in trying to find the balance of upsides and downsides. That balance will likely be different across countries and political systems, as well as across time.

28
Change management

"When you are making the right choice there is no hesitation and no doubt … The decision you make must bring benefits to people, business, and society. Behind a good decision is strong morality."

Li Jinyuan

How does a large business manage a massive change program? At Tiens, the process has been broken down into over 350 individual projects, all of which are categorized according to costs, priorities, and complexity levels. The change program is being planned, overseen, and executed by Dr Han Liansheng (English name Henry), a respected and award-winning master of what is known in China as "projectification management."

With a PhD in management from Nankai University, Han has long been devoted to the study and practice of projectification management theory and is the author of a book titled *Enterprise Projectification Management Paradigm* (China Machine Press, 2016).

Han first met the Chairman three years ago when he was invited to run a training session for Tiens Group.

"When the Chairman met me he said, 'You have to come in and help me!'" Han smiles. He and his dedicated team have been working with Tiens to help make the One Body Multiple Wings strategy a reality.

"Each project is measured on time, cost, and quality, and right now our biggest challenge is an HR one. We have to recruit new people from outside to fit with our needs. Whenever you want innovation and development, talent is a challenge."

But it's about far more than innovation and development. This is change at all levels of the organization, including the re-engineering of systems and processes, major shifts in organizational structure and authority, and, in terms of culture and people, an integration and balance of old and new. And it's all happening within a fast-changing China, which itself is finding its place in a constantly shifting global landscape. Perhaps above all, as the Chairman continually reiterates at the global training sessions involving thousands of the Tiens family from across the world, it is about seeing from a new perspective.

In his own talk at one of those sessions, the Professor highlights the three-part challenge facing Tiens during this time of change. First is a talent challenge which, he says, can be solved with a mix of existing and new staff. Second is the technology that is currently being custom-designed and built to facilitate the marketing and selling of products and services, the global logistics of delivering them, the rewards that are available for those involved in the process, and the linkages to other organizations that offer products and services in association with Tiens. Third is the transformation of the company overall, of the inter-relationship of its various brands, of the connections across different territories of the globe, and perhaps most importantly of the genuine desire of the Chairman for all of the Tiens family to be involved in creating the future of the company as a whole.

The overall message is one that is not specifically Chinese but is, in fact, consistent with the desires of many Western conglomerates.

The intention of many of these changes is to help create economies of scale and to exploit the fact that globally the various Tiens brands already have loyal customers in over 40 million households. Assuming most of these customers currently use only one Tiens product or service, but with more information and a powerful loyalty scheme might happily use two or three, imagine the potential for growth. This is the Chairman's current challenge to the business. In order to meet that challenge, he has set a four-year strategic goal to reach a total of 100 million households.

An experienced branding/PR expert, a Chinese media professional who has worked in the USA, has also been brought in. Her job is to reinvigorate the Tiens brand and all of its subsidiary businesses for the global stage. Just as companies entering China often find their branding requires fine-tuning, or a complete overhaul, to meet expectations of the local market and culture, so too do Chinese businesses looking out-ward. The branding revamp is immediately obvious as logos and fonts become cleaner and simpler, stronger and clearer, leaving behind the detail and complication that so often defines a Chinese logo.

At almost every conceivable level the business is changing, from the surface to deep within its systems and processes. The new data flow and organizational structure will create a powerful stream of information.

Included is a new department known as Global Business Assistant, whose staff are tasked with continuous communication with offices around the globe to gather real-time information about how things are tracking and how processes can be improved. All of this will help Tiens to react more quickly to changes in the market, to identify opportunities, and to predict what customers will want before the customers themselves know.

Many Chinese (and indeed Western) businesses are currently facing a coming of age similar to Tiens, or at least a redirection in changing global markets. As the open economy has matured and Chinese companies are competing around the world, they are realizing a need to modify their culture to suit the globalized markets. It seems ironic that as Western organizations are clawing their way over each other to get into the Chinese market, Chinese businesses at the same time are having to restructure for success in the very markets that Westerners have been trading in for decades.

Chinese businesses are also re-learning their own markets as they change, including coming to terms with ever-increasing rules and regulations that are making the business environment more of a challenge. Zhang Ke, a long-time Tiens staff member and advisor to the Chairman who, in the past number of years has split his time between the USA and China, tells me business in China was much easier some 30 or more years ago, soon after the economy opened up, simply because there were few regulations. All an entrepreneur needed was some business sense, a good idea, and a truckload of courage.

"Now, the market has been very well regulated. There are so many rules they are sometimes very difficult for the government to police," Zhang says. "When he started the business, our Chairman traveled fearlessly into the far corners of so many nations to market and promote Tiens products, driven by the knowledge that he was not only building a business but also improving the health and wealth of the local people. Today, in China and elsewhere, the business environment is becoming much more challenging."

Speaking of regulation and challenge, in early 2019 a government investigation was launched into the entire direct selling industry in China to weed out those businesses utilizing models that engage in misleading advertising and multi level marketing. All 91 Chinese direct sales businesses were put on notice for a 100-day period of investigation and self-reporting.

Companies were told to self-report on certain practices as the government also ran its own investigation. Self-reporting may seem an easy way out, but the penalty for false reporting is likely to be extreme.

At the end of the 100 days, some of the direct sales firms would be shut down and their founders fined or possibly even imprisoned. Others would likely be fined for some transgressions, told to pull their socks up, and would operate under government scrutiny. Others would pass the test with flying colors. The government will also announce new laws and regulations relating to direct selling, and these will likely include a focus on strengthening internal management of direct selling enterprises, strengthening management and control of executives, sales teams, and direct sellers, eliminating misleading marketing and illegal direct sales, and strengthening the quality of health and food products.

Such an occurrence would be a cause of great concern for many business owners, but in typical style the Chairman sees only the positives. These include the purging from the industry businesses that give it a bad name and using the period of change to launch his One Body Multiple Wings strategy.

It all supports Zhang's notion that business success in China today requires greater skill and finesse than it did a few decades ago. I recall also a comment made by Professor Gillis, an American who has worked in business education at Chinese universities for several decades. "In China there's been a 30-year run of 10 percent growth and one of the things about 10 percent growth is it covers up a lot of sins," he said.

"You don't have to be very good at business to make money when the economy's growing at 10 percent. Now, the growth has slowed down to 6 or 7 percent and is maybe heading lower over the next decade, mainly because the planet isn't big enough to sustain that type of growth forever. We will start to see winners and losers in China. It starts to matter whether or not you make the right decisions whereas in the past, in the previous environment of 10 percent growth, everybody and anybody was a winner."

And so the new organizational structure and strategy for Tiens is vital. A business, like an athlete, must remain in perfect shape to hold its place at the front of the pack. And just as it is for an athlete, mindset is as important as physical fitness. This is where a business's leader, or its leadership team, comes in. Restructuring the form of the physical body is meaningless if the mindset of the leader doesn't change at the same time.

29
A changing Chairman

"You need to choose the right thing to pick up and you need to choose the right thing to give up. When you make the decision, you should not hesitate."

Li Jinyuan

When running a large business, it can be useful to be an honored, revered, and sometimes feared leader. There are times when absolute power is a positive, particularly when strong, swift action is required. This is the traditional Chinese way of doing things, but it can be a double-edged sword as managers throughout the business are afraid to flag up serious problems and unwilling or simply not permitted to make important or timely decisions.

As China has propelled itself into the realm of the economic super-power, having adapted, aligned, and developed to operate in a global environment of new complexities and challenges, so too must its companies and its business leaders. This process of adaptation poses some risk and requires personal and corporate bravery.

There is always a concern that the person at the head of an empire, by definition its emperor, will want to retain total power and will not be flexible enough to change with the times. Empires and businesses fail when they lose their ability to foresee and cope with change, particularly when that change is constant and rapid.

But the future of Tiens, Chairman Li tells me, does not rely on him as much as people think. It will instead rely on the organization's ability to create leaders at all levels, to attract and foster entrepreneurial thinkers, and to convince those people that they should care about the business, that they're not just employees. This seems obvious, but thanks to several factors – including the way the people have been taught to think and their absolute respect for authority – it has not been the traditional Chinese way.

"At the very beginning, I was only one man, then we grew into what you see right now," the Chairman says. "Now it is very important that we begin to duplicate more people like myself. I need true partners who can really contribute to the business. So I am trying to duplicate myself and cultivate and nurture more leadership talent. I want people who are like I was when I started this business. These people have to be ready to lead. Once we have more leaders we can work together and go places together. And we especially need more young people in all levels of the business."

Chairman Li has reinvented himself in many ways as China and the world have changed and as his business has adapted. But the shape of the organization and its major decision-making processes have always been his to create and control alone. Since Tiens began as a one-man band it has been his responsibility, and nobody else's, to ensure the company's structure and processes suited the environment in which the business operated.

Over recent times Li has been attempting to alter that single truth, to encourage his senior management team to take responsibility, feel empowered, and make decisions on their own in an increasingly fast-changing world. But old habits die hard, for staff and for leaders, so the journey to greater management autonomy for his leadership team is not yet over.

Senior managers have completed several training sessions in goal setting, project management, and decision making. They have been asked to present at all five One Body Multiple Wings global training sessions. As an aside, for me these sessions have been a cultural eye-opener in terms of presentation style. On stage, some managers – typically those who have not worked in the West – adopt an authoritarian tone, yelling loudly and passionately at the audience instead of speaking in considered tones (several times I have had to put my hands over my ears), and shaking their fists at the sky as they make their point. The Chairman, who rarely raises his voice, regularly interrupts their presentations to make corrections or to add thoughts. He also often mentions quite openly that managers who are not measuring up or can't adapt to the necessary changes will be replaced.

What is yet to be seen is whether the managers truly believe they are empowered to make decisions, to try and potentially to fail, without earning the ire of the person who has made every decision for the past two decades. Only time will tell whether the managers and the

Chairman are able to adapt to the new model. As in most instances of desired change, there will likely be some steps forward and the occasional step backward personally and organizationally. But my sense is that the Chairman and at least some of the senior managers understand that the changes that are occurring are necessary.

Increasingly clear are the many parallels between one man, one company, and one country. As China grows, succeeds, and settles into its new place in the world, so too does Tiens. This is a business whose journey has mirrored that of its nation. And as China takes its place at the global table, creatively adapting to the change in environment, so too must Li, a man who in so many ways embodies China. His greatest challenge right now is to internationalize his own management style, and to engage his people in that change.

"I am always upgrading myself," he tells me, and the evidence would suggest this is true. "Whatever decision you make must fit the particular needs of the time. The business and its leader must fit the particular conditions around them. We need to stand higher and have broader vision. Vision is very important and the way you position yourself is very important."

Interestingly, I also see the company positioning itself to openly recognize the trust issues that have haunted some Chinese businesses in the past when they have sought to go global. "Tiens Group is honest and trustworthy, carries out its business according to the law, promotes the development of the industry and regional economy, and devotes itself to charity," reads the Chairman's letter in the company's 2018/19 annual report. It is not only Western business leaders that have recognized the absolute necessity of being trustworthy and also of being seen to be trustworthy.

Not only has Li shaped the business so that information and advice can arrive more efficiently from below, he is also reaching out to those at his level and above. World leaders, business leaders, and academic leaders, including ex Presidents, ex Prime Ministers and Nobel Prize winners, are being approached for ongoing advice and consultation around the governance of Tiens businesses in particular regions.

New governance structures are being formed to further improve local procedures and structures and to better align with the regulations of relevant countries. This offers business units and territories greater independence, including the ability to utilize local knowledge and expertise to make their own decisions swiftly and efficiently.

"Now it is time for Tiens managers to be brave, to take more responsibility, and to accept greater challenges," Li says. "All leaders should be responsible and accountable and must dare to make decisions and to act quickly, clearly, and effectively."

Exactly how much decision-making power an emperor is willing – or even allowed – to surrender to others is a question that can only be answered with time. But judging by his history of adaptation and change, it would be unwise to doubt the intentions of Chairman Li.

30
Bi-cultural HR: the people perspective

"Managers must know how to act in a genuine manner around other people. Being genuine and authentic will warm many hearts and create an environment in which everybody is comfortable to act sincerely. This is an excellent atmosphere for personal and business development. A truly authentic person is less critical and more understanding and positive."

Li Jinyuan

It would be easy to think that an organization in search of great employees, in a nation with a population approaching 1.4 billion, will never suffer talent shortages. However, the unique shape of the Chinese market and its artificially created "special economic zones" means this fact does not necessarily apply.

The Chairman absolutely must get the people factor right. Arguably his single greatest challenge in pushing his One Body Multiple Wings strategy into play is talent. When a business has had a specific focus and intent for two decades, its personnel and purpose shape themselves very strongly around that focus. It attracts and retains people with particular talents and develops reputations within its markets for being a specific type of employer or brand. Radical organizational change is a monumental management challenge.

At Tiens in Wuqing, an area that is officially part of the city of Tianjin but also not far from Beijing, each morning up to 30 buses of employees roll in. The buses all belong to Tiens, are driven by Tiens drivers, and come from Beijing, Tianjin, and other areas around Wuqing.

These buses are necessary because the Wuqing region was farmland prior to its reinvention as an industrial zone. While it now contains a population nearing 900,000, mostly living in skyscraper-style apartment buildings clumped in groups, the major cities 50 kilometres to the south and 90 kilometres to the north boast headcounts that dwarf

Wuqing's. It's not always easy to convince Beijingers or Tianjiners to work so far outside their own city centers.

Organizations in the West are increasingly familiar with the idea of a battle for talent as ageing populations and other influences whittle down the number of potential staff members. The issue has given birth to an entire genre of academic business study around organizational brand and how businesses become employers of choice. It is fascinating to discover that many Chinese businesses, despite a seemingly limitless pool from which to choose talent, experience the same challenge.

"We set up the Chinese headquarters here in Wuqing because the land was cheap, but talent is severely limited in this area," says Jia Yongqing, a senior manager in HR at Tiens. "But we're in between Beijing and Tianjin, so for head office staff we overcome the limitations by searching for people in those two cities, as well as now across the world."

Jia was brought on board in 2014 and his role, he says, is primarily as an agent of change. As Tiens evolves via its One Body Multiple Wings strategy – weaving together the work of various business units and turning "distributors" into "business partners" who have greater perceived ownership and a broader product remit – so must its people and its HR practices similarly evolve, and in some ways radically change. Particularly since the business's staff numbers and management levels have been cut, Jia's role has been to ensure every staff member is a perfect fit for their role.

"The organization had become very large, as had the organizational chart," he says. "Some of the talent had been buried under a sea of people. You could no longer see where the good people were. Now we have fewer levels of management, we have to dig up the talented people and give them the rewards they deserve. We are finding the great people within the company."

HR management of large teams is a challenge for all corporates. Having that large team spread around the globe and across almost every conceivable culture increases the difficulty level enormously. In Chinese firms that don't have the benefit of a long history of private business practice around the world, or at least a recent history that can be drawn upon, entrepreneurs are learning as they go. Large, state-owned enterprises and government departments have not been set up for great efficiency and high performance, and prior to a few decades ago there was no other type of organization in China. However, things are changing quickly with the contemporary, highly educated workforce in the major cities of China.

Having spent many years working in international markets, including a decade with American multinational Motorola, Jia had exactly the type of experience the business was looking for when the Chairman decided Tiens and its people required a shake-up.

"Even though we have been at this industrial park since 2010, in lovely buildings, and with increasing numbers of staff, somehow the efficiency of our employees was decreasing," Jia says.

After a long period of growth, the Tiens head office was not structured in a way that allowed personnel to be well placed or rewarded for working toward broader organizational goals, as opposed to departmental ones. Departments had grown cumbersome under several levels of management and talent became increasingly difficult to identify. Outside the head office, distributors had been trained only to sell a specific set of products and felt they had little to do with parts of the Tiens business that were not related to that product.

"We began to evaluate what each position was about and whether the right person was in each position," Jia says. "The Chairman has positioned Tiens as a globalized company, so from an HR perspective our challenge is to source the talent that fits this vision, people who will drive the business to greater globalization. We need great talent in the right positions."

An age issue has been identified, for example. The business needs more young people, the Chairman told me, staff from a generation that better understands modern technology and its various uses. At the end of the fourth international One Body Multiple Wings forum, as the Chairman announced the dates of the fifth and final conference, he also asked his international managers to ensure that at least 50 percent of attendees at the following conference would be under the age of 32. I was initially equally shocked and amused at his open addressing of this problem. In a Western business environment he'd be dragged before a tribunal for trampling all over fair employment regulations. But it's also important to note that the very best educated and internationally experienced Chinese staff are the younger ones who have benefited from opportunities their parents dared not even dream about. For many Western companies, the younger ones are also likely the more technologically savvy, a reality that only some Western companies are fully realizing.

Change is always an organizational challenge, but it is often made more difficult when many staff are long-termers. Within Tiens headquarters around 80 staff have been with the business for over 20 years,

170 for over 15 years, and more than 600 for over a decade. Such figures reveal a great deal in terms of positive feelings toward the business. This level of staff retention is the end goal of many corporates, and the knowledge held by these cohorts of long-term staff is priceless. At the same time, implementing change amongst such a long-term group is the modern HR manager's nightmare, no matter what country they are in. To move in a new strategic direction, as the saying goes, businesses have to "either change the people, or change the people."

Even more important than local talent is a consistent organizational culture, Jia tells me. It's not just about fitting local people into positions according to their capability and talents, but also ensuring they are the types of people who will live and breathe the Tiens culture, even in a foreign office, and will promote that culture locally.

"Our corporate culture is unique," he says. "We want our Tiens culture to spread around the world. We educate our employees and business associates about our culture. We do not just allow the culture to be something that is written down and filed away. All of our people need to understand our core values of harmony, responsibility, and prosperity. They must blend our values with their working style, attitudes, and behaviors. We have to make sure they are real Tiens members."

What exactly is the Tiens corporate culture? Simply put, it is about health, humanity, service, and family. In greater detail, it begins with a core philosophy built around Traditional Chinese Medicine and its preventative health measures. It is about the improvement of public health but always with a view to giving back to society.

On the walls of Tiens' offices are several posters and other pieces of wall art containing the words "One world, one family." The "family" part of the business's core values, Jia says, indicates the fact that as soon as an individual begins working for, or representing, Tiens, they are considered part of the company's global family.

Such a philosophy might be considered quaint and mildly amusing, or even lacking authenticity, in the Western business world. But in the Chinese social environment where even a person who illicitly attempted to take over the Malaysian branch of the company was forgiven, and where those who are sacked are protected from public shame, it is as real as it is meaningful. And there's the rub when it comes to employing people from other cultures. Sometimes they're unlikely to understand, believe, or buy into an organizational culture that appears foreign to them. The HR function, in fact, must itself work across cultures and value systems if it is to be effective.

"We are still lacking something important in our HR management at this moment because we're still managing all of the staff under one system," Jia explains. "It is one culture and one management style. But we are moving forward to a multi-cultural system to manage our employees. This needs to be worked on, especially as we're facing some challenges in the global business where we have local managers and local Chinese employees too. We understand that their approaches, their mindsets, and their ethics are different. To manage all of these in a single way is not fair. It does not work and staff will not accept it. So we're now moving toward a multi-cultural system. Some Chinese businesses have what they call a bi-cultural HR system to cover Chinese and Westerners, but that may not be sufficient because we also have people from other cultures such as Africa, Central Asia, and the Middle East."

In fact, many Chinese businesses are now moving to what they describe as a bi-cultural or multi-cultural HR management system, which essentially involves one form of management for Chinese staff and another form of management for foreigners. Such are the differences in workplace behaviors and beliefs, attitudes and motivations, that various ethnic groups require different management styles to encourage high performance.

Some non-Chinese businesses are doing the same. When I speak with a senior manager from American cloud computing giant Salesforce, he tells me of a new internal platform known as "FaithForce." Managed out of Salesforce's Hyderabad offices, FaithForce has been developed specifically to help the company's international workforce understand and appreciate the various beliefs and behaviors within the company and its more than 30,000 staff members.

Having worked in American and Chinese firms, Jia has identified differences in behavior between Chinese and Western staff. Chinese employees, he says, tend to be more emotion-oriented. In other words, they want to have a passion for their job and they tend to be tied to their job through relationships to the people around them, to their colleagues and their manager.

"Foreigners are more economically rational," he says. "They evaluate how meaningful is the career or job and what benefits it can bring them as individuals. They do more of a rational evaluation and justification of the job itself. So there is less emotion in choosing the job, it is purely about what the job can offer them."

It's a massive difference in attitude, so how does a business set up a multi-cultural HR management system? It begins, Jia says, with the absolute basics, including compliance with local rules and policies. Next, it encompasses a meaningful respect for local cultures, living styles, and religious beliefs. Finally, it requires not only the business to get all of this right but for every individual within the business to develop a healthy level of respect for the cultures represented by the people around them.

"No matter how talented a person is, if they cannot fulfill all of these cultural requirements then they are not for us," Jia says.

The Professor adds to this view in some of his comments. "I have seen various non-Chinese people, and some Chinese people who have spent time overseas, come to Tiens and then find the fit was not optimal," he says. "All of these people were talented and motivated, but being able to adapt comfortably to cultural expectations and cultural realities has been difficult for them and for their colleagues. Of course, others have adapted extremely well, largely because they have put in the time to listen, to understand, and to respect cultural differences."

The cultural mismatch can create issues for the Chinese staff and for the foreign employee. One non-Chinese manager told me that while they were flattered to be offered a more senior position very soon after joining Tiens, they were gobsmacked when they discovered that Tiens management had not told the Chinese staff in their territory about the promotion. So the new manager, for many months, was considered junior to the people they would be managing. It was an absurd and unacceptable lack of communication, the territory manager said.

From the Chinese point of view, however, the picture looked very different. Such a process was intended to "protect" the new staff member, Jia says.

"Especially if they are a new hire and previously unknown to staff, when we give somebody a higher position or a new title, whether they are locals or foreigners, the staff are less likely to accept them and to work with them," he explains. "In order to protect new people and to create an initial pathway for them, so that they will eventually become the regional CEO, for instance, they are not immediately announced into the top position. We place them in the region but as there are also a lot of long-serving staff there, we give them a different but important title, such as PA to the Chairman. This creates protection for them so they will be better able to survive the first few months in the region."

It's a different version of saving face, a polite way of offering a person a smoother landing than they otherwise might have experienced in a business that is still transitioning from traditional Chinese to fully globalized.

This also reveals another interesting pattern of employment within a Chinese corporate, the fact that a conversation begins between the business and a potential hire with regards to a specific role, but often ends with an offer of a more senior position in the firm, when management is impressed by the person they meet.

I see this happening again and again during my time at Tiens. I have previously mentioned Stephen Beddoe, who was employed as the General Manager of the Australian business, had New Zealand added to his portfolio within a few months, then, a little more than 12 months later, became responsible for the global direct selling business. An architect originally brought in for a job that involved graphic design of an annual report was soon employed as the Senior Project Manager in Tiens Groups' engineering department. A Mexican professional hired as Director of Customer Service for The Americas was, within a few months, asked to move up by developing and managing the business's global customer service strategy. And another experienced manager, originally from Finland, was brought in as Director of Business Development for Europe but just a few months later became President and CEO West Europe.

"My past experience is with American companies and to come from the West to the Far East, the cultural differences are huge," the manager from Finland said. "I don't think it is a company-specific thing, I think it is a Chinese thing. Normally you would expect to walk into a situation where the job title and responsibilities are clear, but in Chinese business culture they are often not clarified. Anybody walking into the environment of such an organization would need to be prepared for the uncertainty – not around whether you have a job or not, just around the definition of the role itself. It is not always simple or clear cut."

Established Western businesses typically put a great deal of thought into a job description, then carefully employ for that exact role. In China, for the most part, companies instead employ a promising person for a role that is less strictly defined, then allow the person to partially shape that role. It's a quintessentially entrepreneurial approach, a start-up approach, and it's one the Chairman has always been comfortable with. In fact, I often hear him refer to himself as an entrepreneur, but never as a business director, even after two decades in international markets.

For the HR department of a Chinese corporate expanding offshore there are three important issues. The first is the localization of HR management in overseas branches so that people and policies fit the overseas culture, compliance, and religious beliefs, and the like.

The second is how they design their management system to encourage peak performance from all of the talent, all around the world, with their different backgrounds, cultures, and ethics.

"It is very important that we are tolerant of each other," the Chairman says. "Tiens is an international enterprise. We come from different countries and regions and have grown up in different environments with different working and living experiences. So it is common that we may have different opinions about certain things. The key thing is listening to both sides and never being partial toward either side.

"A leader should have an open and tolerant mind, be humble and good at listening to different opinions, particularly those opinions which are the opposite to their own. That way it is easier to come to the right decisions and achieve our objectives easily and quickly."

The third issue is to set up a process that recognizes, trains, and rewards promising young staff who may become future leaders.

These features, at their core, are no different from what Western businesses have to deal with in their operations as well, but they are features that Western businesses can easily forget when they move into foreign markets such as China. Even major Western companies, such as Amazon, appear to have not been able to find the right mix of approaches to ensure success in China, especially in the face of competition. And it can be seen in other major companies as well. For instance, Starbucks failed in its original attempt to enter the Australian market, largely because it sought to impose its one-size-fits-all model, rather than to understand the local knowledge and needs of Australian coffee drinkers.

As new people from around the globe enter Tiens, prove their worth, and bring with them valuable experience from other territories, and as previously siloed business units begin working more closely across brands and as a group, the traditional responsibilities and job descriptions within the business are naturally changing.

"The change does not just happen at one or two levels. It needs to go from top to bottom," Jia says. "The Chairman has now positioned the company as a global corporate so he realizes the business must have more talent from different regions. Therefore he is also changing his mindset about how to cater to them and how to work with them and how to be more open and accepting. Everybody needs to change in order for this to work."

Hence the breadth and depth of change, from practical to philosophical, outlined in the One Body Multiple Wings strategy. Change begins at the very top but it cannot just stop there. It includes all senior and middle management, whether new hires or long-term employees. It affects every partner in every culture around the globe as they are re-trained in, and engaged by, the new direction. The structure and strategy may well have been designed and developed by the Chairman, but it is the people who will make it a success.

31
The future

"We might leave other things, but it is the feelings and thoughts that people have about us after we have gone that are the most important legacy."

Li Jinyuan

I stand before a class of ferociously intelligent students – the "top one percent of the top one percent" is how the Professor describes them – at the University of International Business and Economics in Beijing. I'm struck not only by how sharp they are in their responses to my questions but also by how completely different their lives are compared with those of their parents, indeed with my life, and the lives of students of similar age in Western countries. As discussed earlier, Chinese millennials have not lived through the hunger, suffering, and difficult social change that shaped their parents' views, beliefs, and ways of thinking. They brim with acumen, optimism, and commitment to their country, meaning their feet and hearts are very much in China but their eyes and minds are on the world.

Of course, it's impossible to predict what is in their future and in the future of their nation. Such dramatic generational, social, and economic change has not been experienced anywhere in the modern world. There is no precedent for what is happening in China right now, nor for what will happen as President Xi Jinping leads the country on the ambitious course he has outlined.

A thirty-something Chinese journalist/producer I speak with in Beijing says it's very difficult for any foreigner to understand the depth of the chasm that is forming between two generations – hers and her parents – albeit two generations that still enjoy massive love and respect for each other. "It's as if our parents brought us up to have unswerving faith in a specific religion, in the same religion they and their ancestors always followed, but now my generation has deeply offended them by choosing a different faith," she says. "The shift of thinking around the way we live our lives is as great as a shift of faith, at least in the eyes of our parents."

The "shift of thinking" is what makes China's future so wonderfully exciting. Combine entirely fresh attitudes, opinions, and ideas with high levels of local and international education, and suddenly the talent pool for organizations and government bodies appears very healthy indeed.

Chairman Li is steering his ship into this boundless future, and it will likely be filled with surprises. Nobody can say how it will develop, but we can identify trends.

I ask the university students what types of jobs they see themselves taking on during their careers. Would they prefer, for instance, to work in a Chinese business or a Western one? Every student who responds chooses the latter. I'd expected perhaps 50/50, but the next generation of Chinese leaders appears, according to my quick and dirty research at least, to be very keen on the idea of hitching their careers to foreign wagons. They explain that in their opinion, Western companies tend to have a better structure. Such businesses are not so management-heavy and inflexible and they provide far greater opportunity for recognition and reward related to performance.

"Sometimes, with Chinese companies, it can be very difficult to move up through the structure if you are from the wrong type of family," one student says, and for a moment I make my usual mistake of thinking that this must be unique to China, before realizing she is also describing corporate Britain and its public school and old-boy networks, or the USA and its Ivy League and privileged families networks.

"If you don't have the right social status, then in a Chinese organization your career will be influenced by factors other than your talent and performance," she continues. "If you just come from a normal family, everything will take so much more effort."

Another student tells me about an internship she completed with a state-owned enterprise which, because of the rigidity of the organizational chart and the business's strict and unbending processes, convinced her to change her major so she'd be more suited for work with a private, preferably Western, company.

The Chairman's recent changes, in light of the attitudes of young talent, seem wise and timely. In fact, looking back over the many years of Tiens in business, Li's ability to foresee changes before they happen, and to adapt in time as other companies fall over, is almost uncanny. Tiens Group's new structure, its technology-centric strategy, and its more open and inclusive lines of communication are exactly what the next generation desires. The students I meet don't think they can discover such an environment in a Chinese firm, but it is exactly what the Chairman is creating. The university students I'm meeting with would be pleasantly surprised by Tiens, and would eagerly grasp the innovative changes being put in place.

The experience of Tiens has mirrored the changes occurring more broadly in China. Few people inside or outside of China believed the nation would be as dynamic, vibrant, and full of promise as the one we see today. Yes, there remain many problems of poverty, of perceived control of people, and of perceived role in the world. But just a few decades ago the country was still experimenting with the idea of a free-market economy. Over time, it has changed and adapted, and has borrowed bright ideas from around the globe and improved on them. It has moved at the pace of a much smaller and more nimble entity and continues to test ideas, fearless of failure, and welcoming of innovation.

So much of the Chairman's experience and the Tiens development journey reflects what has been happening at a macro level during the modernization of China that I no longer believe it is a coincidence. Modern China began with strong and autocratic management by Mao Zedong, Tiens began with Li Jinyuan calling all the shots. Even when all of his staff disagreed with the move into direct sales, Li trusted his own judgement and pushed forward. China then began to experiment with opening up its economy to the rest of the world, setting up special economic zones where business could be done differently and more freely. Tiens also experimented with international business, opening offices in various regions, and learning from many valuable mistakes. Modern China finally found a place of comfort with its open economy and quickly became an international economic player, as did Tiens when its international markets began to mature.

When the Chairman started as an entrepreneur he would trade, or swap, goods across China. He would source some goods, take them to where they were needed, swap them for other goods, and take them to another place where they were needed. In many ways, he is still doing that. He sees what is needed in his company, and as he says he is "swapping" or "replacing" one set of approaches with another to meet the needs and the opportunities that he recognizes across the world.

China now has a new strategy – in the form of the Belt and Road Initiative – to become a true global mover and shaker economically and politically. It has put the necessary internal structures in place to support that initiative even as major Western powers take large steps backwards, away from the global sphere. Notably, China actively works with its businesses to create greater success. With its One Body Multiple Wings transformation, Tiens is also altering its internal structures to support its newest strategy, a strong global play with Chinese characteristics, which is absolutely consistent with the Belt and Road Initiative. The organization has been active in nearly 200 foreign markets for two decades, but now plans to become a global business as opposed to a Chinese multinational. Chairman Li is putting functions and processes in place so he can work more closely with his staff and distributors, whom he now increasingly refers to as "partners," to achieve the same goal.

The story of Li Jinyuan and Tiens Group is the story of modern China. When I put this to him during one of our last meetings, he smiles as if I have finally seen the light.

"The two stories are parallel and consistent," Chairman Li says. "Modern China began with absolute power in the hands of its leader, then, as it focused on productivity, it began to be more about the people that worked within, about the individuals who made it great. When Tiens began it was my company, it belonged 100 percent to me. But as I have focused on greater productivity I have followed China's lead and made the business more about the staff and its customers. The business now belongs not only to me but also to the staff, to my partners."

A lot has changed in two decades, he says. From the quality of life in the cities, to the mentality of the people, to their spending power in the market, and to the structure of the market itself. As a result, the strategy of the business has also had to change along the way.

"In China, a lot of villages have been transformed into towns and towns have been transformed into cities. This landscape of transformation creates a new structure for the market," Li says. "It is a new market, and 20 years from now everything will change again in terms of the mentality of the citizens and the cities themselves and the people's spending power. I truly believe the China market will overtake the US market."

It has been a time of enormous change for one man, one company, and one country. But during this period of change, an absolute constant has been the Chairman's passion for the work he does around education and health.

As I speak with the Chairman about the future of China, he wraps his vision of increasingly rapid growth around a story about fast trains. It's an anecdote that is fitting, as I have spent a good amount of time hurtling through the countryside and through urban landscapes at 350 kph, traveling on the world-class fast-train service between Beijing and Tianjin. It turns a stressful two- to three-hour drive into a peaceful, 35-minute train ride and provides an affordable corridor of movement for millions of Chinese. It also creates entirely new choices in employment and accommodation for its passengers and for its potential passengers as it means more people can look for employment in more places. Nobody develops fast-train infrastructure as well as China; it's one of the skill sets that are perceived as most valuable in the nation's Belt and Road Initiative. But according to the Chairman, you ain't seen nothing yet.

"Today we have three vertical, fast-train railway lines from the north to the south of China and another three horizontal lines from the east to the west," the Chairman says. "So currently we have a three-by-three pattern. But the government blueprint within ten years is to have nine vertical railway lines and nine horizontal railway lines. This is the goal, and that target will be achieved. Add to that the fact that the speed of the trains used to be maximum 300 kph, but now the rails and trains are capable of over 400 kph. This means distance is not so much of an issue any more. Combine this with the many Chinese airlines and the new airports being established – in the near future we will have 400 city-level airports and this number will continue to increase – and the interconnectedness of our towns and cities will be complete.

"China has more than 3,000 districts. We are now connecting the districts to the towns and the villages. Many cities are now being transformed into eco-friendly cities that utilize artificial intelligence. Health concerns are always a top priority in China and the government wants to create healthy individuals, healthy communities, and a healthy nation. So you can see that in line with these transformations, civilizations and citizens are being changed. Their spending power is increasing and so is affordability of goods. Twenty years from now spending power will be multiplied several times over compared to the present, as will quality of Chinese products and quality of Chinese life."

What about the availability and quality of education, the Chairman's great passion? Has that improved since his young days in his small hometown?

"There used to be a big gap between urban and rural education levels and things have now improved, but still the gap is there," he says. "Public education has been promoted by the government and the quality of education has improved, from kindergarten to primary school and to secondary school. The quality of education has increased a lot."

Some indication of future directions for China came in 2015. The "Made In China 2025" announcement suggested an innovation-driven change. It outlined a conscious pivot toward intelligent manufacturing and the use of the internet of things to connect businesses involved in mass production, creating efficiencies across the board. At the same time, domestic content of core materials being used in the production process will rise to 40 percent in 2020 and 70 percent in 2025, potentially making up for job losses caused by the greater automation of production processes.

Manufacturing innovation centers, which are regions set up to encourage businesses that push production boundaries and from which other manufacturers can learn, will be created – 15 centers by 2020 and 40 by 2025. Intellectual property rights and regulations, traditionally a major problem in China, will also be strengthened to bring them into line with international expectations, meaning businesses that come up with new processes and products will be offered greater legal ownership and protections for their ideas and inventions.

It's all well and good for the leadership to have a positive plan filled with plenty of stretch-goals for the future, but what about the people of China? What do they hope for when they gaze into the next few decades? I put this question to the younger Chinese people I met to get some idea of general and specific wishes and concerns around the society in which their futures lie.

Edward, one of the students we met earlier, says he's concerned about the ageing population. As with many other nations around the globe, and partly thanks to the one-child policy, China's population is becoming extremely top-heavy, meaning fewer tax-producing workers and more retirees.

"There is going to be huge pressure from the ageing society on a lot of different parts of society," he tells me. "For example, how are we going to pay for people's pensions? The system was designed so that you would save some money in a collective account and after you retire you use the money that you saved. But right now the money that people are saving is used immediately for the people who are at retirement right now. I have seen some data that says in the past two or three years there were 2.9 workers for each retiree. In the near future it will be just 1.5 workers per retiree, so it will create huge pressure if the system does not change in some way. It is going to be a very big problem."

One other young student says education and internet censorship are her big issues. "I think the government can put more funding into basic education, because in remote areas there is an opportunity for children to get a better education," she says. "I would also like to suggest the government stops the restrictions on the internet. For example, I can't find a good way to read *The Economist*. I want to see some publications to help with my learning but right now it is difficult. I am annoyed about these restrictions because I think there is some information we're not seeing. I'm not so bothered about social media, but I don't like being kept away from information about the world."

Another student adds to the internet censorship argument. "Sometimes it is very inconvenient, but I can see why the government does it," he says. "It can shelter Chinese people from unhealthy information from overseas, and from the information that could hurt the country. It works sometimes and I think it is acceptable in some cases. But for students like us it is inconvenient because we always want to find information on the internet. I think the building of the Great Firewall has gone too far."

This is not likely to change any time soon. During his speech at the 2017 Congress, President Xi Jinping said the State would make even greater efforts to control online content to "clearly oppose and resist the whole range of erroneous viewpoints."

A male student says regulation of the finance sector has a long way to go, particularly when compared with other Asian territories such as Japan and Singapore. On this point President Xi agrees. In the same speech he promised stricter regulation of the financial system, including banks, and the stronger containment of financial risks.

Another student says the corruption crackdown must continue. What does corruption look like to him, I ask. "Funds from central government are taken away by officials," he says. "This means people in a remote area cannot enjoy funding from the central government, so their quality of life cannot be improved. Things are improving, but they still need to improve more."

This type of story has been told to me several times. In the past, crooked government officials would fill suitcases with cash and leave the country. The recent corruption crackdown, which launched in 2012, has included the removal of passports from government officers in roles that involve the handling of funds, as well as far stronger checks and balances. Over 1.5 million Party members have been investigated, including 43 members of the powerful Central Committee. Over 100,000 officials have been indicted for corruption and now the anti-corruption body, the Central Commission for Discipline Inspection, has been given increased powers and greater independence from government in its battle against corruption.

As with every nation, in China there is a lot being done and there is a lot more to do. Unsurprisingly, in Tiens similar challenges are being faced and responded to.

"The biggest challenge that we have is the mentality and mindset of Tiens partners and distributors," Chairman Li says. "We need to educate our people to change their mindset and transform themselves for the future. They must be innovative, otherwise they cannot survive. If you stay on your present path you will never move forward.

"For the courageous, nothing will get in the way of what we must do. Along the way we will make mistakes but we will then stand up again and fight a new battle. In terms of our courage and our resolve to succeed, nothing will change."

During the time of emperors, China often saw itself as the center of the world and had little interest in matters outside its own borders, but the nation now sees itself as a vital member of the global community. Along the same lines, the Chairman clearly sees himself as a citizen of the world, but one with a responsibility to his family, his staff, and his customers, no matter where they are located, and including future generations.

On our final day together I ask the Chairman to summarize his thoughts about what is required to create the strong and positive future that he clearly desires.

"We need good health, we need pace and rapidity of innovation, and we need sustainability," he says, without requiring even a moment to consider his response. "We need to see ourselves as partners in our businesses, and businesses must see themselves as partners with their country. This is how we will create global alliances and arrive at our success destinations. This is how we will clearly recognize strategies and achieve great vision. And this is how we will bring benefits to our families, to our communities, to our country, and to all of our friends around the world."

Reflections

Human beings are beautifully and tragically tribal in nature. Whether we choose a sports team, a faith, a national flag, a skin color, a hobby, or a political persuasion, we are always eager to identify with something, to come together with others. We are most comfortable when we are fenced in with a group of similar souls.

This can reveal itself in positive ways. Triathletes come together as a group to exercise, stay healthy, experience friendly competition, and enjoy the outdoors. Buddhists unite via a common belief in the sanctity of all life. New Zealanders bond over a love of their mighty rugby team, the All Blacks.

At the same time, it can manifest in ugly forms. Football fans become violent and clash bloodily with supporters of other teams. Those of a different skin color are considered inferior, or a threat. Wars erupt because of differing political or religious beliefs. Popular media thrives on the exploitation of this innately human need to identify as part of a tribe.

What does this have to do with anything? Near the end of my China immersion the Chairman asked me what I had learned. What had I discovered? I first spoke of experiences, of food, of drink, of people I had met – all of the usual traveler's tales. Then underneath it all was a current of thought that was more difficult to describe, one that caused me to feel shame. For much of my life I had been completely unaware of the real China, I began to explain. I had been swayed by media reports and had made assumptions about certain types of foreignness. I'd believed China was somehow backward and that democratic capitalism was the only road to societal success. With some discomfort, I told the Chairman that I originally thought the Chinese people would not be welcoming to a foreigner such as myself.

All of these beliefs, I discovered during my time in China, were far from the truth. I had considered myself worldly wise and had traveled broadly, but I had never been to the Middle Kingdom. I realized I had been ignorant, but this once-in-a-lifetime China experience had educated me in the truth.

What I had found, I explained to the Chairman, was a technologically advanced nation that, despite its almost unbelievable economic development over the last three decades, still centers itself around family. I had discovered a society guided by strict rules that were based on the thoughts of ancient philosophers, rules that make every interaction both delightful and insightful. And I had thoroughly enjoyed the realization that this culture was so deep that, 18 months in, I had only dipped a toe.

What had I discovered? All of that, and also that there is so much more to learn.

The Chairman simply sat and listened with a knowing smile. He had likely enjoyed similar experiences of his own as he spread his business wings and flew far from his homeland to Russia and Central Asia, to the African continent, the UK and Europe, Latin America, the USA, South-East Asia, and more.

My most important realization about China was that respect is at the core of everything. That is why the Chairman experienced such grand success, because he based every relationship on respect, not on fear, power, envy, or assumption of superiority.

By showing respect, Li Jinyuan wasn't being unique or creative and nor was he innovating or developing a new way of working. He was simply being wonderfully, traditionally, and perfectly Chinese.

Index

Note: *Italic* page numbers indicate photographs.